ALSO BY TARA-LEIGH COBBLE

*The Bible Recap: A One-Year Guide to Reading
and Understanding the Entire Bible*

*The Bible Recap Study Guide: Daily Questions
to Deepen Your Understanding of the Entire Bible*

The Bible Recap Journal: Your Daily Companion to the Entire Bible

*The Bible Recap Discussion Guide: Weekly Questions
for Group Conversation on the Entire Bible*

The God Shot: 100 Snapshots of God's Character in Scripture

Israel: Beauty, Light, and Luxury

THE
BIBLE RECAP

KIDS' DEVOTIONAL

365 REFLECTIONS AND ACTIVITIES FOR CHILDREN AND FAMILIES

TARA-LEIGH COBBLE

BETHANYHOUSE
a division of Baker Publishing Group
Minneapolis, Minnesota

© 2024 by Tara-Leigh Cobble

Published by Bethany House Publishers
Minneapolis, Minnesota
www.BethanyHouse.com

Bethany House Publishers is a division of
Baker Publishing Group, Grand Rapids, Michigan

Printed in the United States of America

Library of Congress Cataloging-in-Publication Data
Names: Cobble, Tara-Leigh, author.
Title: The Bible recap kids' devotional : 365 reflections and activities for children and families / Tara-Leigh Cobble.
Description: Minneapolis, Minnesota : Bethany House, a division of Baker Publishing Group, [2023] | Audience: Ages 8-10 | Audience: Grades 4-6
Identifiers: LCCN 2023030986 | ISBN 9780764242533 (paper) | ISBN 9781493446797 (ebook)
Subjects: LCSH: Devotional calendars—Juvenile literature. | Christian children—Prayers and devotions. | Bible—Devotional use—Juvenile literature.
Classification: LCC BV4870 .C58 2023 | DDC 242/.82—dc23/eng/20230731
LC record available at https://lccn.loc.gov/2023030986

Illustrations by Jayla Jones
Interior design by William Overbeeke

The author is represented by Alive Literary Agency, www.aliveliterary.com.

Baker Publishing Group publications use paper produced from sustainable forestry practices and post-consumer waste whenever possible.

24 25 26 27 28 29 30   7 6 5 4 3 2 1

To my parents,
who raised me in a home where Christ is King
and gave me every opportunity to watch them love Him first.
Because of you, He is part of even my earliest memories.

To my brother Jason,
who led me to Christ when I was four years old
while we played board games on a Saturday night.

*To every parent who prays that their child
will come to know Jesus.
And to every child who picks up this book.*
May you feel the gentle tug of the Holy Spirit,
the kindness of Jesus, and the deep love of the Father.

CONTENTS

A Note to Parents **12**

A NOTE TO PARENTS

How to Use This Book

The Bible is the most amazing book ever written, and we want kids to be excited to dig into it for themselves! *The Bible Recap Kids' Devotional* is designed to help children love God's Word and understand its value in their lives.

Following a 365-day chronological Bible reading plan, it explains and connects the story of Scripture with kid-friendly learning points and fun, engaging activities. Daily Bible reading is a wonderful thing for young and old, but please know that the content in this book can be adjusted to fit your family's schedule and your child's reading level and attention span.

For example, each day starts with a suggested Bible reading that averages three chapters. Your child may want to read the passage on their own, you can read the passage together as a family, or you can listen to an audio version of those Bible chapters. And then it's up to you if your child goes through the rest of the devotional on their own or you do it together. It's also okay if you have to miss a few days or, say, a three-times-a-week schedule works better for your family and child. Every day you're in God's Word is a good day!

One important note: The Bible has mature content in many places. We've included a parental guidance label at the beginning of a few of the chapters to alert parents and teachers that some or all of the  Bible passages for that day may not be appropriate for all children. But there may also be other passages that you may feel are too mature for your child. So we recommend you scan the Bible text before reading it together, or skip over sections as needed while reading.

Just like adults, kids need a solid biblical foundation. And as your child starts reading this book alongside the Bible, you'll all soon learn that no matter where life finds you, "He's where the joy is!" That's a phrase you'll see frequently in this book because we believe it to be true, and we think digging into God's Word is one of the best ways to tap into the joy that He brings.

May you and your family be blessed as you explore the Bible together!

Genesis 1–3

QUICK LOOK: Genesis 1:26—"Then God said, 'Let us make human beings so that they are like us.'"

▷ God creates the world and calls everything He made "good."

▷ God wants to have a friendship with us, so He tells us His name is LORD. And the all-caps name *LORD* represents the Hebrew spelling of YHWH, which sounds like "Yahweh." This is God's personal name.

▷ Adam and Eve sin, but this doesn't surprise God. He has a plan to fix their broken friendship with Him forever.

TODAY'S GOD SHOT

God is our Creator and Lord over everything! When He made people, He made us all to be like Him and to show others what He is like. When Adam and Eve sinned, they had to pay a price for what they had done. Even before they tell God they are sorry, He comes looking for them because He loves them! He's where the joy is!

ACTIVITY

When God made you, He loved you and wanted to be friends with you forever. God knew you would need someone to take the punishment for your sin, so He sent Jesus.

When you believe that Jesus died to take the punishment for your sin, you can be friends with God forever. It's as simple as A-B-C.

A—ADMIT When we're ready to follow Jesus, we need to **admit** that we have sinned. Then we tell God that we are truly sorry.

B—BELIEVE To follow Jesus, we have to **believe** that Jesus died on the cross for us and that God raised Jesus back to life. This is how God made a way for us to be His friends!

C—COMMIT We **commit** to following Jesus by telling Him that we want to follow Him!

Pray this prayer:

*God, I **admit** that I have done wrong things, and I am very sorry. I **believe** in my heart that Jesus died for me and that You brought Him back to life. I **commit** to following You, Jesus. I want You to be the leader and Lord of my life forever. Amen!*

Draw yourself on the world. Color in the word *sin*. Draw a cross over the word *sin* to connect God to the picture of you.

Genesis 4–7

QUICK LOOK: Genesis 6:8—"But the Lord was very pleased with Noah."

RECAP

▷ Adam and Eve have two sons named Cain and Abel. They bring offerings, or gifts, to God to receive forgiveness for their sin. Cain is jealous of Abel's offering and how it pleases God, so Cain kills Abel.

▷ Many more people are born, and God sees how sinful they are. He decides to put an end to everything He made and start over with a man named Noah, who loved Him.

▷ God asks Noah to build a huge boat called an ark to save his family and every kind of animal when the earth is destroyed by a flood.

TODAY'S GOD SHOT

God wants to be friends with everyone He made, but our sin hurts our friendship with Him. From the very first time sin entered the world, God had a plan to fix our friendship. As we read the Bible together, we will learn more about His plan and especially how He's where the joy is!

ACTIVITY

Do you want to live your life in a way that pleases God like Noah did? If you do, color in the word *yes!*

One of the best ways to please God is to spend time with Him every day!

Genesis 8–11

 QUICK LOOK: Genesis 9:17—"So God said to Noah, 'The rainbow is the sign of my covenant. I have made my covenant between me and all life on earth.'"

 RECAP

▷ The flood waters go down, and Noah's family leaves the ark.

▷ God makes a covenant, or a promise, with Noah's family to be faithful to them. He promises to never destroy the earth with a flood again and tells them to fill the earth with people.

▷ Many years later, there are more people on earth, but they all settle in one place and are working together to build a tall tower. God wants them to spread out and fill the world, so He changes their languages to separate them.

 TODAY'S GOD SHOT

God gives us a beautiful reminder of His promise to Noah by continuing to place rainbows in the sky. Every time you see one, stop and think about how much God loves you. He's faithful to keep His promises, and He's where the joy is!

 **ACTIVITY**

Think about three words that describe God and write them on the rainbow.

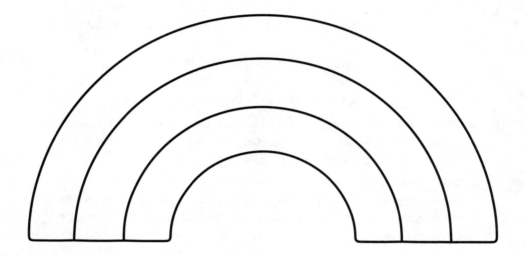

Job 1–5

QUICK LOOK: Job 1:21—Job said, "The LORD has given, and the LORD has taken away. May the name of the LORD be praised."

RECAP

▷ Job is a good and honest man who respects God and stays away from evil. God has given him good things.

▷ God's enemy, Satan, comes to God to talk about Job. He believes that if he can make Job's life bad enough, Job won't respect God anymore.

▷ God allows Satan to cause some very bad things to happen to Job, but God still has a good plan.

TODAY'S GOD SHOT

God is in control over the good things and the bad things that happen in our lives. This can give us comfort. Everything that happens is part of God's good plan for you, and you can praise Him because He's where the joy is!

ACTIVITY

Circle your answers to these questions:

Did Job respect God?

    YES   NO   I'M NOT SURE

Did God allow some bad things to happen to Job?

    YES   NO   I'M NOT SURE

Did God still love Job and have a good plan for his life?

    YES   NO   I'M NOT SURE

Job 6–9

QUICK LOOK: Job 7:17—Job continued, "What are human beings that you think so much of them? What are they that you pay so much attention to them?"

▷ Job loses everything and is heartbroken. Three friends come to visit but do not offer him much encouragement.

▷ When two of his friends try to convince him that he's done something to deserve all the hard things that are happening to him, Job defends himself.

▷ Even though Job has questions for God, he doesn't say anything untrue or unkind about God.

TODAY'S GOD SHOT

God is big and powerful—He created the whole world! And still, He's always thinking about you because He loves you. He sees the hard things that happen in your life, but you can trust that He is in control. He's where the joy is!

ACTIVITY

Think of something that reminds you that God is powerful. Maybe it's a storm, waves in the ocean, or tall mountains. Draw a picture of it below.

Job 10–13

QUICK LOOK: Job 13:15—Job replied, "Even if God kills me, I'll still put my hope in him."

RECAP

▶ Another one of Job's friends speaks up and tells him that he has done something wrong.

▶ Job's three friends say some things that are true about God. But they are wrong when they think the hard things happening are Job's fault.

▶ Even though Job is sad and frustrated, Job knows that God is still in control, and He is the one who can help him.

TODAY'S GOD SHOT

Job has been through so much, but he knows his hope and his help come from God. We can also place all of our hope in God. Hard things do happen, but God is still in control and will help us because He's where the joy is!

ACTIVITY

Unscramble these words that can help us remember who God is and why we can put our hope in Him! God is . . .

LRWEOPFU ....

FHLEPUL ....

DGOO ....

Job 14–16

QUICK LOOK: Job 14:5—Job replied, "You decide how long anyone will live. You have established the number of his months. You have set a limit to the number of his days."

RECAP

▷ As one of Job's friends speaks again, his words continue to make Job feel discouraged and alone.

▷ Job's friends want him to hurry and get over the pain that he's feeling. They think that Job's sadness and frustration mean that he doesn't trust God, but this isn't true. Job speaks up and tells his friends to stop.

▷ Job doubts God's goodness but knows that God is still in control.

TODAY'S GOD SHOT

God is in control of every day of our life. He is powerful, and He is good. This should give us comfort! When we're hurting, we can tell God how we feel and trust that He will make everything right because He's where the joy is!

ACTIVITY

Is there something in your life that feels hard right now? Fill in the blanks in the prayer below to ask God to remind you that He's in control.

Dear God, I'm feeling sad about ....
.... Please help me
remember that You are in control of this and that You will help me
through it. I love You! Amen.

Job 17–20

QUICK LOOK: Job 19:25—Job replied, "I know that my redeemer lives. In the end he will stand on the earth."

▷ Job's friends continue to tell him that the hard things he is facing are a punishment from God.

▷ Even though Job's friends aren't helping, Job points out things that are always true about God.

▷ Job knows that God is alive and calls Him "redeemer."

TODAY'S GOD SHOT

A redeemer is a person who pays a price to get something back that was taken. When God sent Jesus to die on the cross, Jesus became our Redeemer by paying for our sin, which fixed our friendship with God. Jesus is our Redeemer, and He's where the joy is!

ACTIVITY

Imagine someone has taken your favorite thing. How much money would you pay to get it back?

Jesus paid a higher price than all the money in the world to get us back. He gave up His life to pay for our sin. Because He did that, we can be friends with God forever!

Pray or sing the song "God, You're So Good" to thank Jesus for giving His life for us.

Job 21–23

QUICK LOOK: Job 23:10—Job replied, "But he knows every step I take. When he has tested me, I'll come out as pure as gold."

RECAP

▷ Job's friends continue to guess why he is going through these hard things.

▷ Job knows that the way things happen in our lives isn't based on whether we are good or bad.

▷ Job tells his friends that even though things are hard, he still trusts God is there and working in his life.

TODAY'S GOD SHOT

God sees every hard thing you go through. He is always with you and wants to help you trust His plan for your life. God is making everything good because He's where the joy is!

ACTIVITY

Decode the emoji sentences to discover some of the times in your day when God is with you!

....

....

....

....

....

....

Job 24–28

 QUICK LOOK: Job 28:12–13—Job continued, "But where can wisdom be found? Where does understanding live? No human being understands how much it's worth. It can't be found anywhere in the world."

 RECAP

▷ Job tells his friends that he has seen bad things happen to good people and good things happen to bad people.

▷ Job knows he can be angry and sad about bad things, but he still trusts God when things are falling apart.

▷ Job tells his friends that the only place wisdom is truly found is in God.

 TODAY'S GOD SHOT

God is wise, and when we read His Word each day, we grow in wisdom. God promises that when we look for Him, we will find Him. Let's keep coming back to God's Word every day. He's where the wisdom is, and He's where the joy is!

 ACTIVITY

One way we can grow in wisdom is by keeping God's Word in our hearts and our minds. Fill in the blanks with the letter *E* to read and memorize this verse.

J___R___MIAH 29:13—"WH___N YOU LOOK FOR M___ WITH ALL

YOUR H___ART, YOU WILL FIND M___."

Job 29–31

 QUICK LOOK: Job 29:4—Job said, "Those were the best days of my life. That's when God's friendship blessed my house."

 RECAP

▷ Job shows us how much he misses the time before all of the hard things started. He especially misses how close his friendship with God was at that time.

▷ Job misses when people really listened to him and thought he was wise.

▷ Even though Job is not guilty of the things his friends have accused him of, there are still things in his heart that God wants to change.

 TODAY'S GOD SHOT

Job considered God to be his friend. A friend is someone you trust and spend time with. As you spend time with God and learn to trust Him more, your friendship with God will grow! He is worthy of your trust, and He's where the joy is!

 **ACTIVITY**

Draw a picture of something you like to do with your friends.

We can talk to our friends, eat lunch with our friends, and play with our friends. We can also let God be just as involved in our days. God wants us to remember that He is the very best friend we could ever have!

Job 32–34

QUICK LOOK: Job 33:28—Elihu said, "God has set me free. He has kept me from going down into the darkness of the grave. So I'll live to enjoy the light of life."

▶ Elihu, another friend of Job, speaks up. He is angry and tells Job's friends that all of their advice has not been good.

▶ At first, it seems like Elihu has a better understanding of who God is. But then, just like Job's other friends, Elihu accuses Job of doing wrong things too!

▶ Job has lost his work, money, home, family, and health. And four friends have now wrongly told Job that his own actions are the reason for all the bad things happening in his life.

TODAY'S GOD SHOT

God allows you to go through hard things to lead you to something better for your life. God loves you and always knows what's best. As you get to know Him more, you'll learn that He is a good and loving Father and that He's where the joy is!

ACTIVITY

God knows that doing hard things can help you learn that He is good. What is one thing you've learned to do that was hard?

....

Let's pray and thank God for being good when things are hard.

Father God, Thank You for being with me when things are hard. I know You love me and want what's best for me. You are good, and I trust You! Amen.

Job 35–37

QUICK LOOK: Job 36:15—Elihu continued, "But God saves suffering people while they suffer. He speaks to them while they are hurting."

RECAP

▷ As Elihu continues to speak, his words about Job are mean and hurtful.

▷ Elihu tells Job that he can't trade his life of right living for a life of no pain. This is true, but Elihu is wrong in thinking this is what Job has been trying to do.

▷ Job is silent as Elihu speaks. Job may be quiet because he is being humble or because he feels defeated.

TODAY'S GOD SHOT

God always knows what is best. We may not understand what God's plan is while we're in the middle of something hard, but He always has a plan, and it is always good. He truly is where the joy is!

ACTIVITY

When you are going through hard times, God can still give you joy. Circle two things that give you joy:

PLAYING WITH FRIENDS   READING THE BIBLE

EATING A GOOD MEAL   DRAWING A PICTURE

SPENDING TIME WITH YOUR FAMILY   WATCHING A GOOD MOVIE

Now take a moment to thank God for those things, because they are from Him!

Job 38–39

QUICK LOOK: Job 38:33—The LORD said, "Do you know the laws that govern the heavens? Can you rule over the earth the way I do?"

RECAP

▷ God finally speaks!

▷ God's first words don't really address Job's problems. Instead, He reminds everyone of who He is. He created the universe, He set the stars in the sky, He is in charge of everything He created, and He pays attention to every detail in the world He made.

▷ God reminds Job that he is only a man, that he hasn't been alive forever, and that he is not God. God isn't angry with Job—He just wants him to remember what is true.

TODAY'S GOD SHOT

God is patient and loving. He does not get angry with Job for asking questions, but He does remind Job who is in charge. You can ask God questions too, but when you do, remember that He's in control, and He knows a lot more than you do. God is in control, and He's where the joy is!

ACTIVITY

On the lines below, write one question you would like to ask God. Then ask Him!

....

....

....

Job 40–42

QUICK LOOK: Job 42:5—Job replied to the Lord, "My ears had heard about you. But now my own eyes have seen you."

RECAP

▷ God shows Job that he believes God owes him something. Job understands that he was wrong to think this way and says he is sorry.

▷ God tells Job's friends they were wrong for some of the things they said and tells them to apologize. God forgives them and helps them to forgive one another too.

▷ After Job is made right with God and his friends, God blesses Job even more than he had been blessed before his hard times began. He gets back double everything he lost!

TODAY'S GOD SHOT

Nothing you go through, whether good or bad, is ever wasted. When you listen to God and trust Him, He will help you get through hard things. You will be stronger because of them. God works everything out for good because He's where the joy is!

ACTIVITY

After everything Job went through, he saw God more clearly and loved Him more! What are three things you love about God? Write them below.

1. ....

2. ....

3. ....

Genesis 12–15

 QUICK LOOK: Genesis 15:6—"Abram believed the LORD. The LORD was pleased with Abram because he believed. So Abram's faith made him right with the LORD."

 RECAP

▷ God promises to bless Abram and his family with land in a place called Canaan, even though some of God's enemies live there.

▷ Abram waits patiently for God to bless him. He travels with his family to other places, where they face problems and need God's help.

▷ Abram and his wife are very old and have no children, but God makes them another promise—that they will have a son.

 TODAY'S GOD SHOT

God makes Abram promises that seem impossible. Abram has to trust God to do things that he cannot see happening with his eyes. He believes in his heart that God will do them and sees that He's where the joy is!

 ACTIVITY

Draw a ☆ next to the problems you believe God can help you with.

Fighting with a friend or family member

Being jealous

Fearing what will happen

Arguing over who goes first

Believing wrong things about yourself

Did you draw a ☆ by all of them? Do you believe God can help you with each one?

Genesis 16–18

 QUICK LOOK: Genesis 16:13—"She gave a name to the LORD who spoke to her. She called him 'You are the God who sees me.'"

▷ Abram's wife, Sarai, has a hard time waiting for God to give her a son. She sins by taking God's promise into her own hands, and she convinces Abram to have a child with her servant named Hagar.

▷ Hagar obeys her masters and becomes pregnant with Abram's child. Sarai is jealous and sends Hagar away before the baby is born. God sends an angel to help Hagar while she is alone and scared. Later, Hagar gives birth to a son, and Abram names him Ishmael.

▷ God changes Abram and Sarai's names to Abraham and Sarah. Then He sends angels to help them remember the promises He made to them.

 TODAY'S GOD SHOT

Hagar gives God the name El Roi, which means "the God who sees me." Just like God saw Hagar when she was hurt, scared, and alone, God sees you and can speak to you because He's where the joy is!

 ACTIVITY

Write your name in the sentence below.

"GOD SEES .... TODAY!"

God has many names. Here are a few of them and what they mean. Find them in the word search below. Words can go up, down, across, or diagonally.

EL ROI = The God who sees me

ADONAI = My Lord

ABBA = Father

EL SHADDAI = God Almighty

JEHOVAH JIREH = Provider

ELOHIM = Creator

IMMANUEL = God with us

JEHOVAH RAPHA = The LORD who heals

```
J E H O V A H J I R E H U J
I O F S M J P U G M V A A V
I H M A H I L W X G X T H F
E E V G B J H O V H O W P X
L Y T S F B H Q R G J R A I
O O M R V O A M A M W Y R A
H D X T K D I R E X I Q H D
I W N A S O X A Y N G N A D
M G E I M M A N U E L R V A
D H U L I B O E Y C D L O H
F G K E R E L K V L G U H S
N I V A D O N A I X A W E L
H P U O C T I Z O V T M J E
```

If you need help, check out the Word Search Answer Key on page 471.

Genesis 19–21

 QUICK LOOK: Genesis 20:17—"Then Abraham prayed to God, and God healed Abimelek."

 RECAP

▷ God destroys two cities that are full of wicked people. But God saves Abraham's nephew, Lot, and his family who are living there, because God promised Abraham a large family.

▷ Abraham and Sarah meet King Abimelek. He tries to marry Sarah, but God tells him it is wrong. Abimelek returns Sarah to Abraham, and Abraham prays for him to be healed so the king can have children.

▷ Abraham and Sarah finally have a son named Isaac.

 TODAY'S GOD SHOT

God has a forgiving heart and expects us to forgive others too. Abraham prays for Abimelek to show that he has forgiven him. Forgiveness is one way we show God's love to others and help them see that He's where the joy is!

 ACTIVITY

Is there someone you are having a hard time forgiving? God can help you to forgive others, and praying for them is one of the best ways. Pray this prayer now.

Dear God, I've been having a hard time forgiving

.. Help me to forgive them because You

have forgiven me. Amen.

Genesis 22–24

QUICK LOOK: Genesis 22:18—The Angel of the Lord said, "All nations on earth will be blessed because of your children. All these things will happen because you have obeyed me."

▷ The word *sacrifice* in the Bible means to give up something because we've done something wrong. God's people will sacrifice perfect, innocent animals (like lambs or goats) to receive God's forgiveness for their sins.

▷ God asks Abraham to offer Isaac as a sacrifice, and he is willing to obey. Because of Abraham's obedience, God provides a ram to sacrifice instead of Isaac.

▷ Sarah dies, and Abraham buys land to bury her in Canaan. He and his servant pray to find a wife for Isaac who loves God. God answers their prayers when Abraham's servant meets Rebekah.

TODAY'S GOD SHOT

God gives Abraham directions to follow one step at a time. Because Abraham loves and trusts God, he does exactly as God says. God doesn't give Abraham all of the steps at one time, because He wants to walk with Abraham along the way and show him that He's where the joy is!

ACTIVITY

God will speak to you through His Word. Read this verse and write the steps God wants you to take. Remember He is with you as you do!

Matthew 22:37–39

> Jesus replied, "'Love the Lord your God with all your heart and with all your soul. Love him with all your mind.' This is the first and most important commandment. And the second is like it. 'Love your neighbor as you love yourself.'"

1. ....

   ....

2. ....

   ....

Genesis 25–26

QUICK LOOK: Genesis 26:24—The LORD said to Isaac, "I am the God of your father Abraham. Do not be afraid. I am with you. I will bless you."

RECAP

▷ Abraham dies and leaves everything he owns to Isaac.

▷ Isaac and Rebekah have twin sons, Esau and Jacob. Even though Esau is the oldest and should receive the blessing, Jacob is the son who God promises to bless.

▷ Isaac lives near King Abimelek. The king asks Isaac to move away because he is scared of the power and success God gives to him. When Isaac moves away, God promises to be with him and bless him.

TODAY'S GOD SHOT

God loves everyone! He loves us no matter how old we are, where we're from, or what we're like. And God especially cares for those who are not honored and those who are not as popular or talented as others. Everyone needs God, and we do too, because He's where the joy is!

ACTIVITY

Practice loving people like God does every day. As you go throughout your day, say a prayer for as many people as you can.

- As you're riding down the road, you can pray for God to bless the people driving around you with protection.
- At home, you can pray for your parents and siblings to get along.
- At school or at the store, you can pray for each person you see to know that God loves them.

Genesis 27–29

QUICK LOOK: Genesis 28:15—The LORD said, "I am with you. I will watch over you everywhere you go."

RECAP

▷ Isaac wants to bless his oldest son, Esau. But Rebekah helps their youngest son, Jacob, trick Isaac into giving him the blessing instead. Esau becomes angry, so Jacob goes to live with his uncle, Laban, and find a wife who loves God.

▷ Laban promises to let Jacob marry his younger daughter, Rachel, if he commits to work for Laban for seven years. Jacob agrees, but Laban tricks him into marrying his oldest daughter, Leah.

▷ Jacob is upset because he really loves Rachel. He is unkind and hurtful to Leah, but God sees her in her sadness. Leah begins to see that God is enough!

TODAY'S GOD SHOT

God is in control over everything, including the sin we have in our hearts. When Rebekah sins by tricking Isaac, God still uses it to accomplish His plan. When Laban sins by tricking Jacob, God still uses it to accomplish His plan. God knows all the wrong things you will do, but He's still working through it all. He's with you, and He's where the joy is!

ACTIVITY

Memorize today's Quick Look verse by writing it on a small card and putting it in your pocket. Read it throughout the day and remember that God is with you and watching over you!

Genesis 30–31

QUICK LOOK: Genesis 30:22—"Then God listened to Rachel. He showed concern for her. He made it possible for her to have children."

RECAP

▶ Leah and Jacob begin having children. Rachel grows jealous since she does not have a child yet. Eventually, she and Jacob have a son named Joseph.

▶ Jacob wants to return to the land God promised his father, but Laban convinces him to stay. Jacob tricks Laban into giving many of his strong animals to him.

▶ Jacob and his family run away from Laban. But Rachel steals some of Laban's things before leaving, so he chases them down.

TODAY'S GOD SHOT

God is kind to us and hears us, even when we disobey him. He still honors His promises and gives us what we need. He loves and forgives His children, and He continues to help us see that He's where the joy is!

ACTIVITY

God listens to our prayers and is kind to answer. Use the PRAY acronym to talk to God today.

PRAISE—"Thank You for hearing my prayer. You are kind to me."

REPENT—"Forgive me for the wrong things I do. Help me do what is right."

ASK—"Give me .... if it's what You know is best for me."

YES—"I want what You want."

Genesis 32–34

QUICK LOOK: Genesis 32:10—Jacob prayed, "You have been very kind and faithful to me. But I'm not worthy of any of this."

RECAP

▷ Jacob is returning to Canaan but is scared to meet his brother, Esau.

▷ Because Jacob is afraid, He asks God for help. He spends the night alone and wrestles with God. Jacob leaves with an injury, and God gives Jacob a new name, Israel.

▷ Jacob meets Esau, who is excited to see him after such a long time. But then Jacob's daughter, Dinah, is attacked, and his sons plan to get revenge.

TODAY'S GOD SHOT

God draws near to Jacob. He wrestles with him, renames him, and changes him. God often uses hard times to change our hearts too. He's faithful to finish everything He starts, and He's where the joy is!

ACTIVITY

Draw a ☆ beside the ways God is changing your heart.

I have more patience when I have to wait.

My room is clean because it makes my mom happy.

I want to read my Bible and pray.

I show kindness to others.

My friend lied to me, but I forgave him.

Genesis 35–37

QUICK LOOK: Genesis 37:21—"Reuben heard them talking. He tried to save Joseph from them. 'Let's not take his life,' he said."

▷ Jacob moves his family back to the land where his father, Isaac, lives. They get rid of all their idols and build an altar to honor God.

▷ Rachel has a baby boy named Benjamin, but she dies while giving birth to him. Jacob has twelve sons, but Joseph is his favorite.

▷ Joseph and his brothers don't have a good relationship. Joseph tells them about a dream he has where they worship him. They decide to kill him, but his oldest brother, Reuben, saves his life.

TODAY'S GOD SHOT

Reuben shows us a picture of Jesus. Reuben is not perfect, but he points us to the great, saving hand of God in a world where we can't save ourselves. Jesus takes action to fix our friendship with God. He's where the joy is!

ACTIVITY

What are some ways we could be tempted to think we can save ourselves? Draw or write about it below.

Genesis 38–40

QUICK LOOK: Genesis 39:2—"The LORD was with Joseph. He gave him great success."

RECAP

▷ Judah, one of Jacob's sons, gets married and has three sons of his own. Tamar marries his oldest son, but after his two oldest sons die, Judah sends her back to live with her father. Eventually, Judah and Tamar have twin sons named Perez and Zerah.

▷ Joseph, now a slave of an Egyptian official, Potiphar, has found success and blessing even in his difficult situation.

▷ Potiphar's wife tells a lie and accuses Joseph of treating her badly, so Joseph is put in prison, where he is also trusted and finds success.

TODAY'S GOD SHOT

God is a promise keeper! He promised Abraham, Joseph's great-grandfather, that his family would grow large and be successful. God remains faithful to His children and helps them see that He's where the joy is!

ACTIVITY

Unscramble the words below that describe who God is.

RPOMSIE ....

REKPEE ....

Genesis 41–42

QUICK LOOK: Genesis 41:51 NIV—"Joseph named his firstborn Manasseh and said, 'It is because God has made me forget all my trouble and all my father's household.'"

▷ Pharaoh asks Joseph to tell him what Pharaoh's dreams mean. Joseph tells him they will have seven years of plenty, with extra food, and seven years of famine, with no food.

▷ Pharaoh decides that because Joseph is wise, he should be the one in charge of everything in Egypt. Joseph is free after thirteen years in prison.

▷ During the famine, Joseph's brothers go to Egypt to buy grain. Joseph sees his brothers, but they don't recognize him. He accuses them of being spies, throwing one brother in prison and sending the rest home to get Benjamin, his little brother.

TODAY'S GOD SHOT

God is so generous. He sends Joseph to tell the Egyptians that a famine is coming and gives instructions on how to save enough food. He even plans for Joseph's brothers to get free grain! We can know that God will take care of us, even when things feel really hard, because He's where the joy is!

ACTIVITY

List five ways God has been generous to you. Then color in the picture of Pharaoh and Joseph on the next page.

1. ....

2. ....

3. ....

4. ....

5. ....

Genesis 43–45

QUICK LOOK: Genesis 45:5—Joseph said, "But don't be upset. And don't be angry with yourselves because you sold me here. God sent me ahead of you to save many lives."

RECAP

▷ Joseph sees his brothers, including Benjamin, when they get to Egypt. He invites them to dinner at his house. Joseph's brothers leave to go home, but before they go, he puts his cup in Benjamin's bag.

▷ Later, Joseph sends his servants to catch his brothers. They find the cup in Benjamin's bag, and they all go back to Egypt to see Joseph.

▷ Judah takes the blame for the cup and gives a speech. Joseph is very emotional and finally tells his brothers who he is. They make plans for their family to move to Egypt so they can have food.

TODAY'S GOD SHOT

God helps us forgive others when they sin against us, and He helps us forgive ourselves. God isn't surprised by our bad choices. He uses them for His good because He's where the joy is!

ACTIVITY

How hard is it for you to forgive yourself when you make a bad choice?

VERY HARD   KINDA HARD   NOT HARD AT ALL

If God can forgive and love you, you can ask Him for help to forgive yourself when you mess up and sin.

Genesis 46–47

 QUICK LOOK: Genesis 46:4—God said to Israel, "I will go down to Egypt with you. I will surely bring you back again."

 RECAP

▷ Jacob packs up his stuff for the long journey to Egypt. He stops in Beersheba to offer a sacrifice to God.

▷ God promises to make Jacob into a great nation while they're in Egypt.

▷ Even though there is a famine happening, Jacob and Joseph's family gets stronger and is blessed because of God!

 TODAY'S GOD SHOT

God provides for His people and blesses them while they are in Egypt. He keeps His promises, and He's where the joy is!

 ACTIVITY

Circle the things that God provides for you every day.

Genesis 48–50

QUICK LOOK: Genesis 50:20—Joseph said to his brothers, "You planned to harm me. But God planned it for good."

RECAP

▷ Jacob blesses Joseph's two sons before he dies. Usually the special blessing goes to the oldest son, but Jacob gives it to the younger son.

▷ Jacob blesses all of his sons but gives the special blessing to Judah, who will be an ancestor of Jesus.

▷ After Jacob's death, Joseph's brothers are worried that he will be angry with them. Joseph reminds his brothers that God planned all of this to happen to grow and bless their family.

TODAY'S GOD SHOT

Joseph knows that every hard thing he experienced was allowed by God and used for His good plan. He is able to forgive his brothers because he trusts in God's plan. Joseph's forgiving his brothers is like how God forgives us. No matter what we do to Him, He forgives us because He loves us. He's where the joy is!

ACTIVITY

Do you trust that God's plan for your life is good?   YES   NO

If you circled *yes*, pray and thank God for helping you see that His plan is always good.

If you circled *no*, ask Him to help you see what He sees.

Exodus 1–3

QUICK LOOK: Exodus 3:10—The LORD said to Moses, "So now, go. I am sending you to Pharaoh. I want you to bring the Israelites out of Egypt. They are my people."

RECAP

▷ Joseph dies, and the new pharaoh makes God's people, the Israelites, slaves. He orders all of their newborn boys to be killed, but one Israelite woman hides her baby boy, named Moses, in a basket and puts him in the river.

▷ An Egyptian princess finds Moses and raises him in Pharaoh's palace. When Moses grows up, he sees how the Israelites are being treated and is angry. One day, he sees an Egyptian abusing an Israelite, so he kills the Egyptian. Afraid after what he's done, he runs away.

▷ Back in Egypt, the Israelites call out to God for help. Through a burning bush, God tells Moses that He plans to rescue His people, and He wants Moses to go back to Egypt to be their leader.

TODAY'S GOD SHOT

God uses people who are not perfect to accomplish His plan. Moses is an example of someone who doesn't always do everything right, but God still chooses him to free His people! God isn't afraid of our sins and allows us to be a part of His plan because He's where the joy is!

ACTIVITY

Circle the kind of people God uses to accomplish His plan.

SCARED   EXCITED   CONFUSED   HAPPY

SINFUL   EMBARRASSED   NERVOUS

God can use anyone, including you!

Exodus 4–6

QUICK LOOK: Exodus 6:1—"Then the LORD said to Moses, 'Now you will see what I will do to Pharaoh. Because of my powerful hand, he will let the people of Israel go.'"

▶ Moses is afraid to go back to Egypt. God reminds Moses of His power by performing miraculous signs that Moses will perform when he meets Pharaoh. God also tells Moses to take Aaron, his brother, to help him talk.

▶ God explains that Moses is going to ask Pharaoh to release His people but also that God is going to harden Pharaoh's heart. God promises that Pharaoh will listen eventually.

▶ The Israelites worship God when they hear His promise to set them free but quickly lose hope when Pharaoh makes them work even harder.

TODAY'S GOD SHOT

God shows great kindness to Moses when he is afraid by reminding him of His power. God is powerful, and He's also kind, and He's where the joy is!

ACTIVITY

God is powerful and gives us many ways to see His power. Draw a ⭐ next to the way that makes you say "Wow!"

God makes the sun rise and set every day.

God keeps the ocean from swallowing up the land.

God made eyes that see and brains that think.

God had a plan to fix our friendship with Him by sending Jesus to save us from our sin.

Exodus 7–9

QUICK LOOK: Exodus 9:16—God instructed Moses to tell Pharoah, "I had a special reason for making you king. I decided to show you my power. I wanted my name to become known everywhere on earth."

RECAP

▷ Moses and Aaron ask Pharaoh to let the Israelites go free from Egypt, but he says, "No!" God hardens Pharaoh's heart, and he doesn't listen to their warnings.

▷ God punishes Egypt by sending bad things called plagues. Some of them are flies, gnats, frogs, and hail covering the land.

▷ During several plagues, Pharaoh says the Israelites can leave but then changes his mind, exactly like God said he would.

TODAY'S GOD SHOT

God knew that Pharaoh would harden his heart against the Israelites. And of course, God had a plan: to show His great power. God has a purpose for each one of our lives, and it's to make His name known, because He's where the joy is!

ACTIVITY

Thank God for His power and pray this prayer:

Dear God, thank You for making me and showing me Your power! You give my life a purpose, and I want the world to know just how great You are. I love You! Amen.

DAY 33

Exodus 10–12

QUICK LOOK: Exodus 12:51—"On that day the LORD brought the Israelites out of Egypt like an army on the march."

RECAP

- God continues to make Pharoah's heart hard. He refuses to let God's people go after a plague of locusts and darkness.
- God decides to send one final plague but tells His people to have a special meal, called Passover, that includes a lamb, bitter plants, and bread made without yeast. They place blood from the lamb on the sides and the tops of their doors.
- At midnight, God sends the final plague, striking down the firstborn sons of the Egyptians but passing over the houses with blood on the doors. God's people leave in the night, taking gold and silver given to them by Egyptians.

TODAY'S GOD SHOT

All along—even throughout the Israelites' four hundred years of slavery—God had a plan to save His people. When God says the time is right, they march safely out of Egypt, because He saved them! And He wants to save us too! He brings freedom and celebration, because He's where the joy is!

ACTIVITY

Unscramble the words that describe what God gave the Israelites. Praise God that He gives us these good gifts today too.

FESAYT ....

DREOMFE ....

JYO ....

ANSWER KEY: safety, freedom, joy

Exodus 13–15

QUICK LOOK: Exodus 15:2—Moses and the people sang, "The LORD gives me strength and protects me. He has saved me. He is my God, I will praise him."

RECAP

▷ God wants His people to celebrate Passover and a seven-day Feast of Unleavened Bread to remember and teach their children about what He did for them.

▷ God leads His people through the desert with a pillar of cloud during the day and a pillar of fire at night. God is their leader and has chosen to use Moses to speak to the people.

▷ When Pharaoh's army comes, the Israelites don't trust God and are scared. God defeats the army by making a dry path through the Red Sea and closing it on top of the Egyptians. The Israelites praise God with a song!

TODAY'S GOD SHOT

God loves the Israelites so much that He fights any enemy that tries to hurt them. God fights for us in the same way. He wants to get rid of anything that distracts us from following Him and remembering that He's where the joy is!

ACTIVITY

Moses and God's people wrote a song praising God for what He had done for them. Can you come up with a tune? Give it a try!

"The Lord gives me strength and protects me. He has saved me. He is my God; I will praise Him."

Exodus 16–18

 QUICK LOOK: Exodus 16:23—Moses told the people what the LORD commanded: "Tomorrow will be a day of rest. . . . It will be set apart for the LORD."

▷ The Israelites start complaining to Moses, wishing they were back in Egypt, where there was food. God hears them and decides to send food from the sky. He sends manna, a flaky bread, in the morning and meat at night.

▷ God tells them to gather food every day except the Sabbath, which is the seventh day of the week. God wants them to rest and trust Him to give them what they need.

▷ Out of nowhere, an enemy attacks them. Moses has Joshua pull an army together. God helps Joshua win the battle, and Moses gives God the name The LORD Is My Banner.

 TODAY'S GOD SHOT

God loves us so much that He wants us to take a day each week to rest and trust Him. He is a kind and loving God, and He's where the joy is!

ACTIVITY

Moses gave God the name The LORD Is My Banner. A banner is like a flag that armies hold up after they win. Draw a picture of what you think the banner looked like.

Exodus 19–21

 QUICK LOOK: Exodus 20:20—"Moses said to the people, 'Don't be afraid. God has come to test you. He wants you to have respect for him. That will keep you from sinning.'"

 RECAP

▶ Seven weeks after they leave Egypt, God leads the Israelites to Mount Sinai and asks to meet with them. They make themselves clean to prepare for His arrival.

▶ When God comes, a trumpet plays, a storm starts, and smoke covers the mountain as God comes down in fire. He calls Moses to come up the mountain and gives him the Ten Commandments.

▶ God gives Moses additional rules for how to treat people well and keep everything in order.

 TODAY'S GOD SHOT

God's commandments and laws aren't made for you to be afraid of Him. They are there to help you respect, follow, and love Him because He knows the best way to live. Following His laws will bring us joy, because He's where the joy is!

ACTIVITY

God's Ten Commandments are broken up into laws that point to God and laws that point to how to treat other people. Draw a line from each of the Ten Commandments to sort them into whether they point to God or to others. The first one has been done for you:

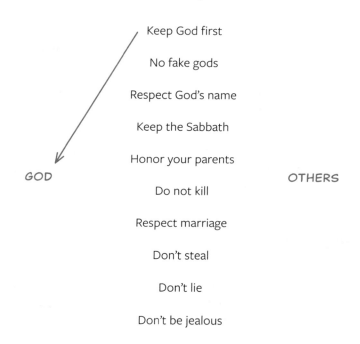

Keep God first

No fake gods

Respect God's name

Keep the Sabbath

Honor your parents

GOD   OTHERS

Do not kill

Respect marriage

Don't steal

Don't lie

Don't be jealous

Exodus 22–24

 QUICK LOOK: Exodus 23:9—The LORD said to Moses, "Do not treat outsiders badly. You yourselves know how it feels to be outsiders."

 RECAP

▶ God talks more about laws and rules to help keep everyone organized and safe while honoring and respecting life.

▶ Many of God's rules protect people who need it, such as the poor, women, widows, orphans, and outsiders—and even enemies. He cares about them all.

▶ God asks Moses to come up on Mount Sinai, where He will give him stone tablets with the laws written on them for the people. Moses stays there for forty days and forty nights.

 TODAY'S GOD SHOT

God wants us to be kind to enemies and outsiders because we were once God's enemy. He showed love and mercy to us even when we rejected Him. He wants us to follow His example and show love and mercy to others, because He's where the joy is!

 ACTIVITY

When have you met someone new who may have felt like an outsider?

....

What is one thing you did to make that person feel loved?

....

Exodus 25–27

 QUICK LOOK: Exodus 25:8—The LORD said to Moses, "Have them make a sacred tent for me. I will live among them."

 RECAP

▷ God asks the people to bring an offering, and they give gold, silver, bronze, and more.

▷ God gives His people directions for making a portable tabernacle, or tent, for Him to live in. He also gives specific instructions for the ark of the covenant, which is covered in gold and holds the tablets of the law.

▷ God's details have a specific purpose, and He gives instructions for the table for holy bread, a lampstand, an altar, and a courtyard.

 TODAY'S GOD SHOT

God goes into a lot of detail describing a place where He wants to meet with His people. He cares so much about meeting with you every day because He's where the joy is!

 ACTIVITY

God wants to meet with you every day. Circle the name of the place where you like to meet with God.

BEDROOM   KITCHEN   OUTSIDE   FAMILY ROOM   CAR   BUS

Exodus 28–29

 QUICK LOOK: Exodus 29:1—The LORD said to Moses, "Here is what you must do to set apart Aaron and his sons to serve me as priests."

 RECAP

▷ Aaron and Moses are from the tribe of Levi, named after one of Jacob's twelve sons. The Levites are set apart by God to be His priests.

▷ Since the priests are the ones offering sacrifices to God for the rest of the people, God is very detailed and serious about what they must wear in His presence.

▷ The priests have to show that they are spiritually clean before they can go work for God.

 TODAY'S GOD SHOT

Because God is holy, the priests had to do a lot of things to make themselves holy so they could be near Him. But God did that for us through Jesus! All we have to do now is believe in Jesus, and we get to be in God's presence. He's where the joy is!

 ACTIVITY

Color a picture of what the priests' robes might have looked like. (Hint: Reread Exodus 28 in your Bible.)

Exodus 30–32

QUICK LOOK: Exodus 32:8—The LORD said to Moses, "They have quickly turned away from what I commanded them. They have made themselves a metal statue of a god in the shape of a calf."

RECAP

▷ God gives more instructions to Moses and Joshua, including instructions for a census, where they count the people. Each person pays a tax of a fifth of an ounce of silver as an offering to God.

▷ God chooses two men who He fills with His Spirit, giving them unique skills for building the tabernacle. God wants everyone to take a day off from work and gives more details about the Sabbath day of rest.

▷ The people have a hard time waiting for Moses to come down from Mount Sinai and beg Aaron to build a gold calf for them to worship. When Moses returns and sees what the people have done, he gets so angry he breaks the stone tablets.

TODAY'S GOD SHOT

God wants us to trust His timing. He always has a plan He is working out to bring us close to Him, and sometimes waiting plays a part in that process. God being close to us is good, because He's where the joy is!

ACTIVITY

Is it hard for you to wait for something you have asked God for? Having patience means waiting with a happy heart! Pray this prayer asking God to help you have patience while you wait.

> *Dear God,* thank You for teaching me to wait on You. I trust Your
> timing to give me .... and will
> be patient by waiting with a happy heart. I love You. Amen!

Exodus 33–35

QUICK LOOK: Exodus 33:16—Moses said to the LORD, "You must go with us. How else will we be different from all the other people on the face of the earth?"

RECAP

▷ God tells Moses it's time for the people to head toward the land He has promised them but says He won't go with them.

▷ Moses talks with God just like a friend. Moses tells God he won't go to the promised land if He doesn't go. God agrees and then shows Moses His glory.

▷ God asks Moses to come up on Mount Sinai so He can write the Ten Commandments on stone tablets again. When Moses comes down from the mountain, his face is shining so much that the people are afraid, so he covers his face with a cloth.

TODAY'S GOD SHOT

God is the one who gives us our identity, making us special and set apart. He uses us to show the world His goodness and mercy. He's where the joy is!

ACTIVITY

Circle the words that describe God.

LOVING   MEAN   MERCIFUL   ANGRY

PATIENT   FRIEND   GOOD

Exodus 36–38

QUICK LOOK: Exodus 36:3—"The people kept bringing the offerings they chose to give. They brought them morning after morning."

▷ God gives specific workers knowledge and skill to build the tabernacle exactly how He wants it. Every morning people bring offerings to be used in it. They bring so much that Moses asks them to stop.

▷ Everything in the tabernacle has special meaning. The washing bowl shows how the people's sins are washed clean. The altar of incense teaches about prayer. The mercy seat is where God rests.

▷ The Israelites work hard and give generously because the tabernacle and God's presence are all they want.

TODAY'S GOD SHOT

God is here with you. He's close to you when things are good, when things are bad, and when you feel like nothing exciting is happening. Even on the not-exciting days, keep spending time in God's Word. Spending time with God, minute by minute, will always be worth the slow days, because He's where the joy is!

ACTIVITY

Which of these habits do you do day after day because it makes your life better?

- Brush teeth
- Put on shoes
- Eat breakfast
- Pray
- Spend time with family
- Read

Getting to know God more and more will happen every day that you spend time with Him. Just like those habits make your life better in the long run, so will time with God!

Exodus 39–40

QUICK LOOK: Exodus 40:35—"Moses couldn't enter the tent of meeting because the cloud had settled on it. The glory of the LORD filled the holy tent."

▷ After the tabernacle is complete, Moses blesses it. This reminds us of creation in the book of Genesis when God sees His completed work and blesses it.

▷ In the Bible, oil represents the Holy Spirit, so Moses places oil on all the furniture to set it apart to be used for God.

▷ God makes Aaron and his family priests.

TODAY'S GOD SHOT

When the tabernacle is completed, God's presence fills it so much that Moses can't even go inside. His presence fills our lives and hearts the same way today! He's where the joy is!

ACTIVITY

You just finished Exodus! Number these events in the order they happened in Genesis and Exodus.

.... The Israelites escape from Egypt.

.... God creates the heavens and the earth.

.... God gives Moses the Ten Commandments.

.... God promises to bless Abraham and his family.

.... Jacob moves his family to Egypt during a famine.

Leviticus 1–4

QUICK LOOK: Leviticus 2:9—The Lord told Moses, "All good things come from the Lord. The priest must take out the part of the grain offering that reminds you of this."

RECAP

▶ Leviticus is a book about our perfect and holy God, who wants to be close to His sinful, imperfect people.

▶ God speaks to Moses and tells him how He is going to help the people use offerings (or gifts) and sacrifices (perfect animals) to cover their sins.

▶ The word *sacrifice* in the Bible means to give up something valuable because we've done something wrong. God's people will sacrifice perfect, innocent animals (like lambs or goats) to receive God's forgiveness for their sins.

TODAY'S GOD SHOT

Even though the people continue to sin, God keeps providing sacrifices for them to give back to Him. God is so merciful and loving. He's where the joy is!

ACTIVITY

Without Jesus's sacrifice on the cross for our sins, we would still have to sacrifice animals like they did in Leviticus. Now, because Jesus sacrificed His life for ours, we simply admit we've done wrong, tell God we are sorry, and commit to changing how we live.

Take a minute to think about any wrong things you keep doing. Tell God you are sorry and receive His gift of forgiveness!

Leviticus 5–7

QUICK LOOK: Leviticus 6:7—The Lᴏʀᴅ said to Moses, "The priest will sacrifice the ram to pay for their sin. He will do it in my sight. And they will be forgiven for any of the things they did that made them guilty."

RECAP

▷ This section talks about being clean and unclean. Being unclean isn't a sin; everyone is unclean at some point.

▷ If a person is unclean, they just can't go into God's presence until they are clean again.

▷ When someone who is poor sins and has to make a sacrifice, God still makes a way for them. He lets poor people offer sacrifices that cost less because they have less.

TODAY'S GOD SHOT

God isn't afraid of our sin. He made a way for us to be with Him despite our sin because He wants to be near us. He loves us, and He's where the joy is!

ACTIVITY

What are your favorite words that describe God? Color the pictures on the next page.

Leviticus 8–10

QUICK LOOK: Leviticus 9:6—"Then Moses said, 'You have done what the LORD has commanded. So the glory of the LORD will appear to you.'"

▷ Moses follows God's rules for preparing Aaron and his four sons to be priests who offer sacrifices to God for the people. This takes seven days.

▷ On the eighth day, God's people have their first tabernacle service where sacrifices and offerings are made. Aaron and Moses bless the people.

▷ Then, the biggest blessing of all happens when the glory of the LORD appears to the people! Fire comes down from heaven and burns up the offering! The people shout for joy and worship God.

TODAY'S GOD SHOT

God's people did everything He asked them to do in preparation for the tabernacle, and they got to experience God's glory! When we spend time with God, He shows us more about who He is, and that makes us more like Him. He's where the joy is!

ACTIVITY

Since you've started reading the Bible, what is one way that you've become more like God? (For example, kinder, wiser, more patient, etc.)

....

....

Leviticus 11–13

 QUICK LOOK: Leviticus 11:44—The LORD said, "I am the LORD your God. Set yourselves apart. Be holy, because I am holy."

▷ God gives Moses rules about what foods to eat and what not to eat.

▷ Since there are no doctors, God gives a lot of details to help Moses and the priests know what to do if someone is sick.

▷ The priests are making sure healthy people stay healthy and sick people get better without infecting others.

 TODAY'S GOD SHOT

God calls Himself holy and asks us to follow His lead: "Be holy, because I am holy." He's the example on how to set ourselves apart, and He's where the joy is!

 ACTIVITY

If you want to live a holy life, you have to have a heart focused on what God wants and be willing to stand out from other people when you do what He says. Pray this prayer and ask Him to make you holy.

Dear God, You are holy and I am not. Give me a heart focused on what You want. Make me holy like You. I love You! Amen!

Leviticus 14–15

QUICK LOOK: Leviticus 14:2 NIV—The LORD said to Moses, "These are the regulations for any diseased person at the time of their ceremonial cleansing, when they are brought to the priest."

RECAP

▷ God is perfect and holy, and we are not. And there are many ways we're not. Some are because of our sin, while others are just because we live in a broken world.

▷ God gives rules for the Israelites to follow when the people have skin diseases, mold in a house, and other sicknesses.

▷ The rules and the sacrifices God asks His people to observe are shaping their hearts to follow Him.

TODAY'S GOD SHOT

God provides everything we need for healing, and as we follow Him, our lives will look different from the world. He's always working for our good because He's where the joy is!

ACTIVITY

Color the star next to the sentences that are TRUE about God.

 God has never sinned.

 God doesn't care about how we live.

 God wants us to be holy and live differently from the way the world lives.

Leviticus 16–18

QUICK LOOK: Leviticus 16:34—The LORD said, "Here is a law for you that will last for all time to come. Once a year you must pay for all the sin of the Israelites."

RECAP

▷ God gives specific instructions to Moses about how Aaron should go into the Most Holy Place, once a year, to offer sacrifices for the priests and the people.

▷ The priests bring two goats to the tabernacle. One goat takes all the people's sins and is sent out into the wilderness. The other is sacrificed to the LORD.

▷ God wants His people to look different from those who don't follow Him.

TODAY'S GOD SHOT

God had a plan all along for Jesus to pay the price to cover our sins, not just for a year but forever! He's where the joy is!

ACTIVITY

Connect the dots to make a cross as a reminder that Jesus paid the price for your sin once and for all.

Leviticus 19–21

 QUICK LOOK: Leviticus 21:15—The Lord said to Moses, "I am the Lord. I make him holy."

▷ God continues to give the Israelites laws and rules on how to organize the people and have peace.

▷ There are three types of laws that can help us understand what we are reading. *Civil laws* explain behaviors and punishments, *ceremonial laws* talk about sacrifices and being unclean, and *moral laws* talk about things that God says are right or wrong.

▷ Civil laws and ceremonial laws are important for the Israelites but not something we have to follow now. Moral laws still apply today.

 TODAY'S GOD SHOT

It can be exhausting reading all the laws and thinking you can never do them all perfectly! Thankfully, Jesus did all the work to keep the laws for us and took our sin so we can be holy with Him. He's where the joy is!

 ACTIVITY

Color the heart and write *Jesus* inside of it. When you give your heart to Jesus, He makes you holy like Him.

75

Leviticus 22–23

QUICK LOOK: Leviticus 22:31—The LORD said to Moses, "Obey my commands. Follow them. I am the LORD."

RECAP

▷ God wants His people to be clean, which means He wants them to stop doing wrong things. He keeps reminding them that He's the one who makes them clean.

▷ God reminds His people about the weekly Sabbath feast and six annual feasts that He wants them to celebrate.

▷ God wants His people to obey His commands.

TODAY'S GOD SHOT

It is impossible for God's people to follow His rules without His help. We're tempted to fix our eyes on ourselves and aim for perfection, but when we do that, we miss the fact that He has provided the perfect sacrifice in our place—Jesus! He's where the joy is!

ACTIVITY

Fill in the blanks for Leviticus 22:31.

"........................ MY .... FOLLOW THEM.

I AM THE ...."

Now read Romans 5:20: "The law was given so that sin would increase. But where sin increased, God's grace increased even more." Praise God for His grace!

Leviticus 24–25

RECAP

▷ God continues explaining how His people should live. They are still learning to trust Him.

▷ God creates a new kind of Sabbath command to let the fields rest every seven years. The number seven is a symbol for completion and perfection.

▷ God defends the poor, provides for the needy, and calls the rich to be helpers. He asks for His people to be kind to those in need.

TODAY'S GOD SHOT

When we remember how generous God is to give us everything we need, we can live openhandedly. We know that the things of this world will never make us happy, and they can never provide safety for us. Only He can do that because He's where the joy is!

ACTIVITY

God is generous, and we should be generous too! Write down one way you can be a helper to someone in need.

....

....

Leviticus 26–27

QUICK LOOK: Leviticus 26:11—The Lord said, "I will live among you. I will not turn away from you."

▷ God explains blessings for keeping the covenant, or promise, and curses for breaking it.

▷ If Israel remains faithful to God's laws and keeps His Sabbath, He'll bless them in clear ways with peace, abundance, and security.

▷ If God's people don't stay faithful to Him, five phases of curses will follow their disobedience. These curses are intended to help them turn from their sin.

TODAY'S GOD SHOT

God is providing an opportunity for His people to turn back to Him. Even when they disobey, if they humble themselves and repent, God forgives them. With God, it's impossible to be too far gone. He's working for our good and for our joy, to draw us back to Himself. He's where the joy is!

ACTIVITY

Think about how many times your parents have forgiven you for doing something wrong. Write them a card to thank them for forgiving you even when you did not deserve it.

Numbers 1–2

QUICK LOOK: Numbers 2:34—"So the Israelites did everything the LORD had commanded Moses."

 RECAP

▷ Today God and Moses meet up to talk again, and God tells Moses to take a census of all the men aged twenty and up from the twelve tribes.

▷ Judah's tribe is the largest of the twelve by far, twice the size of some of the other tribes.

▷ God tells Moses not to count the Levite tribe because their jobs and lives center around the tabernacle. God also gives orders on how to arrange the tribes in camps around the tabernacle.

 TODAY'S GOD SHOT

We see God building the people's trust in Him and His promises. Think of all they've been through since God first promised Abraham that He would give him children. No matter what they do or where they go, they cannot escape God's plan. On the good days and the hard days, He is always with them. He's where the joy is!

 ACTIVITY

In the Hebrew language, this book of the Bible is called In the Wilderness. What do you think of when you hear the word *wilderness*? Write down a few words that come to mind.

....

....

Numbers 3–4

QUICK LOOK: Numbers 3:12—The Lord said to Moses, "The Levites belong to me."

▷ God establishes Aaron and two of his sons as the heads of the tabernacle. The other people from their tribe, the Levites, are there to help them serve the people.

▷ We meet three different groups of people within the Levites: Gershonites, Kohathites, and Merarites. Each group of people has a specific assignment in caring for the tabernacle.

▷ The Levites are much smaller in number than all the other tribes. God gives them a position of honor, putting them right beside Himself and telling them to guard His tabernacle.

TODAY'S GOD SHOT

There are many ways we can serve the church and one another. Oftentimes, people only think about the ways to serve that are very noticeable to others, but God also honors those who serve in ways that no one ever sees. It gives us joy to serve because He's where the joy is!

ACTIVITY

God wants us to serve others. Write two ways you can serve your family today.

1. ....

2. ....

Numbers 5–6

 QUICK LOOK: Numbers 6:24–26—"May the LORD bless you and take good care of you. May the LORD smile on you and be gracious to you. May the LORD look on you with favor and give you peace."

 RECAP

▷ God wants to make sure His people are following His rules and the way of life He has called them to.

▷ God gives rules for people who want to set themselves apart to serve Him for a period of time. They are called Nazirites, and they make promises not to eat, drink, or touch specific things.

▷ God speaks to Moses and tells him how to bless the Israelites, His people.

 TODAY'S GOD SHOT

God loves to bless His people, and Numbers 6:24–26 is a blessing for you! It says, "May the LORD bless you and take good care of you. May the LORD smile on you and be gracious to you. May the LORD look on you with favor and give you peace." He's where the joy is!

 ACTIVITY

Pray this prayer.

Dear God, thank You for blessing me. I'm thankful for the way You take good care of me and smile on me with Your kindness. You give me favor and peace. I love You. Amen!

Numbers 7

 QUICK LOOK: Numbers 7:89—"Moses entered the tent of meeting. He wanted to speak with the LORD. There Moses heard the LORD talking to him."

 RECAP

▷ Moses finishes setting up the tabernacle and anoints it and everything inside with oil to set it apart for the LORD.

▷ Each tribe is assigned one day out of a twelve-day ceremony when its leaders will bring their offerings to the tabernacle.

▷ The Levites need help from other tribes and people. We see God provide for His people. He uses the gift of one to bless everyone.

 TODAY'S GOD SHOT

At the end of this twelve-day dedication period, Moses goes into the tabernacle to hear the LORD speak to him. A holy God is coming close to talk to sinful humans. Through spending time in God's Word, you will feel closer to Him and hear Him speak because He's where the joy is!

 ACTIVITY

Draw a ☆ next to the ways you hear God speaking to you.

I hear God when I read the Bible.

I hear God when I listen to worship music.

I hear God when I get quiet in my room.

I hear God when I go outside for a walk.

Numbers 8–10

QUICK LOOK: Numbers 8:6—The LORD said, "Take the Levites from among all the Israelites. Make them 'clean' in the usual way."

RECAP

▷ God tells Moses to purify the Levites. This is another way of telling him to make them clean.

▷ God gives instructions about celebrating the Passover. He opens up this celebration to the outsiders living among them, including the Egyptians who left Egypt with them. God is so welcoming and hospitable!

▷ God's people begin a new season moving through the wilderness on their way to the land God promised them. They camp where God camps, stay as long as God stays, and follow God wherever He leads them next.

TODAY'S GOD SHOT

God sets apart the Levites even though they're not particularly special, and even though they did nothing to deserve it. This is just God's generous, merciful plan, and He's been working it out all along. God invites all of us—no matter what we've done—to draw near and see that He's where the joy is!

ACTIVITY

What is one thing you learned about God today?

....

....

....

Numbers 11–13

QUICK LOOK: Numbers 11:1—"The people weren't happy about the hard times they were having. The LORD heard what they were saying."

▷ God is angry with His people for complaining about the hard times they are in and sends fire that falls on the camp. Moses prays, and the fire dies down.

▷ Moses tells God how hard it is to lead the people. God sends the power of His Spirit on seventy leaders who help him lead the people.

▷ God tells Moses to send twelve spies to check out the land He promised them. After forty days of scouting out Canaan and seeing how amazing it is, only two of the spies believe God's promise that they can take the land.

TODAY'S GOD SHOT

Even though His people complain, God hears their cries and provides for them. He's where the joy is!

ACTIVITY

Put a check mark by the one thing you complain about the most.

- ☐ Not enough screen time
- ☐ Being bored
- ☐ Doing your chores
- ☐ Homework
- ☐ Wanting a snack

Every time you are tempted to complain, stop and thank God for what you have. He gives you everything you need!

Numbers 14–15; Psalm 90

 QUICK LOOK: Psalm 90:16—"Show us your mighty acts. Let our children see your glorious power."

 RECAP

▷ God's people respond to the spies' report from the promised land with fear. Not only do they want to go back to Egypt, but they also want a new leader.

▷ God's Spirit comes to the tent of meeting. God tells Moses He is ready to kill everyone and start over, but Moses begs God not to. He reminds God of His promises, and God forgives them.

▷ God warns them that enemies are nearby and tells them to move south. They ignore God's directions and lose the battle. Psalm 90 is a prayer where Moses asks for God to be pleased with them and give them success.

 TODAY'S GOD SHOT

God's people are rebellious and disobedient. This could make God change His mind about giving them the promised land, but it doesn't! He says, "You are going to enter the land I am giving you as a home." Despite all their sin, He reminds them that He hasn't changed His mind. He keeps His promise. They're still His people. He's where the joy is!

 ACTIVITY

In Psalm 90:16, Moses asks God to let the Israelites' kids see His power. What is one way you have seen God's power in your life or in the stories your family members tell about their lives?

....

....

Numbers 16–17

QUICK LOOK: Numbers 16:48—"He stood between those alive and those dead. And the plague stopped."

RECAP

▷ Some of the men turn against Moses, disrespecting God's decision for him to be their leader. Moses challenges them to burn incense in cups to see who the LORD chooses to lead the people.

▷ God comes down and says that the people near the tents of the evil men should move. Moses tells the people that what God is going to do to them is not normal. God opens up the ground, and it swallows the evil men.

▷ The next day, the people come against Moses and Aaron again, and God is ready to kill everyone with a plague. Moses has Aaron take incense out and let its holy fragrance cover the people as a sacrifice for their sins.

TODAY'S GOD SHOT

Aaron risks his life to stop the plague and save people from death through this offering to God. This shows us a picture of Jesus, our great High Priest, who intervened, not just risking death, but facing it and defeating it on our behalf. His death makes us alive! He's where the joy is!

ACTIVITY

Unscramble the words that describe who God is.

UTJS ....   ODOG ....

RFAI ....   TIGRH ....

FRCEETP ....

Numbers 18–20

QUICK LOOK: Numbers 20:7–8—"The Lᴏʀᴅ said to Moses, 'Get your walking stick. You and your brother Aaron gather the people together. Then speak to that rock while everyone is watching. It will pour out its water.'"

RECAP

▷ God speaks directly to Aaron. He talks about how the priests and the Levites are supposed to care for the tabernacle.

▷ God gives more laws that have to do with people dying. Miriam, Moses' sister, is one of the people who died.

▷ The Israelites have been traveling for a long time and need water. God gives Moses specific instructions for getting water, but he hits the rock instead of speaking to it.

TODAY'S GOD SHOT

God's character is so consistent. Over and over, we see how He makes His rules, but His people disobey Him. While they have to deal with the consequences of their sins, He's ultimately so merciful, and He's where the joy is!

ACTIVITY

Does God give clear instructions to Moses for how to obey Him? Circle your answer.

YES   NO

God gives us clear instructions on how He wants us to live, but just like Moses, we sometimes disobey God. When we disobey, He is kind enough to forgive us!

Numbers 21–22

QUICK LOOK: Numbers 21:8—"The LORD said to Moses, 'Make a snake. Put it up on a pole. Then anyone who is bitten can look at it and remain alive.'"

RECAP

▷ The Israelites are closing in on the promised land and encounter another food and water shortage. Instead of asking God to help, like they know He can, they complain about Moses and God.

▷ God decides to send snakes to kill the people. When they confess and repent, Moses prays for them, and God shows mercy. God tells Moses to make a bronze snake and put it on a pole, and if anyone is bitten, they can look at it and live.

▷ King Balak of Moab hires a guy named Balaam to cast a spell on the Israelites because he's afraid of their power. God makes Balaam's donkey talk, and it's all a part of His plan to bless His people.

TODAY'S GOD SHOT

The snake on the pole points us to something greater that was to come. Jesus refers to this in John 3:14–15, "Moses lifted up the snake in the desert. In the same way, the Son of Man must also be lifted up. Then everyone who believes may have eternal life in him." That snake could only save people from physical death, offering temporary rescue, but Jesus saves us from spiritual death, giving eternal rescue. He's where the joy is!

ACTIVITY

Pray this prayer.

Dear God, I praise You for being so good to me! Thank You for forgiving me whenever I tell You that I have sinned and done wrong things. Thank You for Jesus's death on the cross and for saving me! Amen.

Count the objects, and write the totals in the circles below.

Numbers 23–25

QUICK LOOK: Numbers 23:21—Balaam said, "I don't see any trouble coming on the people of Jacob. I don't see any suffering in Israel. The LORD their God is with them."

RECAP

▷ The Canaanites believe you can speak things into existence, so King Balak hires Balaam to say bad things about the Israelites. But God gives Balaam a word to speak about them, and much to King Balak's dismay, it's a blessing.

▷ God's people are worshipping other false gods, specifically Baal.

▷ Because of their sin, God sends another plague, and many people die.

TODAY'S GOD SHOT

When God talks about Israel through the words of Balaam, He says things like "I don't see any trouble coming on the people of Jacob." Hasn't God brought trouble on His people? So what is He talking about? God knows He will send Jesus to pay the price for their sins. He sees their past and their future. He's outside of time, and He's where the joy is!

ACTIVITY

What does it mean for God to be outside of time? Circle the correct answer.

    A. God has existed before He created the earth as we know it.

    B. God sees and has planned everything that has and will happen.

    C. Both *a* and *b* are correct. Wow!

Psalm 90:2 says, "Before you created the whole world and the mountains were made, from the beginning to the end you are God." Think about this psalm today and remember how big God is!

Numbers 26–27

QUICK LOOK: Numbers 27:7—The Lord said to Moses, "What Zelophehad's daughters are saying is right. You must certainly give them property. Give them a share among their father's relatives. Give their father's property to them."

RECAP

▷ God tells Moses to count the men, making a list of them by their families. It's time for Moses and Eleazar to divide the land God is giving them.

▷ Zelophehad had no sons to give his inheritance to before he died. His five daughters approach Moses and Eleazar to ask for their father's portion of land, which has never been done before. Moses takes this request to God, and He orders Moses to give them what would've belonged to their father.

▷ God pulls Moses aside and lets him know that he's about to die, just like God promised. God says Moses will get to see the promised land from the top of the mountain before his death. God tells Moses to appoint Joshua as the next leader of His people.

TODAY'S GOD SHOT

God's response to the five daughters of Zelophehad shows us not only His great compassion and generosity but also His fairness. He fights for us to have what is best and right. He's where the truth is, but He's also where the joy is!

ACTIVITY

Reading about God giving Zelophehad's daughters their inheritance shows me that God . . .

....

....

Numbers 28–30

QUICK LOOK: Numbers 29:39—The LORD said to Moses, "Here are the offerings you must present to the LORD at your appointed feasts. They are burnt offerings, grain offerings, drink offerings and friendship offerings."

RECAP

▷ God outlines laws, feasts, and the religious calendar they'll follow once they're in the promised land.

▷ One of God's laws is to remember the Sabbath day. The Sabbath isn't just a day for doing nothing—it's a day for reconnecting with God.

▷ God required His people to make sacrifices. While we no longer offer sacrifices, we still need to be reminded that He's providing for us. There are two things in our lives that serve this purpose: giving to the church and Sabbath.

TODAY'S GOD SHOT

Out of all the Ten Commandments, there are two that God keeps repeating: to have no other gods before Him, and to rest. What other god commands rest? Most of our idols demand more from us—more striving, more trying, more doing. God says, "Nope. Not My people. My people are provided for even when they take a day off to spend with Me." He's where the rest is, and He's where the joy is!

ACTIVITY

Put a check mark next to the ways your family can celebrate a Sabbath day of rest. Remember, this is different for everyone, so choose things that you enjoy and that will help you connect with God and with your family:

☐ Go on a walk
☐ Watch a movie together
☐ Prepare a special meal
☐ Stay in your PJs
☐ Read the Bible together

☐ Play outside
☐ Name what you're thankful for
☐ Play a board game
☐ Eat breakfast together
☐ Go to church together

Numbers 31–32

 QUICK LOOK: Numbers 31:3—"So Moses said to the people, 'Prepare some of your men for battle. They must go to war against Midian. They will carry out the Lord's plan to punish Midian.'"

 RECAP

▷ God gives Moses his final assignment to go to war against the Midianites. They're the ones who led His people astray. Afterward, the Israelites count their men and find that not a single one died in battle!

▷ God's promised land for the twelve tribes is a sliver west of the Jordan River, east of the Mediterranean Sea. It's long and narrow, roughly the size of New Jersey.

▷ Reuben and Gad love living where they are and want to stay, even though this isn't the land God promised them.

 TODAY'S GOD SHOT

God takes our faithfulness to Him seriously. God wants to be first in our hearts, and He knows it's not easy for us to resist making other things more important than Him. He wants our deepest joy to be found in Him because He's where the joy is!

 ACTIVITY

Circle some of the things you might make more important than your relationship with God.

VIDEO GAMES   SPORTS   FRIENDS

PLAYING OUTSIDE   WATCHING TV

Tell God you are sorry for not putting Him first. Ask Him to help you remember how much joy you have when you spend time with Him.

Numbers 33–34

QUICK LOOK: Numbers 33:52—The Lord said, "Drive out all those living in the land. The statues of their gods are made out of stone and metal. Destroy all those statues."

RECAP

▷ Moses remembers and lists all the places where they've camped.

▷ God tells Moses to make sure they drive out all of the people who live in Canaan, the land God promised them. They also need to tear down their altars and their idols.

▷ Nine and a half tribes settle in what was originally known as the promised land, and two and a half tribes settle in the bonus land on the other side of the Jordan River.

TODAY'S GOD SHOT

God defeats His enemies, including other gods. He never denies that there are other gods that people worship. Instead, He says no other gods should get our affection and attention. He's the one true God, and He's where the joy is!

ACTIVITY

We are all tempted to make other things in our lives more important than God, but He is the only one who can truly give us joy. Pray this prayer, and fill in the blank with anything you have been putting before God in your life.

Dear God, thank You for Your love and for always being with me.

Forgive me when I make other things like ....

.... *more important than spending time with You. Help*

me to remember the joy You give me. I love You. Amen!

Numbers 35–36

QUICK LOOK: Numbers 36:6—Moses said, "Here is what the Lᴏʀᴅ commands for Zelophehad's daughters. They can marry anyone they want to. But they have to marry someone in their own family's tribe."

RECAP

▷ While the Levites don't get to inherit land, they still need a place to live and keep their things. God's plan for this is to have each tribe donate a bit of their land to the Levites.

▷ As they continue planning their land divisions, some of the people realize that the five daughters of Zelophehad, who are a part of the tribe of Manasseh, might lose their tribe's inheritance if they happen to marry people outside of their tribe.

▷ The daughters marry within the tribe. Everyone is provided for in God's plan for His people.

TODAY'S GOD SHOT

God cares about the details of our lives. Out of three million people, God pays attention to five women. He writes a new law addressing their situation. He cares. That's one of the ways He keeps us near. With each new need, we should rejoice that He keeps us coming to Him for direction, because He's where the joy is!

ACTIVITY

Circle the emoji that shows how you feel knowing God cares about every detail in your life.

Deuteronomy 1–2

 QUICK LOOK: Deuteronomy 2:7—"For these forty years the LORD your God has been with you. So you have had everything you need."

 RECAP

▷ Deuteronomy is the third most frequently quoted book in the New Testament, and it's one of the most quoted by Jesus. *Deuteronomy* means "second law."

▷ Moses goes over highlights of their time in the desert since leaving Egypt—all God has done for them and all the things that have gone wrong because of their sins.

▷ Moses encourages them about upcoming battles. They're most afraid of the giants in the land.

 TODAY'S GOD SHOT

God blesses anyone He wants to, even if they have not made a decision to be part of His family. For those of us who belong to Him, we are blessed by having a relationship with Him that will last forever. Temporary blessings like land and possessions might bring some level of happiness, but we know *He's* where the joy is!

 ACTIVITY

Write out three ways God has blessed you.

1. ....

2. ....

3. ....

Deuteronomy 3–4

QUICK LOOK: Deuteronomy 4:9—"Don't forget the things your eyes have seen. As long as you live, don't let them slip from your mind. Teach them to your children and their children after them."

RECAP

▷ Our reading today starts out by showing us the battles that were won over King Og of Bashan and King Sihon of the Amorites. We see that even the cities with high walls, gates, and bars are not impossible for God to win.

▷ God tells Moses to encourage and strengthen Joshua for the task ahead of him. Joshua will be the one who leads the people into the promised land.

▷ Moses turns from focusing on their past to focusing on their future. He calls them to obey God's laws and be different from the people around them doing wicked things. God also calls them to remember what He has done for them.

TODAY'S GOD SHOT

God is patient with us while we learn His character. And as we learn it, we find out more and more that trusting God is where the joy is, because *He's* where the joy is!

ACTIVITY

Circle the word that describes God from what we read today!

MEAN   PATIENT   FRUSTRATED   LOUD

Deuteronomy 5–7

QUICK LOOK: Deuteronomy 6:4–5—"The LORD is our God. The LORD is the one and only God. Love the LORD your God with all your heart and with all your soul. Love him with all your strength."

RECAP

▷ Today Moses says God's covenant, or promise, is not with their fathers—it's with them. He is reminding them they have their own relationship with Him.

▷ In chapter 6 we see the beginning of a prayer called the Shema, which means "hear." Religious Jews pray this prayer twice a day.

▷ God is punishing the wicked nations for their rebellion and using Israel as a tool to accomplish that justice. He's protecting the hearts of His people from other gods who are not as great as He is.

TODAY'S GOD SHOT

God is so generous to His people! But He also wants them to remember who gave them everything. He doesn't want them to take it for granted and turn to other gods when they get good things from Him. He wants to remind them of the relationship He's in with them. He's after our hearts, He's after our joy, and He's where the joy is!

ACTIVITY

Write down today's verse on a piece of paper. Stick that paper somewhere that you will see every day—like beside your bed or on your mirror. Then give yourself a challenge to memorize it!

Deuteronomy 8–10

 QUICK LOOK: Deuteronomy 10:14—"The heavens belong to the LORD your God. Even the highest heavens belong to him. He owns the earth and everything in it."

 RECAP

▷ Moses continues talking to the new generation of Israelites before they enter the promised land. He reminds them that the promised land will not be easy.

▷ God gives warnings about pride. Pride makes us forget God and puts our eyes on ourselves or our enemies. We fight these lies by remembering who God is and what He has done.

▷ Moses reminds them that God's rules aren't about taking away their joy and freedom but about increasing them.

 TODAY'S GOD SHOT

God owns everything, yet He still chose to look after and love you. It is not because of any good works you have done; it is because He chose you! If we remember who we are and who He is, we can't help but want to be near Him and spend time with Him! He's where the joy is!

 ACTIVITY

On the next page, find the things that belong to God.

```
G  W  A  H  S  F  R  Z  P  G  V  C
G  A  S  M  O  O  N  I  E  C  X  V
K  L  E  Y  O  A  G  I  O  K  O  K
G  Q  E  Z  U  R  M  E  P  W  L  O
X  P  R  L  T  N  D  H  L  N  D  O
O  T  T  D  L  U  I  N  E  I  N  C
H  E  A  V  E  N  S  V  D  A  I  E
E  A  R  T  H  L  U  T  E  R  W  A
V  D  B  L  K  V  N  N  I  R  L  N
A  V  B  I  R  D  S  Y  P  M  S  Y
V  M  O  U  N  T  A  I  N  S  E  E
S  T  A  R  S  V  Q  Y  Q  U  H  N
```

WORD BANK

HEAVENS	UNIVERSE	OCEAN	MOON	RAIN
EARTH	SUN	TREES	STARS	WIND
PEOPLE	BIRDS	MOUNTAINS	TIME	

If you need help, check out the Word Search Answer Key on page 471.

Deuteronomy 11–13

 QUICK LOOK: Deuteronomy 12:7—"You and your families will eat at the place the LORD your God will choose. He will be with you there. You will find joy in everything you have done. That's because he has blessed you."

 RECAP

▷ God tells the Israelites, and us, to love Him. It is impossible to fully love something or someone that you do not know or even pay attention to.

▷ Moses tells them to pay attention to their hearts, because it could be easy to put other things or people above God if they're not careful.

▷ Even a false prophet can be right, but that doesn't mean we should follow them or seek truth from them. All of these laws are supposed to stop people from rebelling, and the laws are a necessary step in God's plan to restore humanity's relationship with Him. They are meant to protect everyone.

 TODAY'S GOD SHOT

God tells us that we can be filled with joy. He's with us everywhere we go, He blesses us, and He's where the joy is!

ACTIVITY

When you're joyful, it shows on your face and on the faces of those around you. Draw a picture of your family below. Be sure to give everyone a joyful, happy face!

Deuteronomy 14–16

> **QUICK LOOK:** Deuteronomy 15:10—"So give freely to needy people. Let your heart be tender toward them. Then the LORD your God will bless you in all your work. He will bless you in everything you do."

 RECAP

▷ Moses is giving his final speech to the Israelites before he dies and they enter the promised land. He delivers a lot of laws for the people to obey.

▷ God says if they're faithful to His commands, there'll always be enough to go around; the poor will be cared for by the surplus of the wealthy. He'll bless them so much that other nations will borrow from them and they'll never have to borrow.

▷ God calls them to remember where they came from and what He has done for them; it'll keep them humble and grateful.

 TODAY'S GOD SHOT

God wants to bless everything we do. He is after our joy! In Psalm 16:11 David says, "In your presence there is fullness of joy" (ESV). And David is right about God: He's where the joy is!

 ACTIVITY

Circle the words that describe who God is to you:

FAITHFUL   GENEROUS   PRESENT

GOOD   KIND   HUMBLE

Deuteronomy 17–20

QUICK LOOK: Deuteronomy 19:8—"The LORD your God will increase the size of your territory. He promised your people of long ago that he would do it. He will give you the whole land he promised them."

RECAP

▷ Moses has been giving laws for how things will shift once they're no longer camping in the desert. The laws create conflict for the people, so God sets up a court of judges and priests to help carry out justice.

▷ Moses predicts there'll be a day when they look around and think about how all the other nations have kings and decide they want one too! So he establishes laws for the future king.

▷ God is keeping His promise of giving land to Israel. He wants to make sure they know He is the one true God, and He wants Israel to bring justice to the wicked nations.

TODAY'S GOD SHOT

When Moses established the laws for the people, it became obvious that they would disobey them, just as we do today. But God, full of love, made a way for Jesus to take the punishment for every law we have broken and every wrong thing we have done. God is patient with us when we sin against Him and question His heart. Even when we don't believe it or remember it, He's where the joy is!

ACTIVITY

Draw a ☆ next to the times God has been patient with you.

When I show my anger by hitting someone or something

When I get lazy and don't do my homework

When I am disrespectful toward the adults in my life

When I have negative thoughts about myself

Deuteronomy 21–23

PARENTAL
MATURE CONTENT IN TODAY'S BIBLE PASSAGE
GUIDANCE

QUICK LOOK: Deuteronomy 23:5—"The Lᴏʀᴅ your God wouldn't listen to Balaam. Instead, he turned the curse into a blessing for you. He did it because he loves you."

RECAP

▷ Moses continues to share instructions on the laws for the people of Israel. These laws give really clear rules for adults' relationships with each other.

▷ God is meeting the people where they are and giving them a foundation for treating others with respect.

▷ While we don't know all the reasons behind these laws, Bible teachers suggest they're to remind the Israelites of the importance of being set apart from nations that don't follow YHWH.

TODAY'S GOD SHOT

In today's reading, Moses says, "The Lᴏʀᴅ your God turned the curse into a blessing for you, because the Lᴏʀᴅ your God loved you." God took the thing we deserve—what we've fully earned, the curse—and absorbed it Himself through His death on the cross so that we might receive the blessing, just like the Israelites did. He's where the joy is!

ACTIVITY

Do the crossword puzzle on the next page to discover some of the ways God has blessed you.

ACROSS

3. A building for people to live in

4. Things worn to cover your body

6. A road vehicle used to carry people

7. Things you eat

8. A group of people related to each other

DOWN

1. Activities like soccer and football

2. Well-being

5. Where students go to learn

8. Enjoyable, amusing

Deuteronomy 24–27

 QUICK LOOK: Deuteronomy 26:18—"Today the LORD has announced that you are his people. He has said that you are his special treasure. He promised that you would be. He has told you to keep all his commands."

 RECAP

▷ In Moses' final speech, we encounter a wide variety of laws, including the only law about divorce in the Old Testament, and it's very specific.

▷ Other laws show us how God is protective of all human life. He disapproves of slavery and kidnapping and wants to protect the poor.

▷ Moses gives a few instructions for when they enter into the promised land, which is in the near future. He says six tribes will climb Mount Gerizim and six will climb Mount Ebal while the Levite priests declare the curses.

 TODAY'S GOD SHOT

God calls Israel His special treasure, above all the nations He made. He's put His name on them. How beautiful to be treasured, possessed, and loved infinitely by an infinitely lovable God. He's where the joy is!

 ACTIVITY

Have you wondered where Israel is in relation to where you are? God chose His special people to be from a very small country that you can visit today! Spend time praying for God to bless and protect Israel.

Deuteronomy 28–29

 QUICK LOOK: Deuteronomy 29:29—"The LORD our God keeps certain things hidden. But he makes other things known to us and to our children forever. He does it so we can obey all the words of this law."

 RECAP

▷ As Moses reviews the blessings and curses of the covenant, he reminds the people that blessings await them if they obey God.

▷ If they don't follow God, curses will come. And they sound terrible! Covenant curses are typically the complete opposite of the blessings.

▷ Moses encourages the people to do what God has shown them and to trust God with the things they can't see.

 TODAY'S GOD SHOT

God reveals things to His people but also keeps some things hidden. It's good that we don't know everything. It's good that we have to walk in step with Him, trusting His goodness. Regardless of what we know or don't know, He's working for our good. And one thing we do know is that He's where the joy is!

 ACTIVITY

What are some things about God you still don't know?

1. ....

2. ....

3. ....

Take some time over the next few weeks to ask God and also the people you trust to help you know more.

Deuteronomy 30–31

QUICK LOOK: Deuteronomy 31:6—Moses said, "The LORD your God will go with you. He will never leave you. He'll never desert you."

RECAP

▷ Moses gives the people a choice. They can choose life and success or death and harm all by choosing whether to obey God.

▷ Moses wants the people to experience not just the land God promised, but also the life that's only found in friendship with God.

▷ God makes Joshua the new leader of His people and reminds him, "I'll be with you." Joshua will need that reminder soon when Moses dies and the people question God's love and presence.

TODAY'S GOD SHOT

God knows we will doubt and forget Him. But He loves us still. He sets His heart on us. No one else loves like Him—He's where the joy is!

ACTIVITY

Memorize the first part of Deuteronomy 31:6 by filling in the blanks. Write down this verse on a note card and put it on your refrigerator or mirror to help you remember it.

"THE LORD YOUR .... WILL GO WITH

YOU. HE WILL NEVER .... YOU. HE'LL NEVER

.... YOU."

Deuteronomy 32–34;
Psalm 91

QUICK LOOK: Psalm 91:14—"The LORD says, 'I will save the one who loves me. I will keep him safe, because he trusts in me.'"

RECAP

▷ God told Moses to write a song about the Israelites' past, present, and future. It calls for Israel to pay attention to God's greatness.

▷ After Moses sings his song, God tells him which mountain he'll die on. From the top of that mountain, he'll see the promised land. Then he offers a final blessing to eleven of the twelve tribes.

▷ After Moses blesses them, he goes up on the mountain, sees the promised land, and dies, old and strong. Then we see something strange and beautiful: God buries Moses—not on Mount Nebo, where he died, but in the valley in a spot no one knows.

TODAY'S GOD SHOT

As you spend time with God every day, your love for Him will grow. You are learning to trust Him because of who He is. He will keep you safe and give you joy—because He's where the joy is!

ACTIVITY

Do you have a favorite worship song? Spend some time listening to it and thanking God for how great He is just like Moses did!

Joshua 1–4

QUICK LOOK: Joshua 1:9—The Lord said to Joshua, "Be strong and brave. Do not be afraid. Do not lose hope. I am the Lord your God. I will be with you everywhere you go."

▷ Today we step into the first of the history books, and while they do reveal history, their primary goal is to reveal God. Both God and the Israelites tell Israel's new leader, Joshua, to be strong and courageous.

▷ Joshua sends two spies to Jericho, the first city across the promised land's border. The spies have two main goals here: Stay safe and get a good view of the city's layout.

▷ These spies believe in God's promise to give them the land. When they give Joshua the good news, he rallies everyone to cross into the promised land.

TODAY'S GOD SHOT

God repeatedly tells Joshua to be strong and courageous. And every time God gives this command, He follows it with the promise that He'll be with him. True strength and courage come through being mindful of God's presence in our lives. He's where the strength is. He's where the courage is. And He's where the joy is!

ACTIVITY

Memorize Joshua 1:9 by writing each word on a Post-it Note and putting them on your refrigerator or another visible place. Remove a word each day as you practice saying it. Ask a grown-up if you can reward yourself with ice cream, or another favorite treat, when you can say it without help!

Joshua 5–8

 QUICK LOOK: Joshua 6:20—"The priests blew the trumpets. As soon as the army heard the sound, they gave a loud shout. Then the wall fell down. Everyone charged straight in. So they took the city."

 RECAP

▷ The Israelites just set foot in the promised land for the first time as a nation. Their enemies still live there, and the first city they plan to take is Jericho.

▷ As Joshua nears Jericho, he sees a man with a sword. When Joshua asks whose side he is on, the man says that he's not on either side but has come as the commander of the LORD's army. Joshua believes he's in God's presence and bows down in worship.

▷ God tells Joshua that Jericho is theirs but they must follow His special instructions.

 TODAY'S GOD SHOT

As they took their first six trips around Jericho, they probably thought all the walking was a waste of time. Maybe you feel like that some days in our reading plan or in prayer. God is at work, even on the "nothing" days, when obedience feels like we're walking in circles. Listening to Him is the best place to be, even when we don't fully understand, because He's where the joy is!

 ACTIVITY

How many days in a row have you spent time with God? .... The Israelites obeyed God seven days in a row! You can be really proud of yourself for however many days you wrote down! Each day you set aside time for God, He is ready and excited to spend time with you.

Joshua 9–11

QUICK LOOK: Joshua 10:14—"There has never been a day like it before or since. It was a day when the Lord listened to a mere human being. Surely the Lord was fighting for Israel!"

RECAP

▷ The Gibeonites trick the Israelites by asking Israel to enter a protective covenant even though they don't qualify for one. Joshua agrees without asking God, accidentally making a covenant with his enemies.

▷ Instead of killing the Gibeonites, the Israelites assign them to manual labor in the service of the temple. Even God's enemies who have deceived God's people end up serving God's purposes and glory.

▷ God uses miracles—even making the sun stand still so the day is longer—to help Israel defeat six more cities. Joshua is starting to listen carefully to God, and because of God's unique covenant with His people, they continue to see victory in battle when they obey.

TODAY'S GOD SHOT

Joshua set his heart to obey God, but God didn't grant him an immediate victory. In fact, God lengthened his day. Joshua asked for something impossible and God granted it, but it didn't come the easy way. He had to fight longer. Even when it feels impossible, God is still working on our behalf because He's where the joy is!

ACTIVITY

What is something impossible that you are asking God for?

....

....

Joshua 12–15

QUICK LOOK: Joshua 13:6—The LORD said to Joshua, "I myself will drive out those people to make room for the Israelites. Make sure you set that land apart for Israel. Give it to them as their share, just as I have directed you."

RECAP

▷ The Israelites won a lot of wars and took a lot of land. The land divisions are listed in these chapters because this information adds to our faith historically and archaeologically.

▷ Joshua is pretty old, but God says He's not done with him. There's still more land to take, so he's not going to die yet. God will do the heavy lifting for them and drive out the inhabitants Himself. Then Joshua and Caleb, who were sent into the promised land as spies almost forty years earlier, talk about the blessings that come from obeying God.

▷ Judah is the largest tribe by far, so they get the largest plot of land, which is mostly desert. Judah couldn't drive out the Jebusites who were living in Jerusalem.

TODAY'S GOD SHOT

God cares about our obedience. God is at work to shape our hearts, to do us good, and to defeat our enemies. Even when we fail to obey Him, our trust can grow, and joy can be found—because He's where the joy is!

ACTIVITY

When was the last time you obeyed God?

....

Circle the emoji that shows how you felt when you obeyed Him.

Joshua 16–18

QUICK LOOK: Joshua 17:4—"The daughters of Zelophehad went to Eleazar the priest and to Joshua, the son of Nun. They also went to the other leaders. They said, 'The Lord commanded Moses to give us our share of land among our male relatives.'"

▷ Today we encounter all the drama surrounding dividing the land. The allotment for Joseph's descendants takes us back to the day when his dad, Jacob, formally adopted his sons, Ephraim and Manasseh.

▷ Most of the tribes aren't driving out the Canaanites like God repeatedly commanded them to.

▷ In other land-allotment news, the daughters of Zelophehad approach Joshua and Eleazar, giving them a little nudge about the land God promised them, and the new leaders follow God's orders.

TODAY'S GOD SHOT

Jerusalem is surrounded by three valleys that come together to form a sideways number three. To an Israelite, it's clearly the Hebrew letter *shin*, the first letter of the word *Shaddai*, which means "God Almighty." The Israelites regard this letter as God's initial, and it marks their land. God chose to love and mark His people, despite our sins, and He's where the joy is!

ACTIVITY

Do you see the letter *shin*? What do you think it means for Jerusalem to be marked by the first letter of the word that means "God Almighty"?

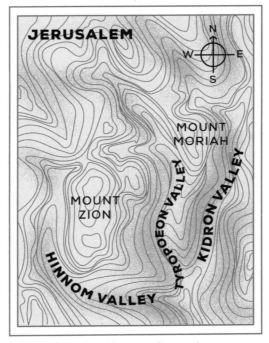

Topographic map of Jerusalem

Letter *shin*

Joshua 19–21

 QUICK LOOK: Joshua 21:45—"The Lord kept all the good promises he had made to the Israelites. Every one of them came true."

 RECAP

▶ Land assignments are very important to God's people. These assignments are marked out to be the home of their tribe.

▶ Since Joshua was one of the two spies who believed God forty-five years earlier, he gets to choose where he wants to live. But he lets everyone else get their land first.

▶ After the land is distributed, cities of refuge are set up where someone who accidentally kills another person can live without fear of someone seeking to kill them in return.

 TODAY'S GOD SHOT

God shows so much of His character by giving the people land and providing cities of refuge. God is generous and faithful. He offers them kindness and forgiveness. He has given them everything they need, but most important of all is Himself—because He's where the joy is!

 ACTIVITY

God keeps His promises. Read the promise below.

I leave my peace with you. I give my peace to you. I do not give it to you as the world does. Do not let your hearts be troubled. And do not be afraid.

John 14:27

What does this tell you about God?

....

....

1

> God will ❤️ me ∞

Your answer:

God will _____ me _____

2

> When I 🙏 , God will always 👂 me

Your answer:

When I _____ , God will always _____ me

3

> God will give me 💪 when I am 😩

Your answer:

God will give me _____ when I am _____

Joshua 22–24

 QUICK LOOK: Joshua 23:14—Joshua said, "The LORD your God has kept all the good promises he gave you. Every one of them has come true. Not one has failed to come true. And you know that with all your heart and soul."

 RECAP

▷ As Joshua nears death, he tells the leaders of the Israelites that while God has accomplished good things for them, they still need to drive out the lingering Canaanites.

▷ God has equipped them with all they need to obey Him; they can drive out the people because God has promised them that land, so they need to do it.

▷ Joshua challenges God's people, telling them they can serve YHWH, or they can serve these other gods. The people respond with a hearty promise that they'll follow YHWH.

 TODAY'S GOD SHOT

For the first time since God called Abraham, the people are living in at least partial fulfillment of all three of the promises He made to them: They've become a great nation, they have a blessed relationship with YHWH, and they're living in the promised land. God hasn't failed. He wasn't failing them in the desert when these things hadn't yet been fulfilled, and He isn't failing them now. He's failproof, and He's where the joy is!

 ACTIVITY

Pray this prayer.

Father God, thank You for the promises You have made to me. I know that You are always working good in my life just like You did for Joshua and Your people. Is there a way I can serve You today? I'm willing to do whatever You ask! In Jesus's name, amen!

Judges 1–2

QUICK LOOK: Judges 2:20—"So the Lord became very angry with the Israelites. He said, 'This nation has broken my covenant. I made it with their people of long ago. But this nation has not listened to me.'"

RECAP

▷ At the beginning of Judges, Israel starts out strong after Joshua's death by asking God for help. They want to get rid of the Canaanites just like God commanded.

▷ God shows up as the Angel of the LORD to tell them they are wrong for keeping Canaanites in their land and there will be consequences for their actions.

▷ God raises up judges from among them to help lead them, but they reject these leaders and continue in wickedness.

TODAY'S GOD SHOT

God is faithful to keep His covenant, or promise, with His people. He is patient and willing to forgive them. He's not trying to force obedience without a relationship. He's after their hearts. Nothing changes unless hearts change. God's love for us prompts our hearts to love Him back because He's where the joy is!

ACTIVITY

God loves us and wants us to love Him with all of our heart. Is there anything you are tempted to love more than God? Circle yes or no.

YES   NO

Tell God you are sorry and ask for His forgiveness and for help to love Him the most.

Judges 3–5

QUICK LOOK: Judges 5:31—Deborah and Barak sang, "Lord, may all your enemies be destroyed. But may all who love you be like the morning sun. May they be like the sun when it shines the brightest."

▷ God is very angry with His people and hands them over to the king of Aram to be slaves. They cry out to God, and He raises up Othniel, the first judge and military leader, to save them. They have peace for forty years.

▷ There are two more judges who rescue God's people after they fall into sin and get captured by their enemies.

▷ The people sin again, and God sells them into slavery for twenty years under King Jabin. God raises up Deborah, the judge who honors Him the most. She sings a song when God gives them victory over the enemy.

TODAY'S GOD SHOT

God chooses unlikely leaders to show who He is. He doesn't just see potential in people—He knows there is potential! We love stories of underdog champions. They bring Him glory, and they bring us joy because they point to Him, and He's where the joy is!

ACTIVITY

Name two characteristics of the leaders God appointed in Judges.

1. ....

2. ....

Thank God for using unlikely leaders to show us His heart for the overlooked.

Judges 6–7

QUICK LOOK: Judges 6:12—"The angel of the LORD appeared to Gideon. He said, 'Mighty warrior, the LORD is with you.'"

RECAP

▷ Forty years after their victory over King Jabin, the Israelites fall into sin again and are so afraid of the Midianites that they hide in caves, and the Midianites eat all their food supply.

▷ God tells a man named Gideon to save Israel from the Midianites, but he is afraid and pushes back. God orders him to tear down the idols and build an altar to God. He obeys but does it in the middle of the night to avoid getting caught.

▷ Gideon struggles with fear and asks God to give him multiple signs that he is to attack the Midianites. God gives Gideon and his army victory!

TODAY'S GOD SHOT

Gideon doubts God a lot, and God never gets angry with him for it. God meets him in his questions. He comes alongside him to give him courage. Gideon needs to hear who God is. God doesn't counter Gideon's doubt by telling him how great he is and puffing him up. Instead, God tells Gideon who *He* is and says, "I am with you." And He's with you. And He's where the joy is!

ACTIVITY

What is one question you have about God?

....

....

Ask God to help you trust Him with your doubt. You can also ask a leader in your life to help you know the answer.

Judges 8–9

QUICK LOOK: Judges 8:34—"They forgot what the LORD their God had done for them. He had saved them from the power of their enemies all around them."

RECAP

▶ Gideon wants to be king. He even names his son Abimelech, which means "my father is king." Abimelech takes over his dad's role, making himself king, and kills all of his brothers except one named Jotham.

▶ The Shechemite leaders make Abimelech "king," but it isn't real. Jotham goes to the top of Mount Gerizim and tells them that Abimelech isn't a worthy king.

▶ God sends an evil spirit that causes a division between Abimelech and his people, showing that even evil bends to God's will. Meanwhile, the Shechemites start to look for Abimelech's replacement, which leads to more fighting.

TODAY'S GOD SHOT

When we love something, we want to defend and protect it. When it comes to God's name and His people, He is very protective. Even in the people's wickedness, He's still protecting them from evil. He's where the joy is!

ACTIVITY

Circle the words that describe who God is to you.

JUST   EVIL   LOVING   MEAN   PROTECTIVE

Judges 10–12

QUICK LOOK: Judges 10:16—"Then they got rid of the false gods that were among them. They served the LORD. And he couldn't stand to see Israel suffer anymore."

RECAP

▷ The Israelites are worshipping other gods. They'll worship anything, it seems. God grows angry and sells them into the hands of two people groups, the Philistines and the Ammonites.

▷ Israel gets rid of the false gods and cries out to YHWH for help. But this time, God is not going to raise up a judge to save them like He's done in the past.

▷ The leaders of Israel appoint Jephthah to lead the battle against the Ammonites. Jephthah is desperate and in a hurry and makes an unwise vow to God in an effort to win the war.

TODAY'S GOD SHOT

God wants what is best for us even more than we do! When the Israelites keep choosing sin, He lets them hit rock bottom, but all the while His heart is sad when His kids are suffering, and He draws near. If you feel miserable from your own sin, remember His great salvation! He's with you, and He's where the joy is!

ACTIVITY

List two things you want to be true about your life:

1. ....

2. ....

You can believe that God wants those things for your life if they are in line with what He knows is best.

127

Judges 13–15

QUICK LOOK: Judges 13:5—The Angel of the Lord said, "He will be set apart to God from the day he is born. He will take the lead in saving Israel from the power of the Philistines."

RECAP

▷ God's people have fallen into sin again and are being ruled by the Philistines. The Angel of the Lord tells the wife of Manoah that she'll have a son who'll help rescue Israel. His name is Samson.

▷ God says Samson must vow to never drink alcohol, cut his hair, or touch dead things. Samson grows prideful and secretly breaks each rule of his vow.

▷ Samson has supernatural strength given to him by God that he uses to overpower the Philistines.

TODAY'S GOD SHOT

Even though Samson is prideful and full of rage, God uses him to defeat Israel's enemy. When God uses sinful people for his righteous plan, He's not telling us that their sin is okay. He's telling us that their sin isn't big enough to ruin God's bigger plan! He uses us and even brings us joy in the process. He's where the joy is!

ACTIVITY

God has a purpose for your life. What do you think that purpose is?

....

....

Judges 16–18

QUICK LOOK: Judges 16:28—"Then he prayed to the LORD. Samson said, 'LORD and King, show me that you still have concern for me. Please, God, make me strong just one more time. Let me pay the Philistines back for what they did to my two eyes. Let me do it with only one blow.'"

RECAP

▷ Samson doesn't seem to take God's call on his life seriously. He doesn't keep his vow to God, and his sin costs him.

▷ At first, Samson refers to God by His generic name, Elohim, not His personal name, YHWH. This shows us how he views God; it's the difference between knowing God and knowing *about* God. When he is in need, on the final day of his life, he calls on YHWH.

▷ A man named Micah tries to use God for selfish gain by setting up a temple in his house and appointing his own priest. The tribe of Dan finds out about his gods and his priest and comes and takes them from him.

TODAY'S GOD SHOT

Samson doesn't call God by His name until the end of his life. God helps him in his hour of need. He doesn't say, "No, you've messed up too many times." God is always coming after us, even when we try to run away from Him! He's where the joy is!

ACTIVITY

Take a deep breath in. Now let it out. What sound do you hear?

YH-WH

Isn't it amazing that the personal name for God, YHWH, is the sound of our breath? When you take breaths today, remember God is close and He loves you!

Judges 19–21

PARENTAL
MATURE CONTENT
IN TODAY'S
BIBLE PASSAGE
GUIDANCE

QUICK LOOK: Judges 21:25 NIV—"In those days Israel had no king; everyone did as they saw fit."

RECAP

▷ In these chapters, a horrible crime happens that proves how wicked the people are. They are living however they want, and a Levite man's actions are proof that something needs to be done.

▷ The tribes of Israel seek justice with the tribe of Benjamin, which leads to a three-day battle. Israel asks God for guidance, and He gives them victory.

▷ Israel makes other decisions without asking God. They don't do things His way, and their decisions lead to a bigger mess.

TODAY'S GOD SHOT

There wasn't much joy in today's reading because there wasn't much God. The last line reminds us that everyone did whatever made them happy. They didn't show love for God in any way. When people do as they please they may be happy for a moment, but it doesn't give lasting joy, because without God, there is no true happiness. He's where the joy is!

ACTIVITY

Pray this prayer.

Dear God, thank You for showing me how to live each day. I know You will help me do what You say is best each time I ask for help. I love You! Amen.

Ruth 1–4

 QUICK LOOK: Ruth 1:16—"But Ruth replied, 'Don't try to make me leave you and go back. Where you go I'll go. Where you stay I'll stay. Your people will be my people. Your God will be my God.'"

▷ A married couple, Elimelech and Naomi, leave their hometown of Bethlehem to go to Moab in hopes of finding food. They have two sons who marry women who worship other gods.

▷ Elimelech and his sons die. Naomi and her daughter-in-law Ruth go back to Bethlehem, where Ruth works in the field of a family member named Boaz. He notices Ruth and praises her for how loving she is.

▷ Several events lead up to Boaz marrying Ruth. They have a baby boy named Obed, who is the grandfather of David.

 TODAY'S GOD SHOT

Both Boaz and Ruth were brought into God's family from other nations and through surprising and difficult circumstances. He became their God, and they became a part of the family line that led to Jesus! God works through every possible situation to bring us into His family and show us His love. He's where the joy is!

 ACTIVITY

God loves families. Draw a picture of yours on the next page.

1 Samuel 1–3

 QUICK LOOK: 1 Samuel 1:27—Hannah said to Eli, "I prayed for this child. The LORD has given me what I asked him for."

▷ Hannah is married to Elkanah but is unable to have children. She goes to the tabernacle to cry out to God, asking Him for a son. The priest hears her passionate prayers.

▷ Hannah becomes pregnant with a son and names him Samuel. True to her promise, she takes him back to God's house and dedicates him to serving God there with Eli, the priest.

▷ Samuel grows up serving in the tabernacle, and one day God speaks to him out loud, but he has no idea what's going on. Eli eventually figures out that it's God and helps Samuel know how to respond.

 TODAY'S GOD SHOT

Hannah is the only female mentioned in the Bible who goes to the tabernacle. She has a real friendship with God. Hannah takes her problem to Him knowing He can be trusted to care for her heart, regardless of the outcome. Hannah goes to God because she knows He's where the joy is!

 ACTIVITY

What problem is on your heart right now? God cares for you, and like Hannah, you can trust Him and take the problem right to him. Take some time to pray and tell Him how you are feeling.

1 Samuel 4–8

QUICK LOOK: 1 Samuel 7:12—"Then Samuel got a big stone. He set it up between Mizpah and Shen. He named it Ebenezer. He said, 'The LORD has helped us every step of the way.'"

RECAP

▷ Israel loses a battle with the Philistines, who capture God's special ark and put it in their temple next to Dagon, the false god they worship. God repeatedly knocks Dagon facedown in front of the ark.

▷ Samuel tells the people to ask God for forgiveness and worship Him. When God gives them victory, Samuel gets a big stone to remind them of God's help.

▷ The people want a king like the other nations. God knows they are rejecting Him but decides to give them a king anyway.

TODAY'S GOD SHOT

God has set this nation apart to be different so other nations will recognize how great He is. They keep rejecting God, the very one who makes them unique. They are driven by fear and not the love of God. They forget what we want to remember: that He's where the joy is!

ACTIVITY

Is there something you can specifically say God has helped you with? If so, go outside, look for a rock, and place it in a visible spot as a reminder. Every time you see your rock—your Ebenezer—thank God for how He helped you!

1 Samuel 9–12

QUICK LOOK: 1 Samuel 12:22—Samuel replied, "But the LORD will be true to his great name. He won't turn his back on his people. That's because he was pleased to make you his own people."

▷ God tells Samuel to appoint Israel's first king. He anoints Saul as king by pouring oil on his head and tells him how God has a plan for him to rescue His people. He gives Saul three signs, and they all come true.

▷ God the Spirit rushes on Saul to equip him for action when the Ammonite king threatens some of the people. Saul has an incredible first victory.

▷ Samuel reminds the people about all God has done for them and begs them to obey God. If they do, things will go well; if they rebel, things won't.

TODAY'S GOD SHOT

After everything God has done for His people, they still reject Him as king. But Samuel says God is pleased to make them His own. No matter what wrong things we've done and no matter what sins we have yet to commit, Jesus has paid the price for all our sins, and He's where the joy is!

ACTIVITY

Connect the dots on the next page to read this truth.

HE'S WHERE THE

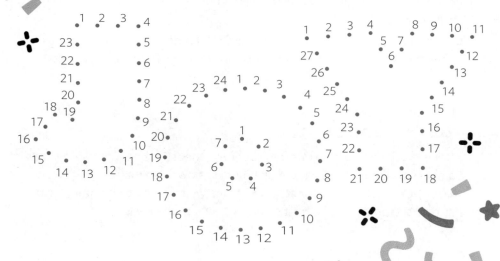

IS!

1 Samuel 13–14

QUICK LOOK: 1 Samuel 13:14—Samuel said to Saul, "But now your kingdom won't last. The LORD has already looked for a man who is dear to his heart. He has appointed him king of his people. That's because you haven't obeyed the LORD's command."

RECAP

▷ Samuel tells Saul to wait for him at Gilgal for seven days. But when the Philistine army gathers to fight Israel, Saul and his men are afraid. Saul grows impatient waiting and offers a sacrifice to God himself, which is against God's law.

▷ Samuel shows up and tells Saul that because of his fear, he doesn't have what it takes to be king. God will raise up someone to replace him.

▷ Saul's son Jonathan is courageous and trusts God as he leads men into battle. Even when Jonathan accidentally sins, he says he's sorry. This shows his honesty and trust in God's control over all things.

TODAY'S GOD SHOT

God is in control over all things, even the timing of things. God also uses all things to accomplish His ultimate will, including Saul's fear and impatience. He's active at every tick of the clock. God owns every moment, and He's where the joy is!

ACTIVITY

Unscramble the sentence below to find something you learned about God today.

DGO SI NI LROTNCO ....

ANSWER KEY: God is in control

137

1 Samuel 15–17

QUICK LOOK: 1 Samuel 16:7—"But the LORD said to Samuel, '. . . The LORD does not look at the things people look at. People look at the outside of a person. But the LORD looks at what is in the heart.'"

RECAP

▷ Samuel tells Saul to wipe out all of the Amalekites. Saul chooses to disobey. God is going to anoint a new king, and the choice for the new king is all about character and integrity (honesty), not about what the person looks like.

▷ Samuel goes to meet Jesse and his sons. God picks the youngest boy, named David, and Samuel anoints him as the new king.

▷ God's Spirit leaves Saul and comes to David, which allows David to later defeat Goliath, the Philistine giant, with just a slingshot and a stone.

TODAY'S GOD SHOT

God's feelings are evident. He's sad over making Saul the king. Even though God is outside of time and knows everything, He's also in each moment with us. When we are in pain, He knows and can give us comfort and joy—because He's where the joy is!

ACTIVITY

Circle the two things God cares about and cross out the things He doesn't.

HOW SOMEONE LOOKS
ON THE OUTSIDE

THAT SOMEONE IS HONEST
AND HAS INTEGRITY

WHAT SOMEONE'S HEART
IS LIKE

HOW TALL OR SHORT
SOMEONE IS

1 Samuel 18–20;
Psalms 11, 59

QUICK LOOK: Psalm 59:10—"You are my God, and I can depend on you."

▷ David is now a local hero, and Saul feels threatened. Saul tries to kill David at least sixteen times, but God prevents all of Saul's plans to harm David.

▷ Jonathan, Saul's son, and David become friends, and Jonathan helps to keep David safe from Saul. God is in control in all things, even over the efforts of an evil king.

▷ David trusts God in the midst of the attacks on his life. He doesn't doubt God's love, despite the testing he's enduring. He remembers God's past faithfulness, reminding himself who God is in the present and will be in the future.

TODAY'S GOD SHOT

God has defeated His and our enemies. He's protecting us and defending His name at the same time. We can depend on Him because He's where the joy is!

ACTIVITY

Memorize Psalm 59:10 by filling in the blanks.

PSALM ....:............—"YOU ARE MY ....,

AND .... DEPEND ON ...."

1 Samuel 21–24

QUICK LOOK: 1 Samuel 24:18—Saul cried, "You have just now told me about the good things you did to me. The LORD handed me over to you. But you didn't kill me."

RECAP

▷ David is on the run from Saul and stops in Nob because he needs food and weapons. Later, Saul gets word of where David is and tries to chase him down, but God tells David to go to another location.

▷ Some people from Ziph tell Saul that David is there. Saul heads that way, but as soon as he gets close to David, Saul gets word that the Philistines have attacked, and he has to rush back to war. David is able to move locations again!

▷ Even though Saul has tried to kill David over and over again, David shows faith in God and respect for the king by only cutting his robe and not killing him when they are both in a cave. David trusts that God is in control and knows Saul's reign as king will come to an end in God's perfect timing.

TODAY'S GOD SHOT

God has incredible timing. He leads and guides us, always making a way to fulfill His plans no matter what attacks the enemy has in mind. He's good to us, and He's where the joy is!

ACTIVITY

What is one thing you learned about God today?

....

....

Psalms 7, 27, 31, 34, 52

 QUICK LOOK: Psalm 34:5—"Those who look to him have joyful faces. They are never covered with shame."

▷ Today we read several psalms David wrote while he was on the run from Saul or in response to that experience. David declares that God is keeping him safe.

▷ Even when he's safe from his enemies, what David really wants is God's nearness. He believes he'll see God's goodness in this life, not just in eternity.

▷ David praises God for delivering him and invites others to trust God too. He reminds us that looking to God delivers us from fear.

 TODAY'S GOD SHOT

You're looking to God, and He is changing and growing your understanding of Him. You're carrying with you a new light and hope that's brighter than it was 105 days ago. Surely your face is joyful, because He's where the joy is!

 ACTIVITY

Draw a ☆ next to a way God is changing you.

You are more loving toward others.

You have joy that comes from knowing God loves you!

You tell God and others you are sorry when you do something wrong.

You haven't changed but are still hoping to.

Psalms 56, 120, 140–142

 QUICK LOOK: Psalm 142:5—"Lord, I cry out to you. I say, 'You are my place of safety. You are everything I need in this life.'"

 RECAP

▷ David sings to God despite everything he is going through. He knows that God is not distant even when we go through hard things.

▷ David is honest with God and tells Him how he really feels.

▷ David asks God to guard his heart and his words. He wants to surround himself with the right kind of people.

 TODAY'S GOD SHOT

David has nothing to offer God but prayer and praise and tears. Our God knows we have nothing to offer Him, but He delights in us still. You can take your needs and your nothing to Him—He's where the joy is!

 ACTIVITY

Pray Psalm 142:5.

Dear God, You are my place of safety. You are everything I need in this life. I love You! Amen.

1 Samuel 25–27

QUICK LOOK: 1 Samuel 25:30—Abigail said to David, "The LORD will do for you every good thing he promised to do. He'll appoint you ruler over Israel."

RECAP

▷ David and his men are protecting the flocks of a rich man named Nabal while he's out of town. When David needs help, Nabal refuses. David and his men plan to attack Nabal.

▷ Meanwhile, Nabal's wife, Abigail, finds out how rude her husband has been and takes supplies to David without telling Nabal. When Nabal dies, David goes back and marries Abigail.

▷ During this time, Saul is still looking for David. David, once again, has the chance to kill him but does not. Saul blesses David.

TODAY'S GOD SHOT

God works through Abigail, granting her wisdom to calm a situation that's about to get out of control. The wise know that joy isn't found in getting our own way—it's found in giving in to God's way, because He's where the joy is!

ACTIVITY

Circle the three ways that you can show wisdom in any situation.

YELL AT SOMEONE   TAKE A DEEP BREATH

THINK BEFORE YOU SPEAK   ASK GOD TO HELP YOU

PUSH SOMEONE DOWN   USE UNKIND WORDS

Psalms 17, 35, 54, 63

 QUICK LOOK: Psalm 63:3–4—"Your love is better than life. So I will bring glory to you with my lips. I will praise you as long as I live. I will call on your name when I lift up my hands in prayer."

▷ Since Samuel anointed David as king, life has only gotten tougher for David, but he trusts that God will come to his rescue.

▷ David knows that God pays close attention to the needy and weak.

▷ David remembers the days when he wasn't living in the desert and could worship God in the sanctuary. He longs for the day when he'll be able to participate in feasts and sacrificial offerings again instead of being on the run.

 TODAY'S GOD SHOT

David clings to God because even though he's far from the tabernacle, God's presence is still with him. He knows these three things are true: (1) God promised he will be king, (2) God is trustworthy, and (3) God will work justice. Even though David is in the desert, he praises God. David knows He's where the joy is!

ACTIVITY

Circle every *I* in Psalm 63:1–8. Then read it and replace each *I* with your name.

Example: So Grayson will bring glory to you with my lips.

Psalm 63:1-8

God, you are my God.
    I seek you with all my heart.
With all my strength I thirst for you
    in this dry desert
    where there isn't any water.
I have seen you in the sacred tent.
    There I have seen your power and your glory.
Your love is better than life.
    So I will bring glory to you with my lips.
I will praise you as long as I live.
    I will call on your name when I lift up my hands in
      prayer.
I will be as satisfied as if I had eaten the best food there is.
    I will sing praise to you with my mouth.
As I lie on my bed I remember you.
    I think of you all night long.
Because you have helped me,
    I sing in the shadow of your wings.
I hold on to you tightly.
    Your powerful right hand takes good care of me.

1 Samuel 28–31; Psalm 18

 QUICK LOOK: Psalm 18:1—"I love you, LORD. You give me strength."

 RECAP

▷ Samuel dies and all of Israel is sad. The Philistines want to attack the Israelites, and Saul doesn't know what to do. He tries to ask God what to do, but God doesn't answer.

▷ Saul wants to talk to Samuel, so he goes to a lady who calls spirits up from the dead. She is shocked when Samuel actually appears. Samuel tells Saul the bad news that Saul and his sons will die tomorrow and that the Philistines will defeat Israel.

▷ David discovers that the Amalekites have burned down the city and taken his family captive. God helps him raid the Amalekites and get everything back!

 TODAY'S GOD SHOT

David wrote Psalm 18 on the day God saved him from all his enemies. He tells of God's goodness even in difficult times. God is the source of all the good things, and He's where the joy is!

 ACTIVITY

What does God give you according to Psalm 18:1?

....

Psalms 121, 123–125, 128–130

QUICK LOOK: Psalm 121:2—"My help comes from the LORD. He is the Maker of heaven and earth."

RECAP

▷ These seven psalms are a part of other chapters known as the Songs of Ascent. *Ascent* means "to go up," which makes sense because Jerusalem, Israel's eventual capital, is at a high elevation.

▷ Up to three times a year, all the tribes of Israel come together to celebrate the holy days. Bible teachers say they sing these fifteen songs as they make their journey.

▷ It's good for God's people to sing these songs, because we know how easy it is for them to forget about all God has done for them.

TODAY'S GOD SHOT

We see that God's forgiveness of our sins inspires respect, awe, and delight—it draws us to Him! That's what the fear of God looks like. No matter what we've done, we can come to Him for forgiveness. He's where the joy is!

ACTIVITY

Play your favorite worship song and thank God for all the ways He helps you.

2 Samuel 1–4

QUICK LOOK: 2 Samuel 3:1—"The war between Saul's royal house and David's royal house lasted a long time. David grew stronger and stronger. But the royal house of Saul grew weaker and weaker."

▷ David is still on the run when he learns that Saul and his sons are dead. The messenger thinks that David will be happy about this, but David is not. He asks God what to do next, and God sends him to Hebron in Judah, where they make David king—but only over their tribe.

▷ Everything goes well until some of Saul's people want to stay in power. They anoint one of Saul's surviving sons, Ish-bosheth, as king over the other eleven tribes, and he makes Abner commander.

▷ Abner's own people spread a rumor that he is going to overthrow the king. Abner is so hurt by this that he makes a promise to help David become king over all twelve tribes.

TODAY'S GOD SHOT

God refers to David as a man after His own heart, and in today's reading we can see glimpses of God's character in David's actions. Though God is the King, He also is gentle—the kind of King we can draw near to, instead of run from. And He's where the joy is!

ACTIVITY

Write one word that describes what God's heart is like.

....

Psalms 6, 8–10, 14, 16, 19, 21

 QUICK LOOK: Psalm 9:1—"LORD, I will give thanks to you with all my heart. I will tell about all the wonderful things you have done."

 RECAP

▷ David is amazed at God's creation and the fact that man gets to be in charge of it.

▷ David praises God for helping him defeat his enemies.

▷ It's clear that David isn't just in this relationship for what he can get from God. He's in this for friendship with God—he doesn't just come to Him selfishly with complaints and needs. He comes to Him with praise!

 TODAY'S GOD SHOT

David says he has everything—all his heart's desires, a crown of fine gold, and a long life—but that his true joy comes from his relationship with God. Despite all David's earthly blessings, he keeps pointing us back to God, reminding us that He's where the joy is!

 ACTIVITY

Psalm 9:1 says, "I will tell about all the wonderful things you have done." Write two wonderful things God has done for you this week:

1. ....

2. ....

1 Chronicles 1–2

 QUICK LOOK: 1 Chronicles 2:1—"Here are the names of the sons of Israel."

 RECAP

▷ First Chronicles starts us back at the beginning—in fact, the first word in the first chapter is *Adam*. This refresher will help us to commit more of the story to memory as well as stir up new things in our hearts.

▷ Don't give up reading if this feels like you've read it before. It's a good thing to realize you've heard something before because that means it's sticking with you.

▷ The second chapter is mostly about the family line of Judah, because David comes from this tribe.

 TODAY'S GOD SHOT

God uses every story, from the great to the terrible to the person whose life won't get written about in history books. We're all written into His story of redemption. He sees us all, and the family names remind us of that. They may be boring, but He's not. He's where the joy is!

 ACTIVITY

Look through 1 Chronicles 1 and 2 for names that are familiar to you and that you have heard before in this book! Write them in the space below.

Psalms 43–45, 49, 84–85, 87

QUICK LOOK: Psalm 84:10—"A single day in your courtyards is better than a thousand anywhere else."

▷ David is struggling and feels far from God, but he tells his heart and mind what to do: Remember who God is and what He has done.

▷ David praises God for the things He's done for his ancestors, not just for him. He remembers that God is the one who grants victory.

▷ The author of Psalm 84 says he never feels more at home than in God's house. When he's away from it, he feels weak, but when he's there, he feels alive.

TODAY'S GOD SHOT

Psalm 87 reveals something important about God. It shows us Israel's unique relationship with God, but it also shows that He invites other nations to make their home among His people. God invites everyone from all nations to be His people. Because He's where the joy is!

ACTIVITY

There are nations in this world that still need to hear the good news of God's love for them. Find the five countries with the most unreached people groups.

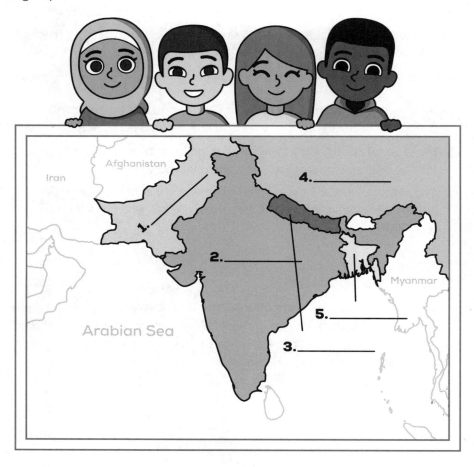

INDIA   PAKISTAN   CHINA

BANGLADESH   NEPAL

ANSWER KEY: 1. Pakistan, 2. India, 3. Nepal, 4. China, 5. Bangladesh

1 Chronicles 3–5

 QUICK LOOK: 1 Chronicles 5:20—"He handed over all those enemies to his people. That's because they cried out to him during the battle. He answered their prayers, because they trusted in him."

 RECAP

▷ We read the prayer of an honorable man named Jabez, who seeks God. He asks God for more land, and God answers his prayer with a yes.

▷ A prophecy from Genesis is being fulfilled with the tribe of Simeon shrinking.

▷ The Levites live spread out among the other tribes. God fulfilled Jacob's prophecy for both Simeon and Levi.

 TODAY'S GOD SHOT

When it comes to His kids, God leaves no prayer unanswered—there's no such thing as an unanswered prayer. He hears them, receives them, and always responds—with yes, no, or wait. He's never busy and He's never bored—He's where the joy is!

 ACTIVITY

Pray and tell God about anything going on in your life! He loves to hear from you!

Psalms 73, 77–78

 QUICK LOOK: Psalm 73:26—"My body and my heart may grow weak. God, you give strength to my heart. You are everything I will ever need."

 RECAP

▷ Asaph, the author of today's psalms, is unhappy with the good fortune of the wicked. His view changes when he goes to worship God—that's when he remembers what has eternal value, and earthly fortune isn't on that list.

▷ Being close to God shapes Asaph's view of the world.

▷ Asaph reminds himself of God's past faithfulness. He points to the fact that God's character can be trusted because those former times weren't easy either, but God came through.

 TODAY'S GOD SHOT

If our eyes are on others, ourselves, or our desires, eventually we'll lose sight of God. Some say comparison steals joy, and here it seems that comparison also steals faith. It prompts us to doubt God's goodness even when we know that He's where the joy is!

 ACTIVITY

Guess the missing words in this verse by naming the emojis.

PSALM 73:26: MY BODY AND MY ♥ MAY GROW WEAK.

GOD, YOU GIVE 💪 TO MY ♥. YOU ARE 🙌 I WILL

EVER NEED.

1 Chronicles 6

QUICK LOOK: 1 Chronicles 6:15—"The Lord took the people of Judah and Jerusalem to the land of Babylon. He used Nebuchadnezzar to take them there as prisoners."

▷ Family trees are listed in the Bible for a few reasons. One reason is to explain historical connections.

▷ God promised to send Israel into exile if they didn't keep the covenant. God eventually raises up an enemy to carry them off into exile. It's all part of His plan to bring them to repentance and to restore all things.

▷ Israel will be in exile for a long time, but then they'll repent and God will bring them back into the promised land. When that happens, these lists of families will be a necessary part of restoring the tribes and families to their rightful allotments.

TODAY'S GOD SHOT

God put all of the family names in 1 Chronicles on purpose. These families were brought to the promised land by His mighty hand. He was so kind to them, and He always had a plan to put them in the land and to bless them! He's where the joy is!

ACTIVITY

This chapter is all about names. Your name is special and unique to you! Do you know what it means? Find out and write or draw about its meaning in the space below!

Psalms 81, 88, 92–93

QUICK LOOK: Psalm 92:12—"Those who do what is right will grow like a palm tree. They will grow strong like a cedar tree in Lebanon."

RECAP

▷ In Psalm 81, people have come from all over Israel to sing praise songs to God, because God has commanded them to keep remembering and celebrating all He's done for them.

▷ We learn that God can handle our frustrations and questions without being threatened one bit. Our prayers don't have to be perfect or polished.

▷ Psalm 93 is a beautiful song of praise for God's reign over His creation. He's always been the King of the earth, and the whole earth knows it! Even the waters worship God and bow to His reign.

TODAY'S GOD SHOT

The people who do what is right are like palm trees that thrive and flourish, always bearing fruit. But palm trees have to stay connected to their supply of nourishment to survive. Thank God, He does all that's required for us to be planted in His house and to bear much fruit. He's where the fruit is, and He's where the joy is!

ACTIVITY

Draw a palm tree with roots. Beside each root, write a way that you can stay connected to God! Some examples of ways to stay connected are to read your Bible, pray, go to church, and sing songs.

1 Chronicles 7–10

 QUICK LOOK: 1 Chronicles 10:13—"Saul died because he wasn't faithful to the LORD. He didn't obey the word of the LORD. He even asked for advice from a person who gets messages from people who have died."

 RECAP

▷ There are more family trees listed here to make historical connections for us. These names serve to track who is a part of which tribe for when they return from exile.

▷ The temple work that is happening isn't just about making sacrifices. So much goes into keeping things running smoothly, and all the people who work there are considered leaders, regardless of their specific task.

▷ Saul was not faithful to the LORD, so He put him to death and turned the kingdom over to David.

 TODAY'S GOD SHOT

God protects His people. God doesn't stand for a leader who is doing things his own way, disregarding the good of the people and seeking selfish gain. He preserves what is most important: our souls and our relationship with Him. He watches carefully when it comes to the things of eternal value. He's where the joy is!

 ACTIVITY

Circle two things that are important to God.

WHAT WE LOOK LIKE   OUR SOULS

OUR RELATIONSHIP WITH HIM   HOW WE SOUND WHEN WE SING

Psalms 102–104

QUICK LOOK: Psalm 102:25—"In the beginning you made the earth secure. You placed it on its foundations. Your hands created the heavens."

▷ Psalm 102 is a song about the writer's personal sadness and trouble. But after he describes his problems, he fixes his eyes on God, which seems to comfort him. By thinking about God's relationship with His people, he reminds himself that God will rescue him somehow, someday.

▷ David then writes a song that praises God for His goodness to His people through the years.

▷ The writer of Psalm 104 praises God as Creator of everything! We read that God made some creatures on earth solely for His enjoyment. There are sea creatures that have lived on the ocean floor since creation that no one has ever seen, but God made them and delights in them.

TODAY'S GOD SHOT

Psalm 104:20 says, "You make darkness" (ESV). Darkness seems to be the absence of something, not the presence of something. How can God create an absence? Maybe it's just poetic language to show that God created everything, but whether it's a great truth or just a great lyric, it gives glory to God. It seems nothing escapes Him. He's everywhere. And He's where the joy is!

ACTIVITY

How cool is it that there are sea creatures that live on the ocean floor that have never been seen! Imagine what one of those sea creatures could look like and draw it on the next page.

2 Samuel 5; 1 Chronicles 11–12

 QUICK LOOK: 1 Chronicles 11:3—"All the elders of Israel came to see King David at Hebron. There he made a covenant with them in front of the LORD. They anointed David as king over Israel. It happened just as the LORD had promised through Samuel."

 RECAP

▷ David is finally anointed king over the other tribes, unifying the nation of Israel.

▷ David eventually takes Jerusalem and makes it the new capital, so they move everything over from Hebron to Jerusalem. David builds his castle there, and if you visit Jerusalem, you can go there—it was discovered a few years ago!

▷ In battle, David has a habit of asking what God thinks and obeying Him, and he sees success in this area. But in his private life—like when it comes to God's holy design for marriage and relationships—he does not ask what God thinks. He has great victories, but Scripture makes it clear that he isn't perfect.

 TODAY'S GOD SHOT

David's greatness doesn't come from himself and doesn't end with him either. Both David's victories and his imperfections point us to an eternal God who is working all things together according to His will, which is also for our joy. Because He's where the joy is!

 ACTIVITY

What is the last thing you asked God to do in your life? How has He answered so far? Remember, there's no such thing as an unanswered prayer. The answers are yes, no, or wait. He knows best and He loves us. Praise God for all the answers He gives us!

Psalm 133

QUICK LOOK: Psalm 133:1—"How good and pleasant it is when God's people live together in peace!"

▷ This is another song that the Israelites sing as they travel on foot all the way to Jerusalem, three times a year. Imagine the whole nation of Israel walking together to one city with their kids and animals in tow—it sounds kinda chaotic!

▷ Millions of people are headed to Jerusalem to remember God's provision and protection, but that kind of road trip is bound to cause some family fights.

▷ This song also points out that living peacefully in the promised land is a lot like being set apart by God.

TODAY'S GOD SHOT

The things David mentions in this psalm represent the best things of life on earth: unity, bounty, peace, blessing, and provision. But God's blessings for His kids don't stop there. The future awaits His kids when He restores all things and we live in that perfect space with Him—that's where real life is found. He's where the joy is!

ACTIVITY

Memorize Psalm 133:1. Knowing this verse will help you to remember that coming to a peaceful resolution when there are disagreements is what God wants for you!

Psalms 106–107

QUICK LOOK: Psalm 107:8—"Let them give thanks to the LORD for his faithful love. Let them give thanks for the wonderful things he does for people."

RECAP

▷ The author of Psalm 106 tells of the sins of Israel's history and confesses a pattern of unfaithfulness to God. Despite their cycle of rebellion and unbelief, God hasn't given up on them, because He is a God of steadfast love.

▷ Psalm 107 describes different kinds of people and their troubles, and all four stories share a common cycle: the problem, the cry for help, God's deliverance, and a call to praise.

▷ God has mercy on all four people. The author of Psalm 107 tells them to thank the LORD for His unending love and for His work on their behalf.

TODAY'S GOD SHOT

Forgetting that God loves us leaves an empty space in our hearts where sin and rebellion sneak in. That's why reading His Word every day and looking for Him on these pages has a way of reshaping our hearts and lives. He loves you, despite you. And He's where the joy is!

ACTIVITY

Read Psalm 107:8, 15, 21, and 31. Unscramble the words below to see what those verses have in common.

VGIE ....

STAHKN ....

ANSWER KEY: Give thanks

1 Chronicles 13–16

 QUICK LOOK: 1 Chronicles 15:28—"So the whole community of Israel brought up the ark of the covenant of the LORD. They shouted. They blew rams' horns and trumpets. They played cymbals, lyres and harps."

 RECAP

▷ David is making plans to move the ark of the covenant to Jerusalem. But there's one problem from the start: David fails to ask what God's rules are for how to treat the ark.

▷ The ark is moved improperly, and a man dies after touching it. David is upset about his death and wants to give up moving the ark.

▷ The ark is carried into the city, and everyone is thrilled except for Michal, David's wife, but as you'll learn in a few days, Michal is not happy with a lot of what David does. The people offer sacrifices, and David feeds them and sings a praise song that's a remix of other psalms.

 TODAY'S GOD SHOT

God never requires something of us that He doesn't tell us about. Many things are outlined for us in His Word, and His Spirit serves as our Guide and Helper, showing us how to apply Scripture in each situation. He knows His plan, and He shares it. He's where the joy is!

 **ACTIVITY**

Color this picture of what the ark of the covenant may have looked like.

Psalms 1–2, 15, 22–24, 47, 68

QUICK LOOK: Psalm 23:1–2—"The LORD is my shepherd. He gives me everything I need. He lets me lie down in fields of green grass. He leads me beside quiet waters."

RECAP

▷ One thing the righteous man thinks about is God's Word—he finds joy in it.

▷ God is holy, and we are not. His standards are higher than we could ever achieve. He shows so much love and mercy in drawing near to us.

▷ We are reminded that God is king of the earth, not just Israel. He is the King over all kingdoms!

TODAY'S GOD SHOT

It's easy to not like stillness and waiting, but God invites us into the calm and the quiet. It's where He can get our attention long enough to remind us He's where the joy is!

ACTIVITY

Memorize Psalm 23:1–2 by filling in the blanks.

PSALM 23:1–2—"THE LORD IS MY ....

HE GIVES ME .... I NEED. HE LETS ME LIE

.... IN FIELDS OF GREEN ....

HE LEADS ME BESIDE .... WATERS."

Psalms 89, 96, 100–101, 105, 132

 QUICK LOOK: Psalm 89:22–23—"No enemy will have the victory over him. No evil person will treat him badly. I will crush the king's enemies. I will completely destroy them."

▷ Jesus is the firstborn of all creation, meaning He is the most important! Israel is the firstborn of a people group, and King David is the firstborn of the kingly line God has established.

▷ Psalm 100 celebrates God's kingship and goodness and reminds us that we belong to Him. Not only are we His creation—all things and people are His creation—but we're also His people and His sheep.

▷ When we focus on God's blessings and character, we can hope when times are tough.

 TODAY'S GOD SHOT

God made a promise to David that He would crush David's enemies. God is in charge of all the details of our lives too. We can trust Him, because He cares about our hearts and He's where the joy is!

 ACTIVITY

Draw a ☆ next to the promise that means the most to you.

I will never leave you. (Deuteronomy 31:8)

I will forgive every wrong thing you have done. (1 John 1:9)

I will save you from your troubles. (Psalm 34:17)

I will take care of you; I know what you need. (Matthew 6:32)

I will save you when you believe in Me. (Romans 10:9)

2 Samuel 6–7; 1 Chronicles 17

QUICK LOOK: 2 Samuel 7:20—David said to the LORD, "What more can I say to you? LORD and King, you know all about me."

▷ As King David is bringing the ark into Jerusalem, a man named Uzzah touches it and dies. David is suddenly afraid of the ark, so he keeps it at the house of Obed-Edom instead.

▷ Then David remembers how God blesses His friends, and he's not afraid anymore, so he brings the ark to Jerusalem. David wants to build a house for God, but God says no. People often say to follow your heart, but even the man after God's own heart doesn't get to follow his heart.

▷ God tells David, "I know you want to build Me a house, but I'm going to build *you* a house. Not an actual house, but a family. And one of your sons will build an actual house for Me."

TODAY'S GOD SHOT

God knows all about David, including the desires of his heart. But God still says no in response to his prayer. If God says no, it is His kindest possible answer. When we trust His heart, we can believe it even when we can't see it. He's where the joy is!

ACTIVITY

Has God said no to a prayer you've prayed? Circle your answer: YES   NO

If God said no, were you able to trust Him even when you couldn't see what He was doing? Circle your answer: YES   NO

God wants us to tell Him all that is in our heart, but He also wants us to trust Him! Ask God to help you trust Him more, especially when He answers your prayers with a kind and good no.

Psalms 25, 29, 33, 36, 39

 QUICK LOOK: Psalm 33:21—"Our hearts are full of joy because of him. We trust in him, because he is holy."

▷ David talks to God about the wrong things he has done. He admits his sin and knows how it hurts his friendship with God.

▷ We can praise God because He is both powerful and peaceful. Praising God is what His children are supposed to do.

▷ David is careful about how and when he talks about his struggles, because he doesn't want to leave a bad impression about God on people who don't know Him.

 TODAY'S GOD SHOT

If you've ever felt joy and happiness when reading the Bible and praying, that almost certainly means you trust God. Keep reading the Bible and praying. God will keep teaching you about Himself, which will help you trust Him more, and you'll be able to confidently say, "He's where the joy is!"

 ACTIVITY

On a scale of one to ten, how easy is it for you to trust God?

1—NOT AT ALL   10—FULL TRUST

1   2   3   4   5   6   7   8   9   10

2 Samuel 8–9; 1 Chronicles 18

 QUICK LOOK: 2 Samuel 8:15—"David ruled over the whole nation of Israel. He did what was fair and right for all his people."

▷ King David leads his army to many victories. He wins these battles because of God's plan and favor, not because of David's strength or ability.

▷ God blesses David with lots of gold and treasure, but David doesn't keep it all for himself. Instead, he uses it to honor God and help the people around him.

▷ David shows kindness to his friend Jonathan's son, Mephibosheth, by offering him a place to live in his palace and inviting him to eat at his table.

 TODAY'S GOD SHOT

The way David treats Mephibosheth because of Jonathan is the way God treats us because of His Son, Jesus. We're invited to live in His kingdom and eat at His table forever! And we could never get there on our own—we're too messed up by our sin. Praise God for making a way for us, because He's where the joy is!

 ACTIVITY

Pray this prayer.

Dear God, thank You for Jesus and for the gift of living in His kingdom and eating at His table forever one day! Help me to love You and do what's right! Amen.

Psalms 50, 53, 60, 75

QUICK LOOK: Psalm 75:1—"God, we praise you. We praise you because you are near to us. People talk about the wonderful things you have done."

▶ The Israelites try to earn God's forgiveness by offering gifts and sacrifices, but God doesn't just want their gifts. Instead, He wants their hearts to trust Him.

▶ We can have freedom from fear and worry when we trust God to take care of us.

▶ When we feel scared that God isn't going to take care of us, we can talk to Him about it! He won't get mad at us for being honest about our feelings. Instead, God will help us see that we don't have to be afraid because He will help us.

TODAY'S GOD SHOT

God wants us to think about Him all the time. We can do that by thinking about all that we are thankful for and telling Him about it! Telling Him that we are thankful connects our hearts to Him, which means we'll be much more likely to follow Him because we know He's where the joy is!

ACTIVITY

Make a list of five things you are thankful for. Put the list somewhere you will see it often, like on your bathroom mirror! This way, when you brush your teeth you can think about all the ways that God is taking care of you, and you can be thankful!

2 Samuel 10; 1 Chronicles 19; Psalm 20

 QUICK LOOK: Psalm 20:4—"May he give you what your heart wishes for. May he make all your plans succeed."

 RECAP

▷ King David wants to keep the peace with his neighboring countries, but they don't trust him. Instead of receiving David's kindness, they are mean to his soldiers and hurt them.

▷ David sends his army into battle. One of his commanders, Joab, encourages another commander, Abishai, that they don't have to be afraid because God is in control. He knows that no matter what happens, God will take care of them. Joab's faith shows that he trusts God.

▷ God will send us help when we need it.

 TODAY'S GOD SHOT

King David knows that God's plans are always the best plans! His ways are perfect, and He's where the joy is!

 ACTIVITY

What is one thing you really want to be true for your life? Pray and ask God to give it to you.

Psalms 65–67, 69–70

QUICK LOOK: Psalm 65:4—"Blessed are those you choose and bring near to worship you."

▷ David knows that his sins are too big for him to fix all by himself. He looks to God to rescue him and forgive him, and then David praises God for His forgiveness.

▷ Since God is everywhere and knows all things, He hears all prayers, even from people who don't love Him. He isn't required to answer everyone's prayers, because He knows that we don't always ask for the right things.

▷ David knows that he isn't perfect, but his enemies are accusing him of things that he didn't do. He asks God to punish them for lying about him.

TODAY'S GOD SHOT ～～～～～～～～～～～～～～～～～～

Do you realize how blessed you are? If you know God, it's because He chose you and He brought you near! It's the greatest blessing of our lives, because He's where the joy is!

ACTIVITY

When we worship God, we tell Him how thankful we are. Have fun filling in this thankful ad-lib as you think about how blessed you are!

THERE ONCE WAS A KID NAMED .... WHOSE FAMILY WAS
(your name)

GOING ON A SAFARI TO SEE THE WILD ....S IN
(your favorite animal)

THEIR NATURAL HABITAT. THEY PACKED UP THEIR SUITCASES AND

MADE SURE TO BRING THEIR .... AND
(favorite gift you've been given)

PLENTY OF .... THEN THEY ALL WAVED GOOD-
(food you're thankful for)

BYE TO THEIR NEIGHBOR, ..., AND SET
(neighbor you're thankful for)

OFF FOR THEIR ADVENTURE! ON THEIR SAFARI, THEIR JEEP WAS

SUDDENLY SURROUNDED BY A PACK OF ....S!
(same favorite animal)

AND .... WISHED THEY COULD GIVE THEM
(name of a family member)

SOME .... FROM .... BE-
(food you're thankful for)   (your favorite restaurant)

CAUSE IT'S THE BEST! BUT .... PRAYED AND ASKED
(your name)

GOD TO SHOW THEM WHAT TO DO. AND GOD DID! ....
(your name)

REMEMBERED THAT THEY HAD A .... IN THEIR
(something in your room)

POCKET, SO THEY USED THEIR .... SKILLS AND
(sport/activity you play)

TOSSED IT TO THE ....S, WHO CHOMPED ON IT
(same favorite animal)

UNTIL .... THE FAMILY DROVE AWAY QUICKLY.
(your favorite time of day)

WHEN THEY ALL GOT HOME, THEY EACH THANKED GOD FOR HELPING

THEM ON THEIR EPIC SAFARI!

2 Samuel 11–12; 1 Chronicles 20

 QUICK LOOK: 2 Samuel 12:8 NIV—The LORD said to David, "I gave you all Israel and Judah. And if all this had been too little, I would have given you even more."

 RECAP

▷ As king, David is supposed to lead his soldiers in battles. Instead, he stays home and disobeys God by stealing another man's wife and acting like she's his own. Then, trying to cover up his sin, David has that man killed in a battle.

▷ God is not happy with David's choices and sends the prophet Nathan to teach David a lesson. David knows that what he did was wrong. God forgives David, but there are still consequences for his sins.

▷ David's baby son dies, but David trusts God's goodness and draws near to worship Him.

 TODAY'S GOD SHOT

David gets greedy and forgets how rich and generous God is. God has already blessed him with more than enough and is still willing to give more. God is a good Father who wants to lavish gifts on His children, and He's where the joy is!

 ACTIVITY

Blessings are all the good gifts that God has given you. And gifts aren't just things, like toys or video games, but people who love you, especially Jesus! Make a list of some blessings in your life:

1. ....

2. ....

3. ....

Psalms 32, 51, 86, 122

 QUICK LOOK: Psalm 32:8—"I will guide you and teach you the way you should go. I will give you good advice and watch over you with love."

 RECAP

▷ David praises God for His forgiveness, because he knows that he has sinned over and over again. He is truly heartbroken over the wrong things that he has done.

▷ David says that his heart feels divided. This means that he knows he should do things God's way, but he really wants to do things his own way. He asks God to teach him the truth and change his heart.

▷ David's sin impacted Jerusalem, so he prays for the city and its people, for peace and security, and he promises that he'll seek its good.

 TODAY'S GOD SHOT

God wants us close to Him. The more we learn to listen to Him, the easier it is to follow Him. And as we follow Him, we realize that He's where the joy is!

 ACTIVITY

Be as still as you can for the next minute. Ask God to speak to you, then write down anything you think He says.

....

....

....

2 Samuel 13–15

 QUICK LOOK: 2 Samuel 15:25—"Then the king said to Zadok, 'Take the ark of God back into the city. If the LORD is pleased with me, he'll bring me back. He'll let me see the ark again. He'll also let me see Jerusalem again. That's the place where he lives.'"

 RECAP

▷ David's kids are fighting with each other. His son Amnon hurts his daughter Tamar, but David doesn't do anything to punish him, so one of his other sons, Absalom, decides to kill Amnon for revenge.

▷ Absalom knows he will get in trouble with his father so he runs away, and they don't speak for two years. During this time, Absalom decides that he wants to be king instead of David.

▷ Absalom convinces David's closest advisors to turn against the king and follow him instead. David has to leave his city of Jerusalem and trust that God will keep him safe.

 TODAY'S GOD SHOT

Even when it feels like everyone is against us, we can trust God's plan. He is in charge and promises to always watch over His people. It feels so good to put our trust in Him because He's where the joy is!

 ACTIVITY

Who is the person in your family who you fight with the most?

....

Most of the fighting we do is over wanting something for ourselves. But God promises to give you what you need. This week when you are tempted to fight with that person, ask God to help you and give you patience instead.

Psalms 3–4, 12–13, 28, 55

QUICK LOOK: Psalm 28:9—"Save your people. Bless those who belong to you. Be their shepherd. Take care of them forever."

RECAP

▷ David is writing about his feelings after his son Absalom has turned all the people against him. David feels a lot of emotions, from anger to sadness to hope.

▷ David feels forgotten by God, but God hasn't forgotten him. This shows us how our feelings aren't always true.

▷ Even though David has been betrayed by his son, is forced to leave his country, and feels scared, he puts his trust in God. He knows that like a shepherd protects his sheep, God will protect him.

TODAY'S GOD SHOT

No matter what is happening in our lives or what we are feeling on the inside, we can trust that God will take care of us. He's our shepherd, we are His sheep, and He's where the joy is!

ACTIVITY

Color the picture of the shepherd with his sheep on the next page and thank God for taking care of you.

2 Samuel 16–18

QUICK LOOK: 2 Samuel 17:14—"The LORD had decided that Ahithophel's good advice would fail. The LORD wanted to bring horrible trouble on Absalom."

▷ King David continues to hide away from his son Absalom, who wants to take away his throne. Several other people try to hurt David, but he waits for God to handle the situation instead of taking action himself.

▷ David has a spy named Hushai who is pretending to support Absalom. Hushai devises a plan to help David return to his kingdom and remove Absalom from power.

▷ David makes his army promise to not hurt Absalom, but the commander of his army, Joab, finds Absalom hanging by his hair from a tree branch and kills him, which makes David very sad.

TODAY'S GOD SHOT

God is just and can be trusted to take care of anything in your life. He brings trouble on Absalom for the way he's treated David, his father. God can be trusted even with the thoughts and plans of our enemies. He's in control, and He's where the joy is!

ACTIVITY

Have you ever been bullied by someone? If so, you know that it can feel like you have to hide from that person. And you know how hard it can be to trust God to make everything right between you and that person. Pray for them right now and know that God is at work in that situation.

Psalms 26, 40, 58, 61–62, 64

QUICK LOOK: Psalm 40:8—David said, "My God, I have come to do what you want. Your law is in my heart."

▷ David talks to God about his sin. He knows that he isn't perfect and that God is his only hope.

▷ People in David's life keep lying to him and hurting him. He talks to God about how that makes him feel, because he knows that God can be trusted with his heart.

▷ David is feeling very sad, but even his sadness doesn't keep him from worshipping God.

TODAY'S GOD SHOT

God wants us to obey Him and His Word because He wants what's best for us, but He cares the most about our hearts. As we grow to love Him more and more, we realize that He's where the joy is!

 **ACTIVITY**

Sometimes it can be hard to hear God's voice to know what He wants for our lives. Here are three ways you can know what God's voice sounds like. Use the key to decode the words:

What God says always agrees with the

God's voice is always

God always tells the

Pray this prayer:

God, *I want to hear Your voice. Help me to know when You are speaking to me. I love You. Amen.*

2 Samuel 19–21

QUICK LOOK: 2 Samuel 19:14—"So the hearts of all the men of Judah were turned toward David. All of them had the same purpose in mind. They sent a message to the king. They said, 'We want you to come back. We want all your men to come back too.'"

RECAP

▶ After David's son Absalom dies, the people aren't sure who they want to follow. They go back and forth deciding to support David as king and then turning against him.

▶ David decides to forgive all of his enemies who turned against him and tried to hurt him. He shows mercy, which is not punishing someone when they deserve it.

▶ David's army is sent to attack a city that will not listen and follow David. Before they can attack, a wise woman offers to help by finding and stopping the man David's army is looking for. She saves the city!

TODAY'S GOD SHOT

When someone hurts you, it would be easy to try to hurt them back. But God wants you to trust Him to work in the other person's heart. He will make things right if you wait and trust Him. He's always working in our lives and in our hearts! He's where the joy is!

ACTIVITY

Is there someone who has hurt you? Can you trust God to work in that person's heart?

Put your hands out in front of you with your palms up. When we open our hands like this, it is a way to show God that we are willing to let go of doing things our way and that we trust His plans. With your hands open, tell God, "I trust You with [name of person]."

Psalms 5, 38, 41–42

QUICK LOOK: Psalm 38:21—"LORD, don't desert me. My God, don't be far away from me."

▷ David is the king, but he calls God his King. This shows his respect for God. He cares about God's opinion and wants to be close to Him.

▷ David is in a lot of pain in his body and his heart. He knows that God can heal him, so he asks kindly.

▷ David feels like God has forgotten him, even though we know this is impossible. He remembers feeling closer to God once before, so he cries out asking God to feel close to him again.

TODAY'S GOD SHOT

At the end of each psalm, David asks God to help him, and he believes with all of his heart that God will come through for him. We can ask God for help with the same humble attitude, knowing that even when God feels far away, He wants us to remember that He's close to us, because He's where the joy is!

ACTIVITY

Be as still as you can for the next minute and ask God to be near you. Here are some things you could say:

● God, I'm so glad You want to be my friend. Help me to talk to You like a friend.

● Please put Your ideas in my mind and guide my heart.

● It's amazing how You sent Your Son, Jesus, to take the punishment for my sin so I can be forgiven and know You.

● Thank You for helping me know that You are close. You haven't forgotten me.

2 Samuel 22–23; Psalm 57

QUICK LOOK: 2 Samuel 22:36 ESV—"You have given me the shield of your salvation, and your gentleness made me great."

RECAP

▷ David is getting older and he knows that he won't live much longer, so he starts to look back over his life and sees the many ways God has worked through all the ups and downs.

▷ David doesn't think of himself as very special. Instead, he knows that it's his relationship with God that gives him meaning and purpose. God brings light and life to his life so that he never has to live in fear.

▷ David has grown to trust God over his life, so when he faces new challenges or fears, his response is to praise God and expect God to deliver him.

TODAY'S GOD SHOT

David says that God's gentleness has made him great. It's been God's mercy and kindness that have helped David and changed him. As David grows closer to God, he becomes more like Him and knows that He's where the joy is!

ACTIVITY

What is one of God's characteristics you saw in today's reading?

God is ....

Psalms 95, 97–99

 QUICK LOOK: Psalm 97:11—"Good things come to those who do what is right. Joy comes to those whose hearts are honest."

▷ God is our Creator and our Shepherd. He gives us life and guides us like a shepherd guides His sheep.

▷ God didn't just make us and then forget about us. He is with us all the time, watching over us.

▷ God gives us everything we need to know Him better and respond to Him with worship. He even forgives us when we sin or do wrong things.

 TODAY'S GOD SHOT

When we sin, God forgives us, and there are also consequences for not living the way God knows is best. When we do what's right and honest, God gives us good things. Sometimes these good things take a little while to show up, but they're coming, because He's where the joy is!

 ACTIVITY

God shows us what is RIGHT. Circle the actions He wants from us and draw a line through the ones that are WRONG.

- Tell the truth
- Complain
- Be thankful

- Be kind
- Tell a lie
- Obey

- Put yourself first
- Work hard/ Do your best

2 Samuel 24; 1 Chronicles 21–22; Psalm 30

QUICK LOOK: Psalm 30:11—"You turned my loud crying into dancing. You removed my clothes of sadness and dressed me with joy."

RECAP

▷ David decides to take a census, which means that he takes an official count of everyone in his army. This isn't a bad thing to do, but David did it because he didn't trust God to win the battle for him.

▷ David is punished for his sin and must offer a sacrifice to God. God sends fire to consume the sacrifice to show that He forgives David.

▷ David tells Solomon how to build the temple.

TODAY'S GOD SHOT

God is so generous, forgiving, and powerful! Sin never gets to win against God and His people; it always ultimately serves God's purposes somehow. We can still praise God when bad things happen because we know He's where the joy is!

ACTIVITY

When David was forgiven for his sins, he praised God and wrote many of the Psalms to show how much God's forgiveness meant to him. Try writing a poem or song for God, praising Him for forgiving your sins.

Psalms 108–110

QUICK LOOK: Psalm 108:13—"With your help we will win the battle."

▷ David feels like God has rejected them and isn't fighting on their behalf anymore. He cries to God for help, trusting He'll come to their rescue.

▷ David tells God how upset he is and doesn't hold back. He asks God to act.

▷ Psalm 110 points us to Jesus. God has Jesus sit at His right hand, the position of honor, and He makes His enemies His footrest.

TODAY'S GOD SHOT

We can't save ourselves by being extra good or even by going to church. God saves us when we accept His Son, Jesus, as our Lord and Savior. Jesus defeated sin and death when He died on the cross and came to life again in three days. When Jesus is our King, our Protector, and our Savior, we can know that He's where the joy is!

ACTIVITY

What problem are you facing right now?

....

....

Tell God about it.

Read Psalm 108:13 and believe God will help you with your problem.

1 Chronicles 23–25

QUICK LOOK: 1 Chronicles 23:25—"David had said, 'The LORD is the God of Israel. He has given peace and rest to his people. He has come to Jerusalem to live there forever.'"

▷ David makes his son Solomon the king. He then offers lots of advice from his years of experience to get Solomon ready for his most important task: building the temple.

▷ The original house of God was called a tabernacle, and it was a tent. This new temple is permanent and a very big deal, so David has lots of instructions for Solomon and for the workers in the temple.

▷ The priests who work in the tabernacle are called Levites. There are certain requirements for someone to be a Levite. David also organizes the musicians who will work in the temple.

TODAY'S GOD SHOT

YHWH is the God of Israel. He has taken His people out of slavery, through the wilderness, and into the promised land, and He has come to live among them! God is good, He's with them, and He's where the joy is!

ACTIVITY

Draw a picture of the tabernacle and what you think it looked like.

Psalms 131, 138–139, 143–145

 QUICK LOOK: Psalm 145:17—"The Lord is right in everything he does. He is faithful in everything he does."

 RECAP

▷ David may have written Psalm 131 when things were really hard for him. He may be confused about the things that are happening and why they are happening, but he trusts God. He knows that God is in control.

▷ David has a personal relationship with God, which he talks about in Psalm 139. David understands that he is known and loved by God.

▷ God shows everyone grace and mercy. Grace is being given gifts that we don't earn or deserve, while mercy is not being punished when we deserve it.

 TODAY'S GOD SHOT

Every answer God gives to every prayer we pray is His kindest possible answer. If He says yes, it's kind. If He says no, it's kind. If He says wait, it's kind. He is kind, and His plans are good. We can trust Him because He's where the joy is!

 ACTIVITY

Fill in the blanks from today's verse.

PSALM 145:17—"THE Lord IS .... IN EVERYTHING

HE DOES. HE IS FAITHFUL IN .... HE

DOES."

1 Chronicles 26–29; Psalm 127

 QUICK LOOK: 1 Chronicles 29:14—David said, "Everything comes from you. We've given back to you only what comes from you."

▷ David continues making preparations for the First Temple. He makes sure that there are gatekeepers keeping everyone safe. David also chooses people to be in charge of the money and special offerings that the people bring.

▷ David reminds the people to seek and obey God always. He also reminds them that God has chosen Solomon for this project and to be king. He charges Solomon to submit his desires and thoughts to God in all things.

▷ David gives his money and gifts generously to the building of the temple. He shows the people how important it is to give with your whole heart.

 TODAY'S GOD SHOT

God is the source of all good things, which means that every good thing we give to God was already His to begin with. Giving our blessings back can remind us to thank Him for all the ways He's blessed us. He's the source, supply, and goal—and He's where the joy is!

 ACTIVITY

Can you show God how much you love Him by giving Him an offering this week?

Count the objects, and write the totals in the circles below.

Psalm 111–118

QUICK LOOK: Psalm 118:20—"This is the gate of the LORD. Only those who do what is right can go through it."

RECAP

▶ When we have a right view of God and how great He is, it makes us say, "Wow!"

▶ Those who delight in God's laws will live them out. He changes our hearts and makes us more like Him.

▶ There's no way to repay God for what He has done, but the author of Psalm 116 commits to praising and serving God forever out of the overflow of gratitude in his heart.

TODAY'S GOD SHOT

Psalm 118:20 says, "This is the gate of the LORD. Only those who do what is right can go through it." Jesus is the way in. He's the gate to the Father. He made us right with God, so we can be in His presence and know that He's where the joy is!

ACTIVITY

Circle the words that describe who God is to you.

GREAT   POWERFUL   KIND   FORGIVING

LOVING   PRESENT   RIGHT   GOOD

1 Kings 1–2; Psalm 37, 71, 94

QUICK LOOK: Psalm 37:4—"Find your delight in the LORD. Then he will give you everything your heart really wants."

▷ David is about to die, and while he has made plans for his son Solomon to be king, his oldest son, Adonijah, decides *he* wants to be king.

▷ Adonijah can't stop God's plans, so Solomon is made the new king after David dies.

▷ David dies as an old man. He didn't live a perfect life, but he knew that God carried him throughout his entire life.

TODAY'S GOD SHOT

We all mess up and sin, so we can't have a relationship with God based on our attempt at being perfect. What a gift to know that all the sins of all God's kids—past, present, future, intentional, confessed, and accidental sins—are covered by Jesus's death on the cross! He's where the joy is!

ACTIVITY

What are two things you really want?

1. ....

2. ....

When you delight in God and enjoy time with Him every day, He hears your prayers and will give you the things you desire if it is a part of His plan. And remember, if God's answer is no, it's his kindest answer and what's best for you. Ask God to help your heart want what He wants.

Psalm 119

QUICK LOOK: Psalm 119:105—"Your word is like a lamp that shows me the way. It is like a light that guides me."

▷ Reading and knowing God's Word, the Bible, keeps us close to God's heart and teaches us everything we need to know about following Him.

▷ We can't change our own hearts, but God can! We can pray, "Open my eyes, teach me, help me understand, lead me, and change my heart."

▷ Loving God doesn't mean that we won't feel pain and loss. But it does mean that we have a safe Person to be with us in our pain. We can ask God to draw near and comfort us.

TODAY'S GOD SHOT

Psalm 119:105 calls God's Word, the Bible, a lamp and a light. This means the Bible is everything we need to see right in front of us, like a lamp. It also means the Bible is everything we need to see all around us, like a huge light. God has generously given it all to us. His Word is where the joy is, because He's in it—and He's where the joy is!

ACTIVITY

God's Word is like a lamp to us in so many ways. Use a yellow marker or crayon to highlight one of the ways God's Word has shown you something.

- I see how my sin hurts others.
- I see how God wants me to give generously.
- I see how I am loved by God.
- I see that I don't have to fear anything because God is always with me.

1 Kings 3–4

QUICK LOOK: 1 Kings 3:9—Solomon answered God, "So give me a heart that understands. Then I can rule over your people. I can tell the difference between what is right and what is wrong."

▷ Solomon's heart is divided between God and other things.

▷ As Solomon is sleeping, God comes to him. Solomon asks God for wisdom to help him be a king who makes the right decisions.

▷ God is glad to answer Solomon. He helps him use the gift of wisdom and blesses him abundantly.

TODAY'S GOD SHOT

God tells Solomon that if he keeps his heart focused on God, He will help him and bless Solomon's entire life. Solomon isn't perfect and his heart gets distracted at times, but God never gives up on him because He's where the joy is!

ACTIVITY

Color the heart and ask God to give you wisdom and help you know the difference between what is right and wrong.

2 Chronicles 1; Psalm 72

 QUICK LOOK: Psalm 72:18—"Give praise to the LORD God, the God of Israel. Only he can do wonderful things."

 RECAP

▷ Psalm 72 is a prayer asking God to help the king do what is right, be fair to the people, and help those who are hurting.

▷ The writer of this psalm, who might be David, prays for God's help for the king, which probably refers to Solomon. God has big plans for this king.

▷ God chooses to bless Solomon more than he even asked for, and He wants to do the same for you.

 TODAY'S GOD SHOT

God is generous and kind and wants to bless His people. Even when we don't know what to ask for, God sees us, knows what we need, and wants to help us. We get to ask God for anything and praise Him for His blessings because He's where the joy is!

 ACTIVITY

Draw or write in the boxes below what you are asking God for.

Song of Solomon 1–8

PARENTAL
MATURE CONTENT
IN TODAY'S
BIBLE PASSAGE
GUIDANCE

QUICK LOOK: Song of Solomon 8:6—The woman said to the king, "Hold me close to your heart where your royal seal is worn. Keep me as close to yourself as the bracelet on your arm. My love for you is so strong it won't let you go."

RECAP

▷ This book of the Bible teaches about God's best plan for the love between a man and a woman.

▷ Throughout the Bible, God uses the love and friendship between a husband and wife to help us remember His never-ending love, friendship, and commitment to us.

▷ When we talk about God's great love and the friendship we have with Him, people will want to learn about Him too.

TODAY'S GOD SHOT

God shows us His perfect plan for dating and marriage between a man and a woman. Even though our world might try to tell us a different plan, God had good things in mind when He gave us rules to obey. God is always showing us how much He loves us, and He's where the joy is!

ACTIVITY

Tell God three things you love about Him:

1. ....

2. ....

3. ....

Proverbs 1–3

QUICK LOOK: Proverbs 3:5—"Trust in the Lᴏʀᴅ with all your heart. Do not depend on your own understanding."

▷ The book of Proverbs is a collection of sayings focused on people who want to be wise and make good decisions.

▷ There are three types of people in Proverbs. *Wise people* love and obey God, *foolish people* don't listen to or obey God, and *simple people* are distracted and don't really know what they believe about God.

▷ When we accept the good gifts of wisdom, knowledge, and understanding that God wants to give us, we can have peace and trust God with every part of our life.

TODAY'S GOD SHOT

God wants us to talk to Him about everything. He cares about every part of our life. God wants us to know He's right there leading and guiding us every step of the way because He's where the joy is!

ACTIVITY

Unscramble the words to see some of the good gifts God gives us.

D I S W M O   W____ ____ D ____ ____

N S T A I G N U D R E D N   U N____ E ____ S T ____ N____ ____ N G

O E G N W K L E D   ____ N ____ W ____ E ____ G E

Proverbs 4–6

QUICK LOOK: Proverbs 6:16–19—"There are six things the LORD hates. In fact, he hates seven things. The LORD hates proud eyes, a lying tongue, and hands that kill those who aren't guilty. He also hates hearts that make evil plans and feet that are quick to do evil. He hates any witness who pours out lies and anyone who stirs up conflict in the community."

RECAP

▷ In these chapters, we can get advice for living a life pleasing to God. The closer we get to God, the more we see how much we really need Him.

▷ We are told more than once to stay away from evil. God gives us freedom when we are obedient to Him.

▷ Walking in wisdom and nearness with God brings peace, but walking outside of His ways brings loss and sadness.

TODAY'S GOD SHOT

There are seven things the LORD hates: pride, lying, murder, hearts that make evil plans, feet that are quick to do evil, those who lie about what they saw happen, and those who cause trouble in the family of God. But He loves humility, honesty, justice, truth, peacemaking, and when we come together in love. He gives us all the things He loves when we ask Him to come into our heart because He's where the joy is!

ACTIVITY

From the list below, draw an X through the things God hates and a around the things He loves.

FIGHTING   GOSSIPING   LYING   SERVING

SHARING   BULLYING   HONESTY   INCLUDING OTHERS

CHEATING   HELPING   KINDNESS   DISOBEYING

Proverbs 7–9

QUICK LOOK: Proverbs 8:17—"I love those who love me. Those who look for me find me."

RECAP

▷ There are three things that are important in our friendship with God: what our eyes see, what our hands do, and having a heart that loves Him.

▷ We can choose a path of foolishness that leads to death or a path of wisdom that leads to life.

▷ Keeping God's Word in front of our eyes and in our hearts helps us choose a life that includes listening to wise advice, being honest, and avoiding sin.

TODAY'S GOD SHOT

God is so happy when we make wise choices. He wants to bless us as we chase after wisdom, because He's where the joy is!

ACTIVITY

Draw a picture of your eyes, hands, and heart below. Ask God to help you use these parts of your body with wisdom.

Proverbs 10–12

 QUICK LOOK: Proverbs 10:17—"Anyone who pays attention to correction shows the path to life. But anyone who refuses to be corrected leads others down the wrong path."

RECAP

▷ The way you live affects others, so learn God's Word, live by it, and see God bless you and those around you.

▷ It is important to understand how the words you say impact your life and the lives of others.

▷ Wise people are humble; they read God's Word and learn from it.

 TODAY'S GOD SHOT

In our friendship with God, we will all make mistakes. The good news is that Jesus's death on the cross made a way for everyone to be forgiven for their sin and live a life that is pleasing to Him. Because God forgives us, we can enjoy time with Him and remember He's where the joy is!

 ACTIVITY

Take some time right now to pray and thank God for sending His Son, Jesus, to this world to forgive us for our sin. Ask God to help you encourage the people around you, speak kind words to others, and become more like Jesus every day.

Proverbs 13–15

 QUICK LOOK: Proverbs 15:29—"The Lord is far away from those who do wrong. But he hears the prayers of those who do right."

 RECAP

▷ Wise people choose their words and their friends carefully.

▷ When we try to do things our own way and rely on our own under-standing, things end poorly. And even if we don't see or understand the bad result, God isn't glorified or honored when we depend on our-selves, and that's still a loss.

▷ God is close to those who do what is right. He hears their prayers.

 TODAY'S GOD SHOT

God tells us over and over again how much He wants to hear from us. Ask God to be close to you today by giving you peace when things are stressful, hope when things feel impossible, or even strength to serve someone who annoys you. God will be near in moments like this, so expect it, and look for it, because He's where the joy is!

ACTIVITY

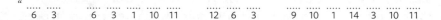

Use the decoder key below to fill in the message that reminds us of how God hears our prayers.

Decoder Key:

1	2	3	4	5	6	7	8	9	10	11	12	13	14
A	D	E	F	G	H	I	O	P	R	S	T	W	Y

" ....
   6   3   6   3   1   10   11   12   6   3   9   10   1   14   3   10   11

   .... "
   8   4   12   6   8   11   3   13   6   8   2   8   10   7   5   6   12

Proverbs 16–18

 QUICK LOOK: Proverbs 16:23—"The hearts of wise people guide their mouths. Their words make people want to learn more."

▷ Speak words that are helpful and kind and not hurtful or mean. More strength is shown in acting peacefully than in acting out in anger.

▷ Get and use wisdom every day by being in God's Word, forgiving others, being grateful, not comparing your life to others', and letting God transform your heart to be more like His.

▷ As we receive God's wisdom in our hearts, we find humility, forgiveness, kindness, and love.

 TODAY'S GOD SHOT

When we feel sad or when fear tries to take over our thoughts, sometimes the only thing we can do is remember how good God is and that He is in control! God cannot be defeated, He is working out His plans for your good, and He's where the joy is!

ACTIVITY

Fill in the speech bubbles as you talk to God using the acronym **P**raise **R**epent **A**sk **Y**es. See Day 22 for an example of praying with this acronym.

Proverbs 19–21

QUICK LOOK: Proverbs 19:17—"Anyone who is kind to poor people lends to the LORD. God will reward them for what they have done."

▷ Having a friendship with God takes time and work, but spending time with God and letting Him guide us is so much better than trying to do life all on our own.

▷ When our sin brings negative consequences, we must remember not to blame God. Instead, we should remember He is patient, slow to anger, and ready to forgive us when we are angry with Him.

▷ As we speak words of knowledge and wisdom to the world that needs it, we must stay humble and give God all the credit.

TODAY'S GOD SHOT

In Proverbs 19:17, God says, "Whoever is generous to the poor lends to the LORD, and he will repay him for his deed" (ESV). We can be generous and trust that God will provide all we need because He's the one who repays what we give. God cares about all of our needs, He's generous, and He's where the joy is!

ACTIVITY

Read the scenarios below and circle a thumbs-up if the kid is giving with a happy heart or circle a thumbs-down if they are not.

 Trevor gives his friend a toy at his friend's birthday party but then cries all the way home because he didn't get that toy too.

 When Taysha brings chalk to the park to share, one of her friends gets mad and breaks her chalk. Taysha asks her friend if she needs help and brings her another piece.

 Alejandro gives up time with his friends to rake his grandma's leaves, even though no one asked him to do it.

 Hana gives her mom flowers and then immediately asks her mom what she's going to give her.

Proverbs 22–24

 QUICK LOOK: Proverbs 23:12—"Apply your heart to what you are taught. Listen carefully to words of knowledge."

▷ Avoiding sin, keeping our attention on God, choosing friends wisely, and being obedient to God are very important things we must choose to do based on God's Word.

▷ Solomon, one of the richest and wisest men, tells us not to focus on trying to get rich, but instead to spend time and energy on the things that God says to do.

▷ Wisdom is knowing how to apply knowledge and understanding to our everyday life and friendship with Jesus.

 TODAY'S GOD SHOT

Proverbs 24:17 says, "Do not rejoice when your enemy falls, and let not your heart be glad when he stumbles" (ESV). God loves us and wants everyone to be part of His family. He says in Ezekiel 33:11, "When sinful people die, it does not give me any joy. But when they turn away from their sins and live, that makes me very happy." Jesus died on the cross for us, and when we ask God into our life, He helps us to see and believe He's where the joy is!

ACTIVITY

Sin is doing, saying, or thinking something that God says is wrong. Use the box below to write down a sin you need to be forgiven for.

- Now ask God to forgive you for that sin and accept His forgiveness.
- Scribble over the sin you wrote down until you can't see it anymore. As you do this, thank God for His Son, Jesus, and how His death and forgiveness completely cover our sin. Hebrews 8:12 says, "I will remember their sins no more" (ESV). How great is our God!

1 Kings 5–6; 2 Chronicles 2–3

 QUICK LOOK: 1 Kings 5:5—Solomon said, "So I'm planning to build a temple. I want to build it for the Name of the LORD my God."

▷ Five hundred years after the Israelites left Egypt, they are finally getting a permanent temple where they can worship God.

▷ Solomon uses his God-given wisdom and riches to build the temple by asking for trees from another kingdom, getting hundreds of thousands of people to help, and gathering precious stones and materials.

▷ God is quick to remind Solomon that impressive buildings aren't what guarantee His presence with them, but that their friendship is based on hearts that love and obey Him.

 TODAY'S GOD SHOT

The temple is built on Mount Moriah. This is the same place where Abraham offered Isaac before God stopped him and provided a ram for a sacrifice (see Genesis 22). The highest point on Mount Moriah is called Mount Calvary, and that is where Jesus sacrificed His life on the cross for us. From beginning to end, God always has been and always will be our Provider, because He's where the joy is!

 ACTIVITY

Color in the truth on the next page.

1 Kings 7; 2 Chronicles 4

QUICK LOOK: 1 Kings 7:21—"Huram set the pillars up at the temple porch. The pillar on the south he named Jakin [meaning "He will establish"]. The one on the north he named Boaz [meaning "in strength"]."

RECAP

▷ Today, the description of the temple is interrupted to zoom in on the construction of Solomon's house and how he uses many of the same things on his house that were used to build the temple.

▷ Solomon hires people like Huram, who are filled with wisdom and understanding, to work on the temple furniture. Huram gives symbolic names to the pillars outside the temple to remind God's people of His strength.

▷ In these verses, we not only see what's happening with Solomon's house, but also his heart. His desire for nice things will eventually become a problem for him.

TODAY'S GOD SHOT

Even though this temple was built to be much more permanent than the tabernacle God's people had before, it will eventually get destroyed. But don't worry! The good news is that God doesn't live in a building anymore; He lives in the hearts and lives of His people. And He's where the joy is!

ACTIVITY

Use the space below to draw a picture of your house. Thank God for your home and the people and things inside of it as you draw.

1 Kings 8; 2 Chronicles 5

QUICK LOOK: 1 Kings 8:27—Solomon said, "But will you really live on earth? After all, the heavens can't hold you. In fact, even the highest heavens can't hold you. So this temple I've built certainly can't hold you!"

▷ The temple is finished, so the Levites begin moving all the holy furniture from the tabernacle to the temple. They also move the ark of the covenant, making sure to carry it the way God said to.

▷ God's presence fills the temple, and Solomon asks God to be in control of everything. He also asks for God to act with justice and mercy toward them, since He alone knows the hearts of all.

▷ The people have a weeklong party, and as it ends they go to their homes full of joy for all of the good things God has done for them.

TODAY'S GOD SHOT

Solomon praises God for keeping His promise. In 1 Kings 8:27, Solomon asks Him, "But will you really live on earth?" He has no idea that Jesus will come to earth to heal people, feed the hungry, raise people from the dead, and do so much more! If you think you understand the joy God gives at this point in the Bible, just wait, because it's only going to get better. He's where the joy is!

ACTIVITY

God kept His promise to Solomon, and He keeps His promises to you. Pray this prayer.

Dear God, thank You for being so big that the highest heavens cannot hold You. You are powerful and keep Your promises. I am in awe of Your love for me. I love You! Amen.

2 Chronicles 6–7; Psalm 136

QUICK LOOK: 2 Chronicles 6:39—Solomon said, "Then listen to them from heaven. It's the place where you live. Listen to their prayer."

RECAP

▷ The temple is complete, so the people celebrate! Solomon begs God, who is always present everywhere, to hear from heaven and answer their prayers.

▷ God's covenant, or promise, with Israel depends on their obedience. God tells Solomon in a vision that they will disobey Him and that He will have to discipline them through drought (no rain), locusts (a type of grasshopper), and disease. If His people return to Him, He will forgive them and never leave them.

▷ Today's reading ends with Psalm 136, where we see the phrase "His faithful love continues forever" repeated. This psalm celebrates God's love and praises Him for His mighty works of creation and salvation, and even for a few acts of destruction.

TODAY'S GOD SHOT

Today Solomon said, "There isn't anyone who doesn't sin" (2 Chronicles 6:36), which is said in different ways throughout the Bible. The fact that every person on this earth sins shows us just how amazing it is that God comes and lives in our hearts even though He knows we mess up. He's here, He's not going anywhere, and He's where the joy is!

ACTIVITY

Look for words that describe who God is.

```
W X B M L D R P H W J V R S
G P R X N G W F M J I J L B
U G E P T E M J O V M U O Z
S R G C N X T K I C S Q V D
G A O X E J E U A C B M I N
W E T N K T V O I E M Y N I
P M N D N M D E J N W F G K
T E D E F J Q L H G G L G T
S K J A R B K P R E S E N T
U A I W J O T O Q G W Q X V
J E F E Q K U K T V E K S G
N T F B U L P S G J D X X L
C O M P A S S I O N A T E N
Z J L V C D X A U Z S M N C
```

WORD BANK

KIND   COMPASSIONATE   LOVING

JUST   PRESENT   GENEROUS

If you need help, check out the Word Search Answer Key on page 471.

Psalms 134, 146–150

 QUICK LOOK: Psalm 150:6—"Let everything that has breath praise the LORD. Praise the LORD."

 RECAP

▷ Today's readings include a psalm of blessing, a psalm of justice, and two psalms commanding all creation to praise God.

▷ The writer of Psalm 146 reminds us not to put our trust in people, but to put our confidence in God, who will never disappoint us and can bring us joy no matter our circumstances.

▷ We are reminded that God delights most in His creation of humanity, especially those people who love and trust in Him.

 TODAY'S GOD SHOT

Psalm 146 lists ten kinds of people that Jesus had relationships with: people treated badly, the hungry, the ones in prison, the blind, the ones who feel helpless, those who love to do what's right, people living in a land they are not from, those without parents, those whose husband or wife died, and even people who do wrong. If you find yourself on that list, how has God shown His love to you? We too can be kind and loving to everyone, like Jesus is, because He's where the joy is!

 ACTIVITY

Use the space below to write your own God shot today. What did you learn about who God is in the reading today, and what does that mean in your life?

....

....

....

1 Kings 9; 2 Chronicles 8

 QUICK LOOK: 1 Kings 9:3—"The Lᴏʀᴅ said to him, 'I have heard you pray to me. I have heard you ask me to help you. You have built this temple. I have set it apart for myself. My Name will be there forever. My eyes and my heart will always be there.'"

 RECAP

▷ Solomon spends twenty years building the temple, his house, and a house for his wife. Then he goes on to build many cities as well as boats with King Hiram to sail across the seas to sell and trade things they have.

▷ God tells Solomon that His eyes and heart will always be in the temple if Solomon obeys His rules and laws. But if he doesn't, the temple will become a pile of stones.

▷ Solomon's heart is becoming greedy and is divided between the ways of the world and following God.

 TODAY'S GOD SHOT

God has rules and a right way for things to be done. He gives them to us for our good. He knows we will make mistakes, and He's always there to forgive us. He is loving in all He does, and He's where the joy is!

 ACTIVITY

Unscramble the word that describes who God is.

IVLOGN ....

Proverbs 25–26

QUICK LOOK: Proverbs 25:2—"When God hides a matter, he gets glory. When kings figure out a matter, they get glory."

RECAP

▷ Today we dig back into the wisdom of Solomon and are reminded that Proverbs isn't a book of biblical laws—it's a book of general life advice.

▷ Both of these chapters talk over and over again about the power and importance of our words and how they can hurt or help those around us.

▷ Solomon tells us how good it is to have self-control and patience in everything we do and that too much of anything other than God is not good.

TODAY'S GOD SHOT

Sometimes God gets more glory when He doesn't tell us everything we want to know. There are things about Him that are mysterious, but He clearly tells us everything we need to obey Him. We can trust He will give us information when we need it, because He's where the joy is!

ACTIVITY

What is one question you have about God that you don't have the answer to?

....

....

....

○ ○ ○

Put the letter of each quality God wants us to have next to the correct definition.

A. HUMILITY   .... thinking before you say or act

B. WISDOM   .... waiting with a happy heart

C. SELF-CONTROL   .... making smart and good choices

D. PATIENCE   .... being friendly to others

E. GENTLENESS   .... putting others before yourself

F. KINDNESS   .... not being harsh with our words or actions

Proverbs 27–29

QUICK LOOK: Proverbs 28:26—"Those who trust in themselves are foolish. But those who live wisely are kept safe."

RECAP

▷ We shouldn't brag about tomorrow, because we don't know what will happen. And instead of bragging about ourselves, we should let other people say good things about us.

▷ As friends of God, we are to think and act differently from the rest of the world, showing grace, compassion, and love to the people around us.

▷ Those who are wise show self-control and patience and think before they speak, but those who are foolish are prideful and act as though they know everything.

TODAY'S GOD SHOT

God knows the future—He's outside of time, so He's already there. He knows the times we won't listen to Him and the times we'll be disobedient, but He never stops trying to have a friendship with us. God loves us so much, and He's where the joy is!

ACTIVITY

Look up these verses and fill in the missing words.

1. PROVERBS 27:6 "WOUNDS FROM A .... CAN BE

   TRUSTED."

2. PROVERBS 28:1 "BUT THOSE WHO DO WHAT IS ....

   ARE AS .... AS LIONS."

3. PROVERBS 29:11 "FOOLISH PEOPLE LET THEIR .... RUN

   WILD. BUT WISE PEOPLE KEEP THEMSELVES UNDER ...."

ANSWER KEY: 1. friend; 2. right, bold; 3. anger, control

Ecclesiastes 1–6

QUICK LOOK: Ecclesiastes 3:14—"I know that everything God does will last forever. Nothing can be added to it. And nothing can be taken from it. God does that so people will have respect for him."

RECAP

▷ The writer of Ecclesiastes, possibly Solomon, is a rich, successful, and powerful man who does an experiment to find out how to have a life full of joy.

▷ The only thing that truly brings joy in life is focusing on God. Everything else is meaningless and doesn't matter.

▷ Through good and bad seasons of life, we can trust God and know He is working everything together for a special purpose.

TODAY'S GOD SHOT

We sometimes work hard to get things that only make us happy for a moment. But everything God does for us will last forever. God is so powerful, and He's where the joy is!

ACTIVITY

Circle the things God says will bring us a life of joy.

GIVING TO OTHERS   BEING LAZY

LYING   GETTING MORE THINGS

BEING KIND   SPENDING TIME WITH GOD

Ecclesiastes 7–12

QUICK LOOK: Ecclesiastes 8:12—"An evil person may be guilty of a hundred crimes. Yet they may still live a long time. But I know that things will go better with those who have great respect for God."

RECAP

▷ Really think about how you are living, and realize that everything is a gift from God.

▷ A little foolishness can make a lot of wisdom useless. We should be wise with our thoughts and words.

▷ We will have tears and smiles, war and peace, pain and joy in our life, but it is always best to enjoy and trust God no matter what.

TODAY'S GOD SHOT

There's no formula for a long and successful life. All we can do is have great respect for God by obeying Him and trusting Him with whatever happens. We can find lasting joy and happiness with God because He's where the joy is!

ACTIVITY

How can you respect God when you . . .

Eat a meal? ....

....

Play with friends? ....

....

Go to bed? ....

....

1 Kings 10–11; 2 Chronicles 9

QUICK LOOK: 2 Chronicles 9:8—The queen of Sheba said to Solomon, "May the LORD your God be praised. He takes great delight in you."

▷ The queen of Sheba does not believe in God, but when she visits Solomon, she sees he is a king with great wisdom and wealth and she gives God credit for it all.

▷ Solomon's heart is eventually turned away from following God. He surrounds himself with women who don't love God, and he gathers up a lot of gold and horses, which God had told him not to do.

▷ Even though Solomon has been disobedient, God keeps His promise to David, Solomon's father. God says that after Solomon dies, ten of the twelve tribes of Israel will be led by Jeroboam, one of Solomon's servants, and Solomon's son, Rehoboam, will be king after Solomon's death.

TODAY'S GOD SHOT

The queen of Sheba blesses God as she sees that God has set Solomon on the throne and given him power on purpose. It's hard for us to see what God might be doing when He puts certain people in charge of things, but that's where we have to trust that God is working out things we can't see and that He's where the joy is!

ACTIVITY

Below are some words that describe who God is. Circle the words you want to describe you, too, and pray to ask God to help you.

LOVING   GENEROUS   GENTLE   WISE   HONEST

BRAVE   JOYFUL   PEACEFUL   PATIENT

Proverbs 30–31

 QUICK LOOK: Proverbs 31:30—"Charm can fool you. Beauty fades. But a woman who has respect for the LORD should be praised."

 RECAP

▷ Proverbs 30 is written by a man named Agur, who tells us that God is more powerful and wise than we are and reminds us to keep reading God's Word.

▷ Agur asks God to keep him honest and to keep him from sin so that he doesn't forget about God and his need for Him.

▷ Proverbs 31 describes a woman who has wisdom in her heart and has godly values.

 TODAY'S GOD SHOT

God gets praise when we are in awe of who He is and rely on Him to make us strong and wise. We aren't the ones who are great, but God is. He gives us strength and wisdom because He's where the joy is!

 ACTIVITY

Pray this prayer.

> *Dear God,* I am in awe of who You are! You give me everything I need to be strong and wise. Help me to fully rely on You to make me great. I love You! Amen.

1 Kings 12–14

QUICK LOOK: 1 Kings 14:12–13—The LORD said to Jeroboam's wife, "Now go back home. When you enter your city, your son will die. All the Israelites will mourn for him. . . . That is because he is the only one in Jeroboam's royal house in whom I have found anything good."

▷ After Solomon dies, his kingdom is divided, leaving his son, King Rehoboam, to take over the southern kingdom. King Jeroboam, who was in Egypt, comes back and leads the northern kingdom.

▷ King Jeroboam knows God's temple is in the southern kingdom of Judah, but he sets up his own worship site in the northern kingdom of Israel, where he worships idols and not God.

▷ God's promise to King Jeroboam depends on his obedience, so eventually, his disobedience leads to consequences that include the death of his son and the kingdom remaining divided.

TODAY'S GOD SHOT

When someone dies, it's hard to understand. God allowed Jeroboam's son to die and said he was the only one in Jeroboam's house who He could find anything good in. The boy escapes the evil world, where his earthly father rules, and goes to the peaceful home of his heavenly Father in heaven. We can trust God with life and death because He's where the joy is!

ACTIVITY

Decode this verse to find out what happens when people who believe in Jesus die.

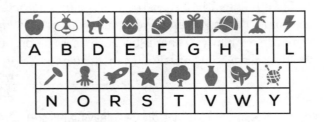

John 3:16 says,

" ___ ___ ___ so loved the

___ ___ ___ ___ ___ that he gave His

___ ___ ___ ___ ___ ___ ___ ___ ___ ___

___ ___ ___. Anyone who

___ ___ ___ ___ ___ ___ ___ ___

in him will ___ ___ ___ ___ ___ ___ but

will have ___ ___ ___ ___ ___ ___ ___

___ ___ ___ ___. "

2 Chronicles 10–12

QUICK LOOK: 2 Chronicles 11:4—"The LORD says, 'Do not go up to fight against your relatives. I want every one of you to go back home. Things have happened exactly the way I planned them.' So the young men obeyed the LORD's message. They turned back. They didn't march out against Jeroboam."

▷ Unfortunately, as King Rehoboam's power grows, his heart turns away from God, which leads his people to turn from God too.

▷ Because King Rehoboam and his people disobey, God sends the Egyptians to take a lot of land and valuable things from the people of Judah. This loss makes them feel weak, so they humbly apologize to God, receiving both His forgiveness and the consequences of their sin.

▷ King Jeroboam put his own priests in power to worship idols and make sacrifices to goats instead of God.

TODAY'S GOD SHOT

God's plan isn't always easy. God told Rehoboam to not fight against Jeroboam even though he had taken some of his people. Rehoboam surrenders to God by obeying Him and sends his soldiers home. We gain things in surrendering to God that we'd never have otherwise. He can be trusted. He's where the joy is!

ACTIVITY

God is happy when we give up doing what we want in order to do what He asks us to do! When was the last time you obeyed? Write about or draw a picture of that time below.

1 Kings 15; 2 Chronicles 13–16

> **QUICK LOOK:** 2 Chronicles 15:2—"The Lord is with you when you are with him. If you really look for him, you will find him."

▷ King Rehoboam, the first king of Southern Judah, dies and is replaced by his son Abijah. Rehoboam didn't follow God, and neither does Abijah.

▷ After Abijah dies, the next king of Judah is his son, Asa. Asa follows God and sets out to make things right in Southern Judah.

▷ After learning an evil king is planning an attack against him, Asa creates his own plan, and he doesn't seek God's counsel. Because God isn't pleased, the consequence of not trusting God for victory is that he'll have many enemies who will go to war against him.

 TODAY'S GOD SHOT

God is with you, and if you really look for Him, you will find Him. That's what you are doing when you study the Bible! Keep seeking Him, because you probably know Him more today than you did yesterday, but not as much as you'll know Him tomorrow. He's where the joy is!

 ACTIVITY

You're been seeking God for at least 176 days. What do you know about God that you didn't know 177 days ago?

....

....

....

1 Kings 16; 2 Chronicles 17

 QUICK LOOK: 2 Chronicles 17:10—"All the kingdoms of the lands around Judah became afraid of the LORD. So they didn't go to war against Jehoshaphat."

▷ Baasha is king in Northern Israel when the prophet Jehu tells him his household will be wiped out. And they are.

▷ Asa's son Jehoshaphat takes over for his dad. God is with Jehoshaphat, because his reign is similar to David's—he seeks God and keeps His laws.

▷ Jehoshaphat tears down the high places and even sends officials and priests throughout Judah to teach people God's truths. Even his enemies are impacted by the way he rules with dignity and honor.

 TODAY'S GOD SHOT

God is sovereign over the hearts of our enemies. Whether He turns those hearts toward Himself or just away from harming His kids, it's the good and right thing, and it serves His purposes. He's a bigger God than we realize, accomplishing far more than we can see, because He does a lot of His work at a heart level and He's where the joy is!

 ACTIVITY

What does it mean that God is "sovereign"? If you need help, ask a grown-up who loves Jesus!

....

....

1 Kings 17–19

QUICK LOOK: 1 Kings 19:11–12—"The LORD said, 'Go out. Stand on the mountain in front of me. I am going to pass by.' As the LORD approached, a very powerful wind tore the mountains apart. It broke up the rocks. But the LORD wasn't in the wind. After the wind there was an earthquake. But the LORD wasn't in the earthquake. After the earthquake a fire came. But the LORD wasn't in the fire. And after the fire there was only a gentle whisper."

▷ Elijah, a prophet who tells people the truth about God, confronts evil King Ahab and tells him that the drought has been caused by Ahab's sin and idolatry. Elijah calls for two bulls and challenges Ahab and his false prophets to meet on Mount Carmel to see whose god will burn up the sacrifice.

▷ The false prophets cry for hours, but nothing happens to their bull. When it's Elijah's turn, God sends fire from heaven, burning up not just the bull and the wood, but also the stones and dirt. The people turn to worship God, and the drought is over.

▷ Ahab's wife, Jezebel, is angry and threatens to kill Elijah. Elijah is afraid and moves to a cave in the wilderness, but then God shows up to talk to him! God tells him to appoint two kings and a prophet named Elisha.

TODAY'S GOD SHOT

Elijah has seen that God can do great big things, and now God is showing Elijah that He can be small too—like a whisper. You have to be really close to someone to hear their whisper. Elijah is so close he has to cover his face. We want the whisper of God's nearness because He's where the joy is!

ACTIVITY

Not only can we talk to God, but He can talk to us! Even though God is in heaven, He can talk to you in so many ways.

Unscramble the words to find out a few of the ways God can talk to you and thank God for talking to you in that way!

LBIEB   B .... L ......

YOHL PRSITI   H .... Y ...... P .... I ......

EPOLEP   P ...... O .... E

1 Kings 20–21

QUICK LOOK: 1 Kings 21:29—The LORD said to Elijah, "Have you seen how Ahab has made himself humble in my sight? Because he has done that, I will not bring trouble on him while he lives."

▷ King Ahab is at war. Following a prophet's instructions, Israel attacks and wins. Afterward, Ahab agrees to leave his enemy alive. This is the opposite of what God commanded him to do.

▷ Ahab's wife, Jezebel, signs a letter with Ahab's seal and uses his name to put together a gathering, presumably to honor God. But her plan is to have Naboth killed so she can take his land for her husband.

▷ God holds Ahab responsible for his wife's sin. God tells Ahab through Elijah that they will all die. This devastates Ahab, and he shows repentance. God shows him mercy.

TODAY'S GOD SHOT

Anytime God makes a promise, He keeps it. The only time He modifies it is for the sake of mercy or grace. We see that with Ahab. God loves to show mercy to people, even the most wicked among us. He's eager to forgive— how can you not love a God like that? He's where the joy is!

ACTIVITY

To repent means to confess and tell God the sinful thing you've done and let Him know that you're sorry and want to do things His way next time. You can trust that God will forgive you, so don't be afraid to tell Him!

Think of a way you have sinned and done the wrong thing this week. Then fill in the blank below as you pray.

> *Dear God,* I know I sinned when I ....
> .... I'm sorry, and I want to do the right thing next time.
> *Thank You for forgiving me.*

239

1 Kings 22; 2 Chronicles 18

 QUICK LOOK: 2 Chronicles 18:33—"But someone shot an arrow without taking aim. The arrow hit the king of Israel between the parts of his armor."

 RECAP

▷ Ahab and Jehoshaphat join armies. Jehoshaphat asks if they can seek God's counsel. Ahab agrees but doesn't like what Micaiah the prophet tells him.

▷ When it's time to go to war, Ahab tries to be tricky and plans to wear a disguise during battle. He tells Jehoshaphat to wear his royal robes, which will make him stand out as a target!

▷ Ahab's plan to disguise himself seems to work at first, because the Syrian archers go after Jehoshaphat in his royal robes, but they withdraw when they see it's not Ahab. Then, one of the archers randomly fires off one arrow that hits and kills Ahab. Just the way Micaiah and Elijah had prophesied.

 TODAY'S GOD SHOT

God will always complete His plan—nothing stops Him. The man who killed Ahab may have shot an arrow without taking aim, but nothing is random where God is concerned. What a great comfort! He's where the joy is!

 ACTIVITY

How does it make you feel that nothing is random with God? Circle all the emojis that you feel.

HAPPY   NERVOUS   THANKFUL   SCARED   SAFE   ANGRY

Tell God how you feel! Don't worry about hurting His feelings. He's your friend, and He wants you to be honest with Him.

2 Chronicles 19–23

 QUICK LOOK: 2 Chronicles 20:12—"We don't know what to do. But we're looking to you to help us."

▷ A group of armies comes to attack Jehoshaphat in Judah. He has the people fast and pray to seek God's will and help. A worship leader prophesies and tells them that the battle is God's and that they will not need to fight.

▷ The worship leaders lead the army into battle, and as they worship God, the attacking armies start fighting each other. Just as God said, they didn't have to fight!

▷ When Jehoshaphat dies, he is followed by three wicked rulers. A priest hides a son born into the family named Joash. He becomes king at seven years old!

 TODAY'S GOD SHOT

Jehoshaphat knew that no matter what terrible things might come their way, they could look to God for help. They have a relationship with a trustworthy God who will ultimately rescue them. He's where the joy is!

 ACTIVITY

God wants to help us no matter what terrible things might happen. What is something that you need God's help with? Write it down below and then pray and ask for God's help. And trust that He will help you!

....

....

Obadiah 1; Psalms 82–83

 QUICK LOOK: Psalm 83:3—"They make clever plans against your people. They make evil plans against those you love."

 RECAP

▷ Enemies come to take over Jerusalem, and the prophet Obadiah tells the Edomites they are wrong for not helping God's people.

▷ Obadiah lets Edom know that God will have justice in this situation. What they have done to others will also be done to them.

▷ God values justice, and He loves to show mercy and kindness to those in need.

 TODAY'S GOD SHOT

God takes it personally when His people are mistreated. He isn't going to sit back and let His people get bullied without doing something about it. He's powerful and protective, and He's where the joy is!

 ACTIVITY

God wants you to show mercy and kindness to those who need your help. Draw a ☆ next to something you can do today!

Speak up for someone who is afraid to speak up for themselves.

Play with, sit with, and befriend someone who doesn't look like you.

When you hear someone say something mean about someone else, do not join in, but do not stay silent. Instead, speak the truth in a loving way.

2 Kings 1–4

QUICK LOOK: 2 Kings 3:17—Elisha announced, "This will happen because the LORD says, 'You will not see wind or rain. But this valley will be filled with water.'"

RECAP

▶ The time has come for Elijah to leave Elisha, but before he leaves, Elisha asks for a double portion of what Elijah has. God gives it to him when he sees Elijah taken to heaven by a chariot of fire.

▶ Israel and Judah team up to go to war with Moab and end up in the desert with no water. They consult with Elisha, and he tells them that God will bring them water and that they will defeat Moab.

▶ Elisha performs many small miracles, like helping a widow provide for her family. God not only uses Elisha to provide for the poor, but He also uses him to provide for the rich.

TODAY'S GOD SHOT

When Elisha prophesies to the kings about how they'll defeat Moab, he tells them that God will provide in a way they will not see. We can't always see what God is doing, but we can trust Him because He's where the joy is!

ACTIVITY

Do you trust that God is working in your life even when you can't see what He is doing?

YES   NO

If you answered yes, pray this simple prayer:

> *God, I trust You are working even though I can't see it. Amen.*

If you answered no, pray this simple prayer:

> *God, please help me to trust that You are working even though I can't see it. Amen.*

2 Kings 5–8

 QUICK LOOK: 2 Kings 5:15—"Naaman said, 'Now I know that there is no God anywhere in the whole world except in Israel.'"

 RECAP

▷ Naaman is a Syrian military commander who has a servant girl from Israel who knows Elisha. She says Elisha can heal his skin disease. Naaman goes to him, and Elisha tells him to take seven baths. Naaman is healed and believes in God.

▷ God gives attention not just to major things like disease but to tiny details like a borrowed axe. When a young prophet loses an axe-head in a river, Elisha miraculously recovers it.

▷ Elisha continues to prophesy, and all of his prophecies are fulfilled.

 TODAY'S GOD SHOT

In Naaman's story, God seeks out His enemy who doubts Him. The God who has been granting Naaman favor all along grants him the greatest favor of all—a forever friendship with Himself. God seeks out His enemies and puts His people in their lives to point them to Him, because He's where the joy is!

 ACTIVITY

Did you know that God wants to use you to point people to Him? That's right. How you respond to people in your life (your parents, your friends, and even the mean kid at school) can point people to God!

2 Kings 9–11

 QUICK LOOK: 2 Kings 10:30—"The LORD said to Jehu, 'You have done well. You have accomplished what is right in my eyes. You have done to Ahab's royal house everything I wanted you to do.'"

RECAP

▷ Prophets are powerful people in ancient Israel. God runs their nation and speaks through the prophets.

▷ Elisha sends a prophet to anoint Jehu as Israel's next king and to tell him to kill all of Ahab's descendants, including King Joram, Israel's current ruler.

▷ Jehu continues this mission until it's complete. It may seem extreme, but this is all part of God's promise to these people.

 TODAY'S GOD SHOT

When we zoom out on God and His plans, we also see the wickedness of rebellious people, and we're reminded of how He has provided for them in the past. But they go their own way. Even when we don't see God, we know He is always working and He's where the joy is!

 ACTIVITY

God sees everything. Even the small details. Can you spot five differences between the pictures on the next page?

2 Kings 12–13; 2 Chronicles 24

QUICK LOOK: 2 Kings 13:21—"One day some Israelites were burying a man. Suddenly they saw a group of robbers. So they threw the man's body into Elisha's tomb. The body touched Elisha's bones. When it did, the man came back to life again. He stood up on his feet."

RECAP

▷ Southern Judah's new king, Joash, is only seven years old. Fortunately, the priest is a wise advisor to him. As long as the priest is alive, he seems to keep Joash in line. Joash's reign goes fairly well until the priest dies.

▷ Meanwhile, in Northern Israel, Jehu's son Jehoahaz is on the throne. He's wicked, but he does seem to recognize what God is doing in Israel. He seeks God's favor, but he's not really seeking God, he's seeking relief.

▷ Elisha dies. Later, as the locals are preparing to bury a dead man, they get distracted and accidentally throw the body into Elisha's open grave instead. When the body hits Elisha's bones, the man comes back to life!

TODAY'S GOD SHOT

We only get a couple of sentences about the accidental resurrection, but they remind us that Elisha's powers don't come from him. They are given to him by God, who—unlike Elisha—is alive and active. He's working even when we can't, and He doesn't need our help. God is going to be good regardless, and He's where the joy is!

ACTIVITY

Like Elisha, God has given you good gifts that are special ways you can serve Him. Can you name at least one gift that He's given you?

....

Thank God for this wonderful gift!

2 Kings 14; 2 Chronicles 25

QUICK LOOK: 2 Chronicles 25:8—A man of God said to Amaziah, "Go and fight bravely in battle if you want to. But God will destroy you right in front of your enemies. God has the power to help you or destroy you."

▷ When King Joash, who became king at age seven, was killed by some of his servants in Southern Judah, his son Amaziah ascended to the throne. He obeys God's commands and refuses to punish children for the sins of their fathers.

▷ Amaziah is a good king, especially at first, but even his good actions aren't done fully following God.

▷ Even without the help of the Israelite soldiers, Amaziah has a significant military victory over Edom. But this God-given victory leads him down a path of pride, because he forgets who granted him success.

TODAY'S GOD SHOT

When the man of God confronts Amaziah for hiring soldiers from outside of Judah, he tells him that God can help him or destroy him. It's in God's hands. Many people like to think of God as not picking sides in anything, but the Bible says He does. We should aim to be on His side, because He is always victorious, and He's where the joy is!

 **ACTIVITY**

How do we know if we are on God's side? He has given us a helper called the Holy Spirit! Five of these things about the Holy Spirit are true and two are false. Think about each one and circle T for true or F for false.

T F He helps you understand what you read in the Bible.

T F He gives you good or bad feelings to help you know the right thing to do.

T F He tries to confuse you.

T F He reminds you of what God says in His Word.

T F He helps you trust God each day.

T F He tempts you to do wrong things.

T F He talks to God for you when you don't know what to pray.

The Holy Spirit will never confuse you or tempt you to do wrong things. The rest of those statements help us understand what a friend we have when the Holy Spirit lives inside of us. Everyone who believes in Jesus has the power of the Holy Spirit in them!

Jonah 1–4

 QUICK LOOK: Jonah 2:8—Jonah prayed, "Some people worship the worthless statues of their gods. They turn away from God's love for them."

RECAP

▷ God tells Jonah to go to the Ninevites and tell them to stop doing wrong things, but Jonah hates the Ninevites and doesn't want them to repent. So Jonah runs and hops on a ship headed in the opposite direction.

▷ A storm hits, the sailors throw Jonah overboard, and then God tells a big fish to swallow Jonah and he's inside for three days and three nights. Jonah prays and thanks God for his life, but he's not sorry for what he's done. The fish vomits him up on the shore, and God tells him to go to the Ninevites and tell them to repent.

▷ So Jonah, unrepentant, goes to Nineveh to tell *them* to repent. He is full of pride, bitterness, and self-pity. Jonah is so focused on himself that he can't be happy when Nineveh repents!

 TODAY'S GOD SHOT

When we chase after the things that only make us happy, they can leave us feeling empty a lot of the time. But when we seek to do what God wants us to do, we're always met with His love—it's been there all along, and He's where the joy is!

 ACTIVITY

It's easy to say yes when an opportunity is easy or fun, but when it's hard, that's a whole other story! Has there been a time when you felt like God wanted you to do something, but it just seemed too hard?

Now pray this prayer:

Father God, even when it's hard, I say yes to doing what You want me to do. Thank You for loving me no matter what!

2 Kings 15; 2 Chronicles 26

 QUICK LOOK: 2 Chronicles 26:5—"As long as Uzziah obeyed the LORD, God gave him success."

▷ King Azariah takes over after his father's death. After his people have a series of military victories that make him rich and famous, Azariah grows prideful and decides he wants to burn incense in the temple in Jerusalem, which is an act reserved only for priests.

▷ The priests are shocked and tell Azariah to stop, but he's unrepentant and grows angry with them. God strikes him with leprosy, and he has to leave the temple immediately.

▷ Northern Israel has five short-lived kings and is beginning to fall apart.

 TODAY'S GOD SHOT

When God strikes Azariah with leprosy in the temple, it shows God's holiness. He punishes Azariah's rebellion and removes him from the throne without killing him, which also demonstrates His mercy. So many of God's attributes are on display in this one story—He's righteous, merciful, and wise, and He's where the joy is!

 ACTIVITY

God is so good! Search and find some of God's attributes on the next page!

```
F O R G I V I N G W O R
M T R K Q Q V Z E L L Z
J N F O N U L E G U V L
Y E J R O E G D G F I U
R I G H T E O U S I C F
W T Q L Q X J U U C T R
K A G U S M Y E W R O E
M P N F A T L I Q E R W
M H I Y P Q O Q R M I O
O W V O Y N H V O V O P
I A O J N F Q I V K U W
G H L W I S E Z Q L S L
```

WORD BANK

HOLY	MERCIFUL	WISE	LOVING
RIGHTEOUS	VICTORIOUS	JOYFUL	
POWERFUL	PATIENT	FORGIVING	

If you need help, check out the Word Search Answer Key on page 471.

Isaiah 1–4

QUICK LOOK: Isaiah 4:5–6—"The LORD's glory will be like a tent over everything. It will cover the people and give them shade from the hot sun all day long. It will be a safe place where they can hide from storms and rain."

▷ Isaiah is writing to Southern Judah and addresses what's been happening in Northern Israel and how God is dealing with their sins.

▷ Isaiah says Assyria's attack on Israel is punishment. God is after their hearts, so He describes what a changed heart would look like, which includes caring for the poor and needy in their society.

▷ Judah grows fearful, making agreements with other nations to protect themselves, but Isaiah says their safety is fake. He tells them they are like prideful women and says God is about to destroy all the things they find their pride in.

TODAY'S GOD SHOT

Our reading ends with a beautiful reminder that God is a place of protection and refuge—just like the tabernacle and the temple, where God came to dwell with them. God wants to be with us, and He sent the Son and the Spirit to be with us forever because He's where the joy is!

ACTIVITY

In today's verse, God is like a tent or shade on a hot, sunny day. Draw a picture below of yourself in a tent under the shade, and thank God for being a safe place.

Isaiah 5–8

QUICK LOOK: Isaiah 6:6–7—"A seraph flew over to me. He was holding a hot coal. He had used tongs to take it from the altar. He touched my mouth with the coal. He said, 'This has touched your lips. Your guilt has been taken away. Your sin has been paid for.'"

▷ Isaiah writes a poem to God's people, comparing God to a vine keeper and the Israelites to wild grapes. He highlights six ways they stink and pronounces a punishment corresponding to the bad things they are doing.

▷ Isaiah 6 is an awesome look into God's throne room. Imagine yourself as Isaiah. God's people are sinning, and you don't even want Him to forgive them sometimes. Isaiah has to have a proper view of God, and he needs God's mercy too. This vision is God's way of reminding him of that.

▷ When Southern Judah gets into military trouble, King Ahaz is likely tempted to make foreign alliances for protection, but Isaiah says to trust God for deliverance.

TODAY'S GOD SHOT

We can see Jesus show up in the throne room vision. When the seraph takes a burning coal from the altar and touches it to Isaiah's lips to purify him, it refers to the altar of sacrifice. What's on the altar of sacrifice that purifies us from our sin? Jesus! Thank God for the burning coal and for the death of Jesus, because He's where the joy is!

ACTIVITY

Jesus took your punishment by dying on the cross. Three days after Jesus died, God raised Him back to life to show everyone that He is stronger than sin and death! God did this for you so that you can be saved from having to spend forever apart from God. God wants to give you the gift of living forever with Him!

Amos 1–5

QUICK LOOK: Amos 3:6—The LORD said, "When someone blows a trumpet in a city, don't the people tremble with fear? When trouble comes to a city, hasn't the LORD caused it?"

▷ God gives Amos eight judgments for Israel and Judah.

▷ God has already used less-harsh ways to get His people to repent— drought, famine, locusts, mildew, disease, death—but none of it has turned their hearts.

▷ God has been patient with His people and begs them to seek Him and live, to hate the evil things that break His heart, and to love the things that align with Him.

TODAY'S GOD SHOT

God takes ownership of disaster here. This can be hard to understand, but it's okay to wrestle with those thoughts. It may seem comforting to think of bad things as coming only from the enemy, but we don't actually want the enemy to be in control, do we? God's judgment for sin is always deserved and often even delayed, because He's patient. He wouldn't be a good, trustworthy God if He ignored evil. God's judgment on His people is for restoration, because He's where the joy is!

ACTIVITY

Is there something that you feel God keeps trying to get your attention about? Maybe it's that feeling in your tummy after you say something rude to a friend or disrespect your parents. Repent today and ask God to forgive you!

Amos 6–9

QUICK LOOK: Amos 8:9–10—"The LORD and King announces, 'At that time I will make the sun go down at noon. The earth will become dark in the middle of the day. I will turn your holy feasts into times for mourning. I will turn all your songs into weeping.'"

▷ Amos calls out the leaders who relax in luxury, pay no mind to the needy and the poor, and fail to notice what's happened in their relationship with God. God shows Amos visions that tell about future destruction.

▷ Twice Amos pleads with God to wait, and He does. But when the third vision appears, Amos realizes it can't be avoided and is a necessary part of God's process to turn His people's hearts back to Himself.

▷ They've earned destruction, but God promises mercy. Of all the people in this story, those who get mercy are the only ones who don't get what they deserve.

TODAY'S GOD SHOT

When Amos describes this particular judgment of the Lord, it sounds just like the day when God the Son died. Everything God is about to put Israel through, He went through Himself. He went through it for them, and He went through it for us too. Does sin require harsh punishment? Yes. Does it seem unfair? Absolutely. And the most unfair thing of all is that we'll never receive that punishment ourselves, because Jesus took it for us and He's where the joy is!

ACTIVITY

What is SIN? Sin is any wrong thing we do instead of doing what God says is right.

Circle the actions below that God says are RIGHT for us to do and draw a line through the ones that are WRONG. Ask God to help you to do the right thing today!

TELL THE TRUTH   COMPLAIN   BE THANKFUL   BE KIND

TELL A LIE   OBEY   PUT YOURSELF FIRST   WORK HARD/ DO YOUR BEST

2 Chronicles 27; Isaiah 9–12

 QUICK LOOK: Isaiah 9:7—"His rule will be based on what is fair and right. It will last forever. The LORD's great love will make sure that happens. He rules over all."

 RECAP

▶ King Uzziah has just died, and his son Jotham, one of Judah's good kings, takes over the throne. After Jotham dies, his son Ahaz takes over the throne, and he is not a great king.

▶ We see God's anger coming for the wicked, and just because people are part of the kingdom of Israel doesn't mean they're part of the kingdom of God.

▶ Isaiah prophesies about Jesus's birth, saying He's a great ruler who will bring peace.

 TODAY'S GOD SHOT

God's anger is real, and sin has to be punished. And the only person who doesn't deserve God's anger stepped up to pay for our sin with His death so we don't ever have to face God's anger. Jesus took all our punishment on the cross. We get the love and the joy, because He's where the joy is!

 ACTIVITY

Have you ever gotten angry at your parents? Does that mean you don't love them? Of course not! It's hard to be angry at someone you care about. And God cares a whole lot about you. He loves you so much that His son, Jesus, took all of your punishment.

Let's thank God right now with this prayer!

Dear God, thank You for caring about me so much that You want me to make the right choices. Help me to make the right choices today to follow You. Amen.

Micah 1–7

 QUICK LOOK: Micah 5:4—"That promised son will stand firm and be a shepherd for his flock. The LORD will give him the strength to do it. The LORD his God will give him the authority to rule. His people will live safely. His greatness will reach from one end of the earth to the other."

 RECAP

▷ The prophet Micah tells the people that God is about to take action against their sins. Micah tells them how to grieve and be sad privately so that their enemies will not be happy.

▷ Micah says the rulers, priests, and prophets are all wicked. The people think these leaders will avoid consequences because they're too powerful, but Micah says they won't escape.

▷ Micah offers several warnings but always follows with a reminder that destruction and exile aren't the end for them, and God will establish a kingdom of peace on the earth. Micah reminds the people that God is after their hearts and calls them to repent.

 TODAY'S GOD SHOT

God's greatness, not our own, is where our only peace and security are found. When He increases and we decrease, that's where we find our greatest peace, because He's where the joy is!

 ACTIVITY

When we follow God and do what He wants us to do, He increases in us, and our friends and family can see Him in our actions and hear Him in our words. Write down two ways that your friends or family can see God through your actions and what you say.

1. ....

2. ....

2 Chronicles 28; 2 Kings 16–17

QUICK LOOK: 2 Kings 17:14—"But the people wouldn't listen. They were as stubborn as their people of long ago had been. Those people didn't trust in the LORD their God."

▷ Because of Judah's sins, God allows them to be defeated by Syria and Israel. Then Judah is attacked again. Ahaz, the king, is fearful, but instead of going to the King of the universe for help, he goes to the king of Assyria.

▷ The Assyrian king pretends he'll help but doesn't. So Ahaz sacrifices to more foreign gods.

▷ Meanwhile Northern Israel is under the leadership of wicked King Hoshea. Assyria's king has been collecting regular payments from Hoshea, but one year Hoshea skips out on that payment, and the Assyrian king finds out that Hoshea has been talking with the king of Egypt, which he's not happy about. The Assyrian king takes over Samaria and holds it captive.

TODAY'S GOD SHOT

God shows a lot of patience with His people. He has sent them multiple warnings over many, many years, and they continue to disobey Him. Now He has brought captivity to reveal what really holds their attention: idols. This may feel like punishment for Israel, but it's an act of great mercy. He's patient, He's merciful, and He's where the joy is!

ACTIVITY

To be patient means to wait with a happy heart. It's really easy to complain when we want something right away and a lot harder to wait patiently for it. What is something that you are patiently waiting for? Ask God to give you a happy heart while you wait.

Isaiah 13–17

QUICK LOOK: Isaiah 16:9—"Jazer weeps for the vines of Sibmah. And so do I. Heshbon and Elealeh, I soak you with my tears!"

▷ Isaiah prophesies against other nations that worship other gods, starting with Babylon, a ruling power of the ancient world. God will use their sinful ways to work out His long-term plans to bless His people—initially through discipline, then through restoration.

▷ Next is Assyria, who will destroy Northern Israel. God will punish them, and the burden they've placed on Israel will be broken, freeing Israel. Then Isaiah reminds the Philistines that God has only promised to preserve and protect His people, so even if they see relief, it won't last.

▷ Moab's prophecy has a different tone from the other nations', because God mourns over Moab's destruction. And last, the prophecy for Damascus says it'll be a heap of ruins.

TODAY'S GOD SHOT

It's incredible to see how tenderhearted God is toward Moab, a nation that has rejected Him. Some people may not expect to see that in the Old Testament, but His character has always been the same—God the Father, God the Son, and God the Spirit. He's the same yesterday, today, and forever because He's where the joy is!

ACTIVITY

God does not change! That is something we can have confidence in. Write three things you have learned about God since you started this reading plan.

1. ....

   ....

2. ....

   ....

3. ....

   ....

Those things you learned were true when the Bible was written, and they are true now! Thank You, God!

Isaiah 18–22

 QUICK LOOK: Isaiah 19:3—The LORD said, "The people of Egypt will lose hope. I will keep them from doing what they plan to do."

▷ Isaiah gives more prophecies to the nations surrounding Judah. There is a mystery nation, and Isaiah warns them that God is about to bring judgment.

▷ Next is Egypt, and God promises to confuse their wisdom, to bring hard things on them the way they've brought hard things on others, and to turn them against each other. But God says that Assyria and Egypt, two of the most powerful enemies of God's people, will worship Him!

▷ Finally, Isaiah is devastated by what he has to tell Jerusalem. Jerusalem will be attacked and destroyed, but when they realize destruction is coming, they still won't repent.

 TODAY'S GOD SHOT

When God talks to Egypt and tells them that He is going to confuse their wisdom, the thought of God being able to change our minds can be confusing. But it can also be so encouraging. If God couldn't do that, how else could God the Spirit guide us into all truth, or remind us of what Jesus said? He is willing and able to help us understand His thoughts and His Word, because He's where the joy is!

 ACTIVITY

The way you think affects the way you act. When a thought comes to your mind, ask yourself these questions before you do anything with that thought.

Is it true?

Is it right?

Is it respectful?

God, what do You want me to do?

Isaiah 23–27

 QUICK LOOK: Isaiah 26:12—"LORD, you give us peace. You are the one who has done everything we've accomplished."

 RECAP

▷ The last batch of judgment for foreign nations begins with Tyre and Sidon, Phoenician cities that specialize in international trade. They're wealthy, influential, popular, and prideful. It seems like their hearts don't actually turn to God, but He still uses them to bless His people.

▷ Chapter 24 describes the judgment of the whole earth—from destruction to restoration. God can be trusted because He has a perfect track record.

▷ The destruction scenes aren't the end. God puts death to death, there'll be no more tears, and He'll throw a big feast on the holy hill of Mount Zion!

 TODAY'S GOD SHOT

God the Son has fulfilled all of God the Father's requirements to cover our sin debt. And as if that weren't enough, God the Spirit is equipping and allowing us to fulfill God's specific plans for us in our lives. God is at work in you! He's creating both the desire in you and the actions through you that please Him. He does the doing, and He's where the joy is!

 ACTIVITY

God has a special plan for your life, and He has given you special gifts! What gifts do you think He has given you? Circle two from the list below (or add your own on the line), and ask God how He wants you to use those gifts!

GENEROSITY   CREATIVITY   COURAGE   LEADERSHIP

WISDOM   SERVING OTHERS   FAITH   ENCOURAGEMENT

2 Kings 18; 2 Chronicles 29–31; Psalm 48

 QUICK LOOK: 2 Chronicles 30:9—The messengers said, "The LORD your God is kind and tender. He won't turn away from you if you return to him."

▷ While Judah's King Ahaz was terrible, his son Hezekiah is one of Judah's best kings. He helps rebuild the temple and points people back to God. They're finally beginning to admit they have done wrong things. When you repent, you turn away from wrong things to do things God's way.

▷ The Assyrians attack Judah, taking over cities and demanding money. They tell them not to trust God because He's not real, and they even promise to give them wealth and prosperity if they follow Assyria instead. But the people don't respond.

▷ As Judah reinstates all the long-forgotten practices, this is a reminder to teach God's ways to all generations.

 TODAY'S GOD SHOT

God is kind and quick to forgive. Hezekiah knows God's heart, so in his letter of invitation, he promises the people that God will not turn away from them if they return to Him. They are finally seeking God, and He's where the joy is!

 ACTIVITY

On a scale of one to ten, how easy is it for you to admit you've done something wrong and turn back to God, asking Him to forgive you? Circle your answer below.

EASY   HARD

1   2   3   4   5   6   7   8   9   10

It might be hard to admit you've done something wrong, but you can trust that God will not be mad at you when you tell Him. He will forgive you!

Hosea 1–7

 QUICK LOOK: Hosea 1:10—The LORD said, "But the time will come when the people of Israel will be like the sand on the seashore. It can't be measured or counted. Now it is said about them, 'You are not my people.' But at that time they will be called 'children of the living God.'"

 RECAP

▷ The people's hearts have grown away from God, so He sends Hosea to give them a message reminding them that they belong to Him.

▷ Hosea experiences the rejection of his wife, Gomer, which is an image throughout the book of the way God's people have rejected Him.

▷ The leaders and elders were commanded to teach the people about YHWH, but they failed to do that. No one knows who God is anymore.

 TODAY'S GOD SHOT

God comes to us right where we are and redeems us by taking the punishment for our sins and putting it all on Jesus. When we didn't belong to God, He made a way for us to be His children. And He's where the joy is!

ACTIVITY

When you decide to follow Jesus, you become a part of God's family. Fill in the characteristics that are unique to you in the picture below. Write your name.

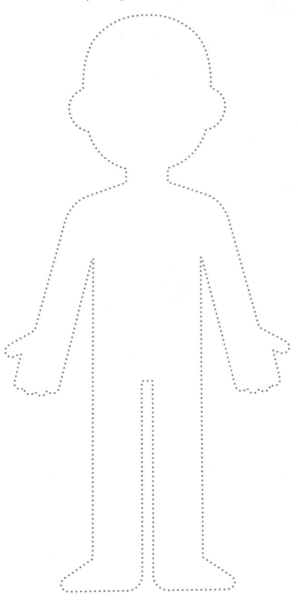

.... — CHILD OF GOD

Hosea 8–14

 QUICK LOOK: Hosea 11:7—The LORD said, "My people have made up their minds to turn away from me. Even if they call me the Most High God, I will certainly not honor them."

 RECAP

▷ Hosea reminds God's people that there are consequences for their sins.

▷ Nearness to God impacts every area of our lives, and so does turning away from Him.

▷ The story of Hosea and Gomer and the story of God and Israel show us that God's love is bigger than our sins!

 TODAY'S GOD SHOT

Because of Jesus, God's anger toward sin doesn't land on us. Jesus received that punishment for us. We get the relationship with God and all its benefits: provision, hope, discipline, mercy, grace, and of course, joy. He's where the joy is!

 ACTIVITY

Tell God how thankful you are for Jesus in your own words, or pray this prayer.

Dear God, thank You for sending Jesus to take the punishment for all my sin. Thank You for being my friend and being so good to me! Amen.

Isaiah 28–30

QUICK LOOK: Isaiah 30:21—"You will hear your Teacher's voice behind you. You will hear it whether you turn to the right or the left. It will say, 'Here is the path I want you to take. So walk on it.'"

▷ Today we read about three of the six woes, or troubles, coming for Israel. The overarching theme is that we shouldn't rely on our own strengths.

▷ God warns us against walking in our own wisdom. He promises to teach and guide us.

▷ God wants His people to come to Him and trust Him.

TODAY'S GOD SHOT

By being in God's Word every day, you're starting to recognize the kinds of things He says, you're developing a deeper awareness of His personality traits, and you're storing up His Word in your heart and mind. Based on what you know from His Word, listen for His voice today. He's where the joy is!

ACTIVITY

Draw a picture of yourself walking on the path toward God's ways. Then complete the crossword puzzle about God's ways on the next page.

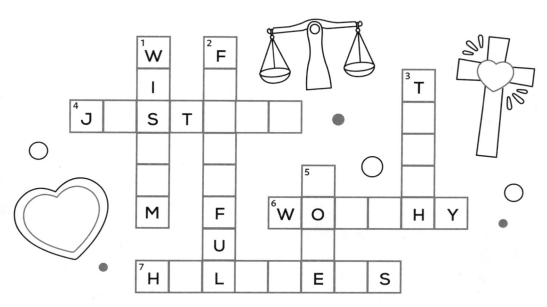

ACROSS

4. Fairness, doing what's right
6. Deserving, having merit and value
7. Sinless perfection

DOWN

1. Ability to discern what is right or true
2. Reliable and trustworthy, keeping promises
3. Fact, reliable, not false in any way
5. Tender and caring affection for others

Isaiah 31–34

QUICK LOOK: Isaiah 32:17—"Doing what is right will bring peace and rest. When my people do that, they will stay calm and trust in the LORD forever."

▷ Today we read the final three of six woes (troubles) that are coming.

▷ Isaiah tells about a day when God's people will finally turn to Him and destroy their idols. In that future day, a righteous king will reign. That king is Jesus.

▷ God promises to bring judgment to all the nations of the earth.

TODAY'S GOD SHOT

God gives us the Holy Spirit, who helps us do what is right. When we obey God, we have peace and rest. Obedience to God helps set our hearts at peace and helps us trust God forever. What a great relief! He's where the joy is!

ACTIVITY

Today's verse is a good one to memorize. Fill in the blanks to see if you can remember it.

ISAIAH 32:17—"DOING .... IS .... WILL

BRING .... AND .... WHEN MY

PEOPLE DO THAT, THEY WILL STAY .... AND

TRUST IN THE .... FOREVER."

Isaiah 35–36

 QUICK LOOK: Isaiah 35:4—"Say to those whose hearts are afraid, 'Be strong and do not fear. Your God will come. He will pay your enemies back. He will come to save you.'"

 RECAP

▷ God made a specific promise to a specific people, and He fulfilled that promise. God can be trusted to keep His word.

▷ The Assyrians confront the leaders who work for King Hezekiah and try their best to intimidate the people into doubting God and following them instead.

▷ King Hezekiah is wise and tells his people not to respond to what the Assyrians are saying.

 TODAY'S GOD SHOT

The prophecies of chapter 35 point to the faithfulness of our promise-making, promise-keeping God. He tells us He will come and save us. He's where the joy is!

 ACTIVITY

Color in the heart next to the promise you need to remember today.

♡ God will love you forever. (Psalm 136:1)

♡ God will never leave you. (Hebrews 13:5)

♡ God will comfort you. (Isaiah 49:13)

♡ God will help you. (Psalm 121:1–2)

Isaiah 37–39; Psalm 76

 QUICK LOOK: Isaiah 37:26—"But I, the LORD, say, 'Haven't you heard what I have done? Long ago I arranged for you to do this. In days of old I planned it. Now I have made it happen.'"

 RECAP

▶ King Hezekiah turns to God when King Sennacherib threatens them. God lets him know He is planning to put an end to this evil king.

▶ When King Hezekiah becomes sick, he cries out to God asking for more time to live. God answers his prayer by adding fifteen years to his life.

▶ Psalm 76 praises God for saving His people from their enemies.

 TODAY'S GOD SHOT

God is in control over what happens with King Sennacherib. We don't have to worry because God has already set His very good plan into motion. He arranges everything, and He's using it to bless us and bring glory to Himself. He's where the joy is!

 ACTIVITY

Decide if the statements below are true or false.

TRUE   FALSE   Everything in my life is a mistake.

TRUE   FALSE   God is in charge of life and death.

TRUE   FALSE   God heard Hezekiah's prayer.

TRUE   FALSE   God is in control of every detail of my life.

Isaiah 40–43

 QUICK LOOK: Isaiah 41:8—"The LORD says, 'People of Israel, you are my servants. Family of Jacob, I have chosen you. You are the children of my friend Abraham.'"

 RECAP

▷ Israel's exile ends, they've been brought back to their land, and God is comforting them.

▷ God's people struggle with trusting and praising God. They act like God can't see their actions and their hearts and like He's being mean to them.

▷ God promises to provide for and protect His people, which should set their hearts at ease.

 TODAY'S GOD SHOT

God's people are special to Him, and even though they sinned and rebelled, He still has a purpose for their lives. There are no perfect people for God to use. He has written us into His story, and He blots out our sins because He loves us! What an incredible God and Father! He's where the joy is!

 ACTIVITY

Pray this prayer.

Father God, I praise You for making me a part of Your family. Even though I am not perfect, You forgive me, love me, and give my life a purpose. Help me to trust You each day. I love You! Amen.

Isaiah 44–48

QUICK LOOK: Isaiah 45:19—The LORD said, "I have not spoken in secret. I have not spoken from a dark place. I have not said to Jacob's people, 'It is useless to look for me.' I am the LORD. I always speak the truth. I always say what is right."

RECAP

▷ God is the one true God, and to put anything else above Him is a sin.

▷ God is in charge of everything, and everything He says is right and true.

▷ God wants us to know Him.

TODAY'S GOD SHOT

Even though you may not understand everything you read about God, you can be sure He sees your desire to understand. He's the one who gave you that desire to begin with! As you look for God and listen for His voice, He will surprise you, because He's where the joy is!

ACTIVITY

Circle the words that describe who God is to you.

God is . . .

WRONG   FAITHFUL   TRUTHFUL

HIDING   RIGHT   IN CHARGE

2 Kings 19; Psalms 46, 80, 135

QUICK LOOK: Psalm 135:5–6—"I know that the LORD is great. I know that our Lord is greater than all gods. The LORD does anything he wants to do in the heavens and on the earth."

RECAP

▷ Hezekiah reads a threatening letter from the Assyrian king. He prays, asking God to save His people.

▷ God sends a message to Hezekiah from the prophet Isaiah to let him know how He will defeat the Assyrian king. The Angel of the LORD goes into the Assyrian camp and kills their entire army, giving God's people victory.

▷ Psalms 46, 80, and 135 tell about how great God is and how He provides for and protects His people.

TODAY'S GOD SHOT

God is in control of everything, even evil. And He is always working things out—the good things and the bad things—for the good of everyone who loves Him. God does whatever He pleases! It makes Him happy to save us and make us part of His family. Wow! He's where the joy is!

ACTIVITY

Read Psalm 46 on the next page and circle all the things you see about who God is and what He does.

Psalm 46

God is our place of safety. He gives us strength.
   He is always there to help us in times of trouble.
The earth may fall apart.
   The mountains may fall into the middle of the sea.
   But we will not be afraid.
The waters of the sea may roar and foam.
   The mountains may shake when the waters rise.
   But we will not be afraid.
God's blessings are like a river. They fill the city
      of God with joy.
   That city is the holy place where the
      Most High God lives.
Because God is there, the city will not fall.
   God will help it at the beginning of the day.
Nations are in disorder. Kingdoms fall.
   God speaks, and the people of the earth melt
      in fear.
The LORD who rules over all is with us.
   The God of Jacob is like a fort to us.
Come and see what the LORD has done.
   See the places he has destroyed on the earth.
He makes wars stop from one end of the earth
      to the other.
   He breaks every bow. He snaps every spear.
   He burns every shield with fire.
He says, "Be still, and know that I am God.
   I will be honored among the nations.
   I will be honored in the earth."
The LORD who rules over all is with us.
   The God of Jacob is like a fort to us.

Isaiah 49–53

QUICK LOOK: Isaiah 53:10—"The LORD says, 'It was my plan to crush him and cause him to suffer. I made his life an offering to pay for sin. But he will see all his children after him. In fact, he will continue to live. My plan will be brought about through him.'"

RECAP

▷ God chooses Israel to be a special nation. The Messiah, who will save people everywhere, will come from these special people.

▷ God reminds His people that even though they feel forgotten by Him, they are not. They are engraved on the palm of His hand.

▷ Prophecies about Jesus point to how He will help people who are tired and hurting.

TODAY'S GOD SHOT

God the Father, God the Son, and God the Holy Spirit are of equal value and work together for the same purpose and plan to fix our friendship with God. The Father is the supreme authority, and the Son and Spirit carry out the Father's good plan because they all work together in unity. Jesus died willingly and was on board with God's plan so that we could be friends with God forever, because He's where the joy is!

ACTIVITY

On another sheet of paper, trace your hand and draw a heart inside it. Write the name of someone you love in the heart and give it to them. When you do, tell them about how much God loves them!

Isaiah 54–58

 QUICK LOOK: Isaiah 57:18—God said, "I have seen what they have done. But I will heal them. I will guide them. I will give those who mourn in Israel the comfort they had before."

▷ God promises to bless His people and reminds them they have nothing to fear because He will protect them.

▷ God has good plans for His people. He has ideas that humans don't even have the brain capacity to come up with!

▷ God can never be disappointed in you. He knows the wrong things you do, but because Jesus paid the price for those things, He has already forgiven you.

 TODAY'S GOD SHOT

When we sin by doing wrong things, God doesn't run away from us. He has compassion for us and will help us. Even though God sees our sin, He will heal us! He's where the joy is!

 ACTIVITY

Color the star next to the statement that is true about your relationship with God.

 When I do wrong things, I don't feel bad because I don't care what God thinks.

 When I do wrong things, I run to God, knowing He loves me.

 When I do wrong things, I run from God because He's disappointed in me.

Isaiah 59–63

QUICK LOOK: Isaiah 63:7—"I will talk about the kind things the Lᴏʀᴅ has done. I'll praise him for everything he's done for us. He has done many good things for the nation of Israel. That's because he loves us and is very kind to us."

RECAP

▷ Our sin hurts our friendship with God, making us feel distant from Him.

▷ God promised to send Jesus to take the punishment for our sin. Jesus's death and resurrection made a way for us to be friends with God.

▷ God does many good things for His people because He loves us.

TODAY'S GOD SHOT

God is so good to us! We see that in how He provided a way for us to have a relationship with Him. He loves us and wants us to enjoy being with Him because He's where the joy is!

ACTIVITY

Write one way God has shown His love to you.

....

....

....

....

Isaiah 64–66

 QUICK LOOK: Isaiah 66:19—The Lᴏʀᴅ said, "But when I act, those I send will tell the nations about my glory."

 RECAP

▷ When we sin, we may feel like God has hidden His face from us, but He's not hiding.

▷ Our sin hurts our friendship with God, and that feeling is what makes us want to tell Him we're sorry. He is always there, ready to forgive us.

▷ God will make a new heaven and a new earth one day, and we will live with Him there forever. He sends people to tell everyone in the world how great He is!

 TODAY'S GOD SHOT

God goes above and beyond to share the good news of His love with all people, including people who hate Him. God is on a mission to bring people from every nation into His family. And He's where the joy is!

 ACTIVITY

The good news of the gospel was sent out and has made its way to you and your family! Color the world map on the next page and draw a ☆ for where you are!

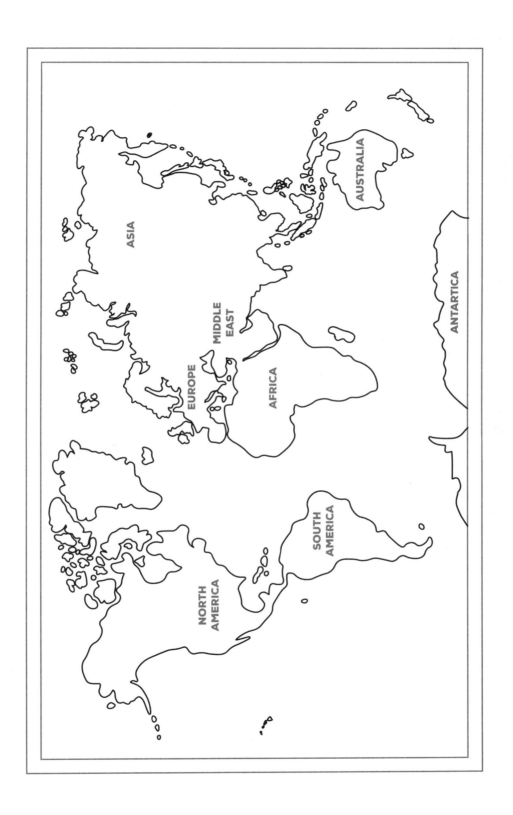

2 Kings 20–21

 QUICK LOOK: 2 Kings 20:5—The LORD said to Isaiah, "Go back and speak to Hezekiah. He is the ruler of my people. Tell him, 'The LORD, the God of King David, says, "I have heard your prayer. I have seen your tears. And I will heal you."'"

 RECAP

▷ Hezekiah prays and asks God to give him more years to live. God hears his prayers and gives him fifteen more years!

▷ God uses our prayers to accomplish His plan for us.

▷ Both Hezekiah's son and grandson become king after him, and they lead the people to worship false gods and do terrible things.

 TODAY'S GOD SHOT

God is very kind to Hezekiah. He hears his prayer and gives him more years to live! We can know God hears our prayers and that He's where the joy is!

 ACTIVITY

Write or draw one thing you are asking God for today.

2 Chronicles 32–33

 QUICK LOOK: 2 Chronicles 33:12–13—"When Manasseh was in trouble, he asked the LORD his God to help him. He made himself very humble in the sight of the God of his people. Manasseh prayed to him."

 RECAP

▷ King Sennacherib and the Assyrians decide to attack Jerusalem.

▷ Hezekiah develops a plan to outsmart the Assyrians and reminds the people in his army that God is with them and they can have hope!

▷ God sends an angel to completely wipe out the Assyrian armies and saves the people of Jerusalem.

 TODAY'S GOD SHOT

Manasseh is Hezekiah's son who repented from doing wrong things and turned to God. God has compassion for him and answers his prayer by blessing him. Manasseh knows that the LORD is the one true God and that He's where the joy is!

 ACTIVITY

Circle the words that describe who God is to you.

God is . . .

JOY   GOOD   MEAN   AFRAID   COMPASSIONATE   SAFE

Nahum 1–3

 QUICK LOOK: Nahum 1:7—"The LORD is good. When people are in trouble, they can go to him for safety. He takes good care of those who trust in him."

RECAP

▶ Nahum is a prophet whose message is that God will always judge people who do evil.

▶ God judges Assyria for the way they have treated His people.

▶ God defends and blesses those who trust in Him.

 TODAY'S GOD SHOT

God not only has His eyes on us but also on wicked people who do evil. He will punish those who bring harm to others, and He will bless those who belong to Him. We can put our hope in God and know that He's where the joy is!

 ACTIVITY

Memorize today's verse by filling in the blanks.

NAHUM 1:7—"THE LORD IS .... WHEN PEOPLE

ARE IN ...., THEY CAN GO TO HIM FOR

.... HE TAKES GOOD .... OF

THOSE WHO .... IN HIM."

2 Kings 22–23;
2 Chronicles 34–35

 QUICK LOOK: 2 Chronicles 35:22—Josiah "wanted to go to war against Necho. He wouldn't listen to what God had commanded Necho to say. Instead, Josiah went out to fight him on the plains of Megiddo."

 RECAP

▷ Josiah is eight years old when he becomes king. He does what is right in God's eyes.

▷ Josiah repairs the temple and finds the book of the law, which is likely the scroll of Deuteronomy. He makes a covenant to obey God, and the people join in.

▷ At the end of Josiah's life, he doesn't believe his enemy, Necho, who God uses to speak to him.

 TODAY'S GOD SHOT

God speaks to us in various ways, including through the mouths of people who don't love Him. God can use anyone to point to His truth. We need to pray and ask Him for wisdom to know the difference between truth and lies. He will always help us, because He's where the joy is!

 ACTIVITY

Circle one of the ways that God has spoken to you.

Zephaniah 1–3

QUICK LOOK: Zephaniah 2:7 csb—"The Lord their God will return to them and restore their fortunes."

▷ Zephaniah warns the people about God's judgment for the way they have worshipped Him while also worshipping false gods.

▷ God gets rid of all our fears through the power of His nearness.

▷ Even though the people sin against God, He promises to save them and give back what they have lost.

TODAY'S GOD SHOT

God hates sin and will punish it. But He loves His people, and His grace and mercy extend to all who believe and trust in Him. God is faithful to keep His promises. He wants to give us good things because He's where the joy is!

ACTIVITY

What is one good thing you can thank God for today?

....

....

Jeremiah 1–3

QUICK LOOK: Jeremiah 1:5—The LORD said to Jeremiah, "Before I formed you in your mother's body I chose you. Before you were born I set you apart to serve me. I appointed you to be a prophet to the nations."

RECAP

▷ Jeremiah is called the weeping prophet because God gives him sad messages to deliver to the people.

▷ God has a specific purpose for Jeremiah and promises to be with him.

▷ God begs the people to turn away from doing wrong things and to turn back to Him.

TODAY'S GOD SHOT

God tells Jeremiah that He not only created him like a potter shapes clay, but He also knew him and set him apart before he was born. God has a plan for each of us! And *He's* where the joy is!

ACTIVITY

Even though you may be young, you can know God has created you for a purpose. What is one thing you think God made you to do?

....

....

ACROSS

3. A person who cooks food at a restaurant
5. A person who puts out fires
6. A person who flies planes
7. A person who grows crops
9. A person who helps sick people
10. A person who cleans buildings
12. A person who helps sick animals

DOWN

1. A person who helps students learn
2. A person who makes bread and cakes
4. A person who fixes teeth
8. A person who repairs cars
11. A person who makes paintings and drawings

Jeremiah 4–6

 QUICK LOOK: Jeremiah 5:25—The LORD said to Jeremiah in a message to the people, "But the things you have done wrong have robbed you of these gifts. Your sins have kept these good things far away from you."

 RECAP

▷ Jeremiah continues to tell the people of Judah and Israel to repent and turn away from doing the wrong things.

▷ God doesn't just want His people to change their actions, He wants them to change their hearts.

▷ God is patient because He knows Jesus will take the punishment for the sins of all people: past, present, and future.

 TODAY'S GOD SHOT

God picked Jeremiah to be the one to tell His people to turn away from doing wrong things. God continually sends this message, showing how patient He is. He doesn't want anything to get in the way of our friendship, because He's where the joy is!

 ACTIVITY

Circle some of the wrong things that you sometimes do and need forgiveness for.

LYING   SAYING MEAN THINGS   SELFISHNESS   PRIDE   HATE

Jeremiah 7–9

QUICK LOOK: Jeremiah 9:24—"But here is what the one who brags should boast about. They should brag that they have the understanding to know me. I want them to know that I am the Lord. No matter what I do on earth, I am always kind, fair and right. And I take delight in this."

RECAP

▷ The people have come to worship God inside the temple, but outside the temple walls, they're sacrificing to false gods, as though God can't see them.

▷ God calls His people to change the way they treat others and the way they treat Him and promises to bless them if they do.

▷ God continues to point out that He wants their hearts, not their bad attitudes toward obedience.

TODAY'S GOD SHOT

God leads with love. And He delights in being kind, fair, and right. God does what He loves, and He IS what He loves. And He's where the joy is!

ACTIVITY

Unscramble the words to find three words that describe God.

DINK ....

RFAI ....

IRHTG ....

ANSWER KEY: kind, fair, right

Jeremiah 10–13

 QUICK LOOK: Jeremiah 10:23—Jeremiah prayed, "Lord, I know that a person doesn't control their own life. They don't direct their own steps."

▷ Jeremiah reminds the people that their idols are made of everything God made and they have no power.

▷ Jeremiah complains to God about his life and how hard it is. God reminds Jeremiah that He is with him.

▷ God allows His people to experience consequences for their sins. He still loves them and keeps His eyes on them.

 TODAY'S GOD SHOT

God is with us in every small step we take. We don't control our life, He does! He wants us to listen to Him and do what He says. He knows all about your life. He's there to help you and guide you. And He's where the joy is!

 ACTIVITY

Draw arrows on the clock to show the time that you read this recap.

Ask God to direct your steps at every hour of the day today.

Jeremiah 14–17

 QUICK LOOK: Jeremiah 17:22—"Do not bring a load out of your houses on the Sabbath day. Do not do any work on that day. Instead, keep the Sabbath day holy. Do as I commanded your people of long ago."

 RECAP

▷ The people cry out to God. They aren't crying because they are sorry for how they've acted—they are crying out for His help.

▷ God sees and judges everything.

▷ God wants us to set aside one day a week to rest and focus on Him.

 TODAY'S GOD SHOT

God wants us to slow down and set aside one day a week to spend extended time focusing on Him. He wants us to rest in trusting He is in control, because He's where the joy is!

 ACTIVITY

Circle the day of the week that you will set aside to spend more time resting and focusing on God.

SUNDAY   MONDAY   TUESDAY   WEDNESDAY

THURSDAY   FRIDAY   SATURDAY

Jeremiah 18–22

QUICK LOOK: Jeremiah 22:3—"The LORD says, 'Do what is fair and right. Save those who have been robbed. Set them free from the people who have treated them badly.'"

▷ God sends Jeremiah to see a potter making jars. God tells him, "I'm the potter. The people are the clay."

▷ God wants His people to repent but knows that they won't.

▷ God has called Israel and Judah His people, but the Bible says repeatedly that God's people are made up of people from every nation—anyone whose heart turns to follow Him.

TODAY'S GOD SHOT

God says to know Him is to do what He says. Obeying God is where the joy is because obeying God is where we connect with God on the deepest level. And He's where the joy is!

ACTIVITY

What is one rule you always obey? Thank God for helping you do what is right.

....

....

Jeremiah 23–25

QUICK LOOK: Jeremiah 23:6—The LORD said, "In his days Judah will be saved. Israel will live in safety. And the Branch will be called The LORD Who Makes Us Right With Himself."

RECAP

▷ God promises to raise up a righteous king from the line of David. This is a prophecy of the coming of Jesus.

▷ The false prophets are leading God's people to sin, but He's watching their every move.

▷ God will pour out anger across all nations for their sins.

TODAY'S GOD SHOT

God promises to raise up a new king named "The LORD Who Makes Us Right With Himself." Even here in the Old Testament, Jesus is marked as God and King and Savior. We have no righteousness of our own, but our God-King-Savior came down and gave us His. He's where the joy is!

ACTIVITY

Fill in the blanks from Jeremiah 23:6.

THE LORD SAID, "IN HIS DAYS JUDAH WILL BE SAVED.

ISRAEL WILL LIVE IN .... AND THE

BRANCH WILL BE CALLED THE .... WHO MAKES

US .... WITH HIMSELF."

Jeremiah 26–29

QUICK LOOK: Jeremiah 29:23—"'I know what they have done. And I am a witness to it,' announces the LORD."

RECAP

▷ God sends Jeremiah to prophesy to people going to the temple, the kings of five nations, and also to the prophet Hananiah. Each time, the people accuse Jeremiah of things that aren't true, but God keeps protecting him.

▷ Jeremiah tells God's people that even though they will be sent away to another country for seventy years, they should make the most of the time by trying to bless the people who have taken them captive.

▷ God reassures the people that He has a good plan but that it's going to be seventy years until they can go back home.

TODAY'S GOD SHOT

God keeps proving Himself to Jeremiah, and all Jeremiah has to do is stand firm on God's word. He has to trust God in the place where God put him, which is what he tells the exiles to do too. That's so much easier to do when we know the God who knows—that's what God calls Himself in 29:23: "I know what they have done." He's with you. He knows. And He's where the joy is!

ACTIVITY

Circle the emoji that matches how it makes you feel to know that God is with you, knows you, and has a good plan for you.

Jeremiah 30–31

 QUICK LOOK: Jeremiah 31:12—The Lord said, "They will come and shout for joy on Mount Zion. They will be joyful because of everything I give them."

▷ God tells His people all the good things He will do for them. These are a few of them: "I will save you," "I am with you," "I will discipline you," "I will heal your wounds."

▷ God promises His people many things, but here He makes a new promise, or covenant, that will last forever. This new promise points to Jesus and how He will forgive our sin.

▷ God tells the people that they should have joy because He gives them everything they need.

 TODAY'S GOD SHOT

God wants to give us every good thing. When we have God, we have all we need because He's where the joy is!

 ACTIVITY

Make a list of three of the good things God has given you.

1. ....

2. ....

3. ....

```
K D L P G J B D Y X X O S R
Z L L I P I R L B Y F F T K
E N V N O F R J R F Q T N Z
B Q E I S N Q A I S R A A B
R M L U N M W E F J F D H F
A E C B Z L A K J F S N P B
T M F G P Z M E W Y E A E C
A L L I G A T O R P U P L I
T J Y V K S V S Z V W O E P
L O K M H W R E A N N E Q S
U N C G Q Q L M O N K E Y H
T I G E R A S W B K E E C A
Z H Z S P O W A X Q P J T L
K R U S M R W E D N A R O N
```

WORD BANK

ELEPHANT	ZEBRA	LION	RHINO	ALLIGATOR
PANDA	TIGER	MONKEY	GIRAFFE	APE

If you need help, check out the Word Search Answer Key on page 471.

Jeremiah 32–34

 QUICK LOOK: Jeremiah 33:16—The LORD announced, "In those days Judah will be saved. Jerusalem will live in safety. And it will be called The LORD Who Makes Us Right With Himself."

 RECAP

▷ Jeremiah is in prison because the king doesn't like the prophecies, or messages from God, that Jeremiah is telling the people. While there, Jeremiah is afraid and has doubts, but he takes his questions and doubts to God.

▷ God shows that He wants to talk to Jeremiah and patiently reminds him that everything happening is a part of God's plan. God even says, "I am the LORD. I am the God of all people. Is anything too hard for me?"

▷ God tells Jeremiah that He is going to keep His promise to save His people. It's Jesus, our Lord, who makes us right with God!

 TODAY'S GOD SHOT

God promised to do everything necessary for us to be made right with Him. That's why He sent Jesus to take the punishment for our sin. There's nothing we can do to earn this forgiveness. He gives it to us for FREE because He's where the joy is!

 ACTIVITY

The name of God we learned today in Jeremiah 33:16 is The LORD Who Makes Us Right With Himself. Write about what it feels like to be forgiven and made right with God.

....

....

Jeremiah 35–37

QUICK LOOK: Jeremiah 35:13—Jeremiah said, "The LORD who rules over all is the God of Israel. He says, 'Go. Speak to the people of Judah and Jerusalem. Tell them, "Won't you ever learn a lesson? Won't you ever obey my words?"'"

RECAP

▷ God tells Jeremiah to write down everything He's told him.

▷ King Jehoiakim asks to have the scroll with God's words read to him. When he hears the warnings from God, he tears up the scroll and throws the pieces into a fire, believing they will not come true if he destroys them.

▷ Jeremiah gets thrown into prison but continues to give messages from God to King Zedekiah.

TODAY'S GOD SHOT

God wants people to hear the words He has to say because He wants us to know Him! And nothing can stop God from communicating with us. God's words are powerful and true, and they will last forever because God is forever. He's where the joy is!

ACTIVITY

On a scale of one to ten, with one being the easiest and ten being the hardest, how hard is it for you to obey God's words?

EASY   HARD

1   2   3   4   5   6   7   8   9   10

Jeremiah 38–40; Psalms 74, 79

 QUICK LOOK: Psalm 79:9—"God our Savior, help us. Then glory will come to you. Save us and forgive our sins. Then people will honor your name."

 RECAP

▷ The local officials throw Jeremiah into an empty well to keep him from sharing God's messages with the people.

▷ A man named Ebed-Melek uses ropes to get Jeremiah out of the well.

▷ Asaph, the psalmist who wrote Psalm 79, reminds the people that there are consequences for their sin. He begs God to help them because he knows that God is powerful and good.

 TODAY'S GOD SHOT

We see how desperate God's people are in Psalm 79. Their cry to be saved was answered with a yes when Jesus died for the sins of God's people—past, present, and future. We can praise God and honor Him because He's where the joy is!

 ACTIVITY

Pray Psalm 79:9 but make it personal.

*God **my** Savior, help **me**. Then glory will come to You. Save **me** and forgive **my** sins. Then **I** will honor Your name.*

2 Kings 24–25;
2 Chronicles 36

QUICK LOOK: 2 Kings 25:29—"So Jehoiachin put his prison clothes away. For the rest of Jehoiachin's life the king provided what he needed."

RECAP

▷ Babylon destroys Jerusalem just like Jeremiah prophesied, taking away the people and the treasures of the temple and setting it on fire.

▷ Everything the LORD spoke to Jeremiah comes true. The land of Israel is deserted. It isn't farmed for seventy years.

▷ Cyrus becomes king, and God inspires him to build a temple in Jerusalem where God's people can go to worship.

TODAY'S GOD SHOT

Jehoiachin is an enemy to the king of Babylon, but in 2 Kings 25:29, we see how the king has mercy on Jehoiachin, allowing him to go free, giving him new clothes, and letting him eat at his table. This is a beautiful reminder that God does this for us! He's where the joy is!

ACTIVITY

God gives you everything you need. Discover what some of those things are in the word find.

```
H W C M M V K S A Y D I A R
L A S V B F J V F O D C Q C
S S I Q Q V X L O V E B F L
D R H R P Z R Y G Z I S O O
D G P E O T M C E M H D O T
E S H F L P X M M O Q N D H
D Y K Q G T H O G N J E T E
O T E Y L Z E E F E Q I L S
A E Q J X W Q R S B Z R W M
N F B R G S X P Z R N F A N
W A T E R L F H A L U I R N
V S C Z A E U A Q M M A M J
D G N C V E E P W P B L T X
H B V F J P R L M Z H X H Z
```

WORD BANK

FOOD	WATER	SHELTER	AIR	CLOTHES
SLEEP	SAFETY	WARMTH	FRIENDS	LOVE

If you need help, check out the Word Search Answer Key on page 471.

Habakkuk 1–3

QUICK LOOK: Habakkuk 3:18–19—"But I will still be glad because of what the LORD has done. God my Savior fills me with joy. The LORD and King gives me strength. He makes my feet like the feet of a deer. He helps me walk on the highest places."

RECAP

▷ Habakkuk is a prophet who talks to God on behalf of the people, telling Him about the terrible ways people are being treated.

▷ Habakkuk feels like God isn't listening to his prayers since God isn't doing what he asks for, but God is listening and gives Habakkuk His perspective on what He is doing.

▷ God warns His people about putting their hope in money, safety, power, pleasure, and control. He knows that trusting in those things instead of Him leads to all kinds of sin.

TODAY'S GOD SHOT

Even when everything seems to be going wrong, Habakkuk decides to be glad because God fills him with joy and strength. He even says that God makes his feet like the feet of a deer who can climb dangerous, steep cliffs to get to higher, safer places because of how strong God made its feet. Habakkuk recognizes that his strength is from God because He's where the joy is!

ACTIVITY

Thank God for filling you with joy and strength that come from Him.

Jeremiah 41–45

QUICK LOOK: Jeremiah 43:7—"So the Jewish leaders disobeyed the LORD. They took everyone to Egypt."

▶ Judah's governor, Gedaliah, is killed by a member of the royal family named Ishmael. He takes everyone captive, leading them to Babylon. On the way, Johanan fights him and wins, freeing God's people.

▶ The people want to flee to Egypt in hopes of protection, so they seek counsel from Jeremiah and promise to do whatever God says. Jeremiah tells them to stay, but they don't listen to him.

▶ They continue on to Egypt and don't feel sorry for disobeying God. They continue to worship idols, and Jeremiah says the scariest thing he's ever said: "Go ahead. Worship your idols. God is done with you."

TODAY'S GOD SHOT

God promises that His Spirit will tell us when we sin by disobeying Him. When you feel that you have disobeyed God, that is evidence of God's love for you. Don't resist that feeling. Instead, say you are sorry, and He will forgive you because He's where the joy is!

ACTIVITY

Have you ever felt the Holy Spirit tell you when you've done something wrong?

YES   NO

How did it make you feel?

SAD   MAD   NO FEELINGS   SORRY

Take some time to pray and thank God for loving you and helping you feel sorry when you have done wrong things.

Jeremiah 46–48

 QUICK LOOK: Jeremiah 46:18—The LORD said, "I am the King. My name is the LORD Who Rules Over All."

▷ Jeremiah has messages from God for Israel and also for the enemy nations like Egypt, the Philistines, and Moab.

▷ The Israelites have disobeyed God and are hiding in Egypt. Even though they've disobeyed, God is gentle with them.

▷ God reminds the Israelites not to be afraid because He is with them.

 TODAY'S GOD SHOT

God sends prophets, or messengers, to talk to His people as well as His enemies. God is in charge of everyone, everywhere, all the time. There's no other God but Him, and He's where the joy is!

 ACTIVITY

Decode the name of God we learned about today.

Jeremiah 49–50

 QUICK LOOK: Jeremiah 50:20—The LORD said, "At that time people will search for Israel's guilt. But they will not find any. They will search for Judah's sins. But they will not find any. That is because I will forgive the people I have spared."

 RECAP

▷ God judges the nations that have come up against His people. God tells them that bad things will happen because of what they've done, but He also promises to restore them and take care of their orphans and widows.

▷ God is everywhere, and we see that this is good for God's people because they experience His blessings, but this is not good for God's enemies because they experience His judgment.

▷ When God destroys Babylon, it will also end the captivity of His people who are there.

 TODAY'S GOD SHOT

Even though we sin and do wrong things, God will forgive us! When we decide to follow Jesus, His death on the cross cancels out all the wrong things we've done and will ever do, and we are completely forgiven. Then God doesn't see our sins anymore! He's where the joy is!

 ACTIVITY

Use a pen or black marker and blot out the actions below that are sins. When you are finished, thank God for His forgiveness!

LYING   PLAYING   BEING MEAN   COOKING

STEALING   SWIMMING   DISOBEYING   CAMPING

Jeremiah 51–52

QUICK LOOK: Jeremiah 51:19—The Lord said, "I give my people everything they need. I can do this because I made everything, including Israel. They are the people who belong to me. My name is the Lord Who Rules Over All."

▷ While they're in Babylon, God reminds His people that He is with them and will bring them back to their land.

▷ God says that He is going to punish Babylon for everything it did to His people and that nothing, no matter how strong it seems, can stop His plans. God tells His people not to be afraid when they hear about this happening in the land.

▷ God blessed King Jehoiachin for his obedience even though he was an evil king.

TODAY'S GOD SHOT

God is able to give His people everything they need. There's nothing better for us than Him! He's where the joy is!

ACTIVITY

List three things you need that God gives you.

1. ....

2. ....

3. ....

Lamentations 1–2

 QUICK LOOK: Lamentations 2:19—"Get up. Cry out as the night begins. Tell the Lord all your troubles. Lift up your hands to him."

RECAP

▷ The book of Lamentations is a book of poems that express the extreme sadness the people feel over the horrible things that have happened to them.

▷ God's people forget what He has done for them in the past and what He has promised for their future.

▷ The prophets no longer receive messages from the LORD.

 TODAY'S GOD SHOT

God wants us to tell Him how we feel. He wants us to be honest with Him, even when we are sad, angry, or confused. He loves and cares about us! In our saddest, hardest moments, He's where the joy is!

 ACTIVITY

Fill in the blank and pray this prayer.

Heavenly Father, I am sad because ....
.... Please help me. Thank You for loving me and caring about the things that bother me. I trust You. Amen.

Lamentations 3–5

 QUICK LOOK: Lamentations 3:22–23—"The LORD loves us very much. . . . His great love is new every morning. LORD, how faithful you are!"

 RECAP

▷ The author of Lamentations, who is possibly the prophet Jeremiah, reminds us that God's love for us never ends.

▷ Challenges are good for us because they teach us to trust God and wait on Him.

▷ God's people tell Him what they've done wrong, and they repent (turn away from wrong things in order to do things God's way). When they do this, they feel how close God is, and He tells them not to be afraid.

 TODAY'S GOD SHOT

God always knows and does what is best, even when He disciplines us. He is compassionate, and His love never ends. He wants to give us joy because He's where the joy is!

 ACTIVITY

Color the verses from Lamentations on the next page and think about how God loves you every single day.

Ezekiel 1–4

QUICK LOOK: Ezekiel 3:9—The LORD said to Ezekiel, "I will make you very brave. So do not be afraid of them. Do not let them terrify you, even though they refuse to obey me."

RECAP

▷ Ezekiel reminds us that God does the things He has planned so His people will know Him.

▷ God gives Ezekiel a vision of a windstorm, four creatures with wings, a man on a throne, and other things. The things Ezekiel sees are hard for him to explain.

▷ God uniquely made Ezekiel to be the one who would give a message to His people to stop sinning. God says He will make Ezekiel brave and tells him not to be afraid of the people.

TODAY'S GOD SHOT

God is intentional about how He makes each of us. His design for each one of us goes along with His purpose for our lives. God's design is not only intentional, it is also KIND. His plans for us are good, and He's where the joy is!

ACTIVITY

God made you unique! What is one quality you love about how He made you? Thank God for how He made you with this quality.

I am ....

Ezekiel 5–8

QUICK LOOK: Ezekiel 6:9—The Lᴏʀᴅ said to Ezekiel as a message for His people, "You will be taken away to those nations as prisoners. Those of you who escape will remember me. You will recall how much pain your unfaithful hearts gave me."

▷ God tells Ezekiel to shave off all the hair on his head and divide it into three parts. These parts represent the three bad things God will use to punish His people for disobeying Him.

▷ God judges His people but also shows mercy to a small group of people, the remnant, whose hearts He is turning toward Himself.

▷ God's people reject His patient love.

TODAY'S GOD SHOT

Our sin has broken God's heart. We deserve His punishment, but instead, He sent Jesus to take our punishment and die in our place. God loves us, and He's where the joy is!

ACTIVITY

Finish the sentence.

Dear God, I'm sorry for .... Thank You for sending Jesus to take the punishment for my sin.

Ezekiel 9–12

 QUICK LOOK: Ezekiel 10:19—"They stopped at the entrance of the east gate of the LORD's house. And the glory of the God of Israel was above them."

 RECAP

▷ God judges His people who are worshipping other gods.

▷ God's presence leaves the temple, rests on the cherubim chariot, and heads east toward Babylon, where His people are headed.

▷ God sends His people to Babylon, but He promises to bring them back one day.

 TODAY'S GOD SHOT

Even though God's people are leaving their own country, God is not leaving them. He is with us wherever we go. He's where the joy is!

 ACTIVITY

Draw a picture of one place you will go today, knowing that God is with you.

Ezekiel 13–15

 QUICK LOOK: Ezekiel 13:22—The LORD said, "I had not made godly people sad. But when you told them lies, you made them lose all hope. You advised sinful people not to turn from their evil ways. You did not want them to save their lives."

 RECAP

▷ God gives Ezekiel messages for false prophets who are telling the people lies and whatever they dream up in their own minds. God says that their messages are not from Him and that He is against them.

▷ Some leaders who are not worshipping God come to Ezekiel for advice from God. God knows their hearts, and He wants to help them. He wants them to learn to come to Him for help instead of their idols.

▷ God shows that He is persistent. He shows us where to go, then He patiently walks us there step by step.

 TODAY'S GOD SHOT

God wants His people to be at peace and to walk in truth. And God wants the wicked to hear the truth too, and turn from their wicked ways. Because God cares so deeply about those things, He says He will punish those who discourage His people. He is so protective! He's where the joy is!

 ACTIVITY

Draw a ♡ around the things that are true about who God is:

PROTECTIVE   CARING   RUDE   PERSISTENT

LIAR   WITH US   DISCOURAGING   ENCOURAGING

LOVING   FATHER   FAKE

Ezekiel 16–17

QUICK LOOK: Ezekiel 16:1–2—"A message from the LORD came to me. The LORD said, 'Son of man, tell the people of Jerusalem the evil things they have done. I hate those things.'"

RECAP

▷ God uses a metaphor to explain His relationship with Israel. He says that Israel is an abandoned orphan, unloved and left to die. But then someone, the King of the universe, rescues her and nurses her to health.

▷ God points out the heart issue behind Israel's sin—pride. God had given them so much, but they lived in luxury without caring for the poor and needy.

▷ God says He will plant a small tree in Israel, and it will grow up into a cedar that will bear fruit and make shade and be a home for all kinds of birds. This points to Jesus and His coming kingdom.

TODAY'S GOD SHOT

Israel did evil things, and God hates those evil things. They broke the promise they made to obey Him. But God made a promise, or a covenant, that will last forever. His excessive love is shocking and is something we should praise Him for because He's where the joy is!

ACTIVITY

Think about a promise you have broken in the past. Were you worried about what would happen because you didn't keep it? Circle your answer below.

YES   NO   KINDA

Pray and tell God you are sorry for breaking your promise. Thank Him for forgiveness and for how He always keeps His promises.

Ezekiel 18–20

QUICK LOOK: Ezekiel 20:44—The LORD said, "People of Israel, I will deal with you for the honor of my name. I will not deal with you based on your evil conduct and sinful practices."

▷ God says He will judge each person individually. While we may feel the effects of other people's sin, we will not be judged for it.

▷ God reminds the Israelites of how He has provided for them for years, but they continue to rebel and disobey.

▷ God reminds His people of how wicked they've been. But because God is so kind, He then reminds them that He's going to restore things in the end. He is talking about sending Jesus to fix our friendship with God once and for all!

TODAY'S GOD SHOT

God sees our sins and the times we disobey Him. Because of His love, He sent Jesus to take the punishment for us all. When we choose to follow Jesus, we get a new heart! And having a new heart allows us to know God and see that He's where the joy is!

ACTIVITY

Pray this prayer.

> **Dear God,** thank You for Your love and kindness. You have given me a new heart, and I want to obey You every day. I love You! Amen.

Ezekiel 21–22

QUICK LOOK: Ezekiel 22:30—The Lord said, "I looked for someone among them who would stand up for Jerusalem. I tried to find someone who would pray to me for the land. Then I would not have to destroy it. But I could not find anyone who would pray for it."

▷ God doesn't see anyone who is doing what is right.

▷ God delivers a pretty strong message to Ezekiel, telling him He's pulling out a sword to use on the people.

▷ God hates sin but made a way for us to be made right with Him through the gift of Jesus.

TODAY'S GOD SHOT

Our sin affects our friendship with God. It doesn't affect the truth that we belong to Him. He always loves us. God showed us His love by placing all of His anger toward our sins on Jesus. Jesus made a way for us to always be right with God. He's where the joy is!

ACTIVITY

What is sin? Sin is doing things our own way instead of God's way.

Below are some things we can do God's way or our way. Look at each one in the list, then draw a line to God's Way if you think it's doing things God's way, or draw a line to My Way if it's doing things your own way.

Ezekiel 23–24

QUICK LOOK: Ezekiel 24:14—The LORD said, "I have spoken. The time has come for me to act. I will not hold back. I will not feel sorry for you."

RECAP

▷ **Ezekiel 23 is not appropriate for children to read or hear. Skip this chapter.** In chapter 23, God tells a story about two sisters who represent Samaria and Jerusalem who are unfaithful to Him and use their bodies in sinful ways that God hates.

▷ God's people continue to reject Him in horrible ways. He warns them about how much this hurts Him.

▷ When God's people don't listen to God or put Him first, He punishes them.

TODAY'S GOD SHOT

All the punishment for all the sins of every person God made was placed on Jesus when He died on the cross. Because of God's plan to save us through the gift of Jesus's life and death, we can have a friendship with God! He's where the joy is!

ACTIVITY

Circle the actions below that help your friendship with God grow. Draw a line through the actions that hurt your friendship with Him.

- Tell the truth
- Complain
- Be thankful
- Be kind

- Tell a lie
- Obey
- Put yourself first
- Work hard/do your best

Ezekiel 25–27

QUICK LOOK: Ezekiel 25:6–7—"The Lord and King says, 'You clapped your hands. You stamped your feet. Deep down inside, you hated the land of Israel. You were glad because of what happened to it. So I will reach out my powerful hand against you.'"

RECAP

▷ The enemy countries that hate Israel are happy to see them destroyed.

▷ God judges the enemy countries, because He is against the people who are against His people.

▷ Prophecies aren't always fulfilled in obvious ways.

TODAY'S GOD SHOT

God's protective nature and His promise of justice are good news for us—because of them, we don't have to take things into our own hands! We can trust Him to be just. God is our defender, and He's where the joy is!

ACTIVITY

We can worship God because He is our defender. Listen to the song "Defender" by Rita Springer or write your own song and sing it.

....

....

....

....

Ezekiel 28–30

 QUICK LOOK: Ezekiel 28:25—"The LORD and King says, 'I will gather the people of Israel together from the nations where they have been scattered.'"

 RECAP

▷ God opposes the pride of Israel's enemy nations.

▷ God promises to bring Israel back to their land to live there in safety.

▷ People who take credit for their own strengths steal the credit from God, the Giver of those gifts.

 TODAY'S GOD SHOT

When we praise God, it kills pride, which God hates, in our hearts. It helps us to focus our eyes on our Father—and He's where the joy is!

 ACTIVITY

Circle the situations that show pride in our hearts.

BRAGGING   SHOWING LOVE

MAKING FUN OF OTHERS   OPENING THE DOOR FOR SOMEONE

PUSHING OUR WAY TO THE FRONT

FORGIVING SOMEONE   GETTING EVEN

Ask God to get rid of any pride in your heart.

Ezekiel 31–33

QUICK LOOK: Ezekiel 33:11—The Lord said, "Tell them, 'When sinful people die, it does not give me any joy. But when they turn away from their sins and live, that makes me very happy.'"

RECAP

▷ Ezekiel is only responsible for his obedience to God. He isn't responsible for how other people respond to God *or* him.

▷ God tells Ezekiel to remind the people that no matter how wicked they've been, it's never too late to repent! True repentance is a sign of a new heart.

▷ God is happy when we turn from our sin and do what is right.

TODAY'S GOD SHOT

God's happiness and joy are expressed in saving sinful people. When sinners repent and turn to Him, we see His delight. We see His joy and affection in the spotlight. His delight is one of the best things that has ever happened to us. He's where the joy is!

ACTIVITY

Check the box that represents how often you feel God's happiness with you.

☐ Every single second   ☐ Never
☐ Sometimes   ☐ Only when I do something good

Pray this prayer:

God, *thank You for being happy to save me from my sin! Help me to trust that You always love me no matter what! Amen.*

On the next page, complete the color-by-number.

326

| 1 | Yellow | 2 | Blue | 3 | Red | 4 | Green |
| 5 | Black | 6 | Brown | 7 | Orange | 8 | White |

Ezekiel 34–36

 QUICK LOOK: Ezekiel 36:11—The LORD said, "I will help you succeed more than ever before. Then you will know that I am the LORD."

 RECAP

▷ God calls the wicked kings to account. He compares them to shepherds who have not looked over their flock. God has set up a Good Shepherd who will take care of His sheep.

▷ God uses eighteen verbs to tell how He'll begin, sustain, and fulfill His plan for restoring His people.

▷ God is the author of heart change and obedience. He will remove the heart of stone, and He will give the heart of flesh. God is saying He'll take their stubbornness and give them hearts that want what He wants.

 TODAY'S GOD SHOT

"I will help you succeed more than ever before" (Ezekiel 36:11). This is what God is saying to the people who are currently rebelling against Him. Who is like that? Only YHWH. Only the God who has always been good would look at a bunch of sinners and promise to be even better. He's where the joy is!

 ACTIVITY

God wants you to be successful. What are two things you want to be good at?

1. ....

2. ....

Write the last part of Ezekiel 36:11 (see Quick Look) on a note card and put it in a place where you can see it.

Ezekiel 37–39

 QUICK LOOK: Ezekiel 39:29—"'I will no longer turn my face away from the people of Israel. I will pour out my Spirit on them,' announces the LORD and King."

 RECAP

▷ Ezekiel has a vision of a bunch of dry bones in a valley that represents the twelve tribes—the people of both Judah and Israel.

▷ God commands breath to come into the dry bones, making them alive again.

▷ God is bringing His people back to their land and will set one Shepherd over them. He will pour out His Spirit on them.

 TODAY'S GOD SHOT

God is always working to take what the devil meant for evil and turn it into something good. Nothing God's people have done has earned them anything but separation from Him. But He doesn't just forgive us for turning away from Him, He gives us His Spirit, who helps us obey. There's no one like Him! He's where the joy is!

 ACTIVITY

Take some time to ask God to pour out His Spirit on you.
Pray something like this.

Father God, thank You for loving me and taking everything in my life and turning it into something good! I want to trust You in everything. Please pour out Your Spirit in my life. I love You. Amen!

Ezekiel 40–42

QUICK LOOK: Ezekiel 40:3—"I saw a man who appeared to be made out of bronze. He was standing at the gate of the outer courtyard. He was holding a linen measuring tape and a measuring rod."

RECAP

▷ God gives Ezekiel visions of what the new temple will look like with the help of a man made out of bronze.

▷ The temple wall isn't there to keep people out but to make a clear entrance that points to Jesus being the only way to get to God.

▷ God designs the temple with very specific details that help us know more about who He is.

TODAY'S GOD SHOT

God gives Ezekiel a vision of a new temple while His people are still exiled in Babylon. He gives him very specific measurements and other important details. It is like God is saying, "I know you've lost everything. I know the First Temple was destroyed, the one Solomon built, but I want you to know I've got a plan for your future." God's plans are always good, and He's where the joy is!

ACTIVITY

What is one thing you learned about God today?

....

....

....

Ezekiel 43–45

QUICK LOOK: Ezekiel 44:4—"I looked up and saw the glory of the LORD. It filled his temple. I fell with my face toward the ground."

RECAP

▷ Ezekiel sees the glory of the LORD and falls on his face to the ground in worship.

▷ God has Ezekiel do two main things: (1) write down all the dimensions of this temple and tell the people about it and (2) write down all the laws God gives and command the people to obey Him.

▷ God is holy. That means He is perfect and not like us. God's holy presence is so powerful that the priests have to change clothes after they have been in it.

TODAY'S GOD SHOT

God keeps pursuing His rebellious people in their sins, so it's easy to forget what a big deal His holiness is. In His perfection, He made a way to be close to us. He is powerful and present, and He's where the joy is!

ACTIVITY

Unscramble the words to describe God's holiness.

GOD IS .... (REPFETC)

GOD DOES NOTHING .... (ORNWG)

GOD ALWAYS .... (EVOLS)

GOD IS .... (UTSJ)

GOD .... (RGIFOSVE)

Ezekiel 46–48

QUICK LOOK: Ezekiel 48:35—"The city will be six miles around. From that time on, its name will be 'The LORD Is There.'"

▷ God gives Ezekiel specifics on how each person will exit the temple differently from how they entered it. This represents the change that takes place in us when we come before God to worship Him.

▷ Ezekiel sees a vision of fresh water flowing from the temple, through what is currently desert, and into the Dead Sea.

▷ God is not specific on when this temple should be built. Bible teachers tell us there are three different views on what that might mean.

TODAY'S GOD SHOT

God makes it clear that whenever this vision comes to pass, He will be there! There will be no more trekking through the wilderness, no more captivity or exile. God promises to stay there forever because He's where the joy is!

ACTIVITY

Fill in the blanks for the name of God we learned today.

"THE .... IS ...."

Joel 1–3

QUICK LOOK: Joel 2:29—The LORD said, "In those days I will pour out my Spirit on those who serve me, men and women alike."

RECAP

▷ Joel is another prophet chosen by God to give messages to His people.

▷ God sends a plague of locusts to destroy the land of Judah. He wants His people to repent and tell Him they are truly sorry for their sin.

▷ God has pity on His people and promises to give them food and many other wonderful things, including His Spirit.

TODAY'S GOD SHOT

God says He will pour His Spirit out on people who serve Him. His Spirit is powerful, giving us hope and helping us see that He's where the joy is!

ACTIVITY

Ask God to pour out His Spirit on you today by praying this prayer.

Dear God, I am amazed by Your power. You are great, and I want to know You more and more! Please pour out Your Spirit on my life. Help me to serve You today! Amen.

Daniel 1–3

QUICK LOOK: Daniel 2:23—Daniel said, "God of my people of long ago, I thank and praise you. You have given me wisdom and power. You have made known to me what we asked you for. You have shown us the king's dream."

RECAP

▷ Daniel and his three friends are taken to Babylon by King Nebuchadnezzar (King Nebby), who gives them special training. God gives them wisdom, and He also gives Daniel a gift for interpreting dreams and visions.

▷ The king has a dream about a large statue and wants to know what it means. Daniel prays and asks God to help him understand it. When he tells the king the meaning, he puts Daniel in a position of authority.

▷ King Nebby sets up a ninety-foot gold statue and orders everyone to worship it, but Daniel's three friends resist. King Nebby throws them into a furnace of fire, but they don't burn up. The king is amazed and worships YHWH, the one true God.

TODAY'S GOD SHOT

God answered Daniel's prayer, and Daniel praises him for it! When we ask God to give us wisdom and power, He hears us and will answer. He is worthy of our praise, and He's where the joy is!

ACTIVITY

List three things you can praise God for today:

1. ....

2. ....

3. ....

Daniel 4–6

QUICK LOOK: Daniel 6:27—King Darius said, "He sets people free and saves them. He does miraculous signs and wonders. He does them in the heavens and on the earth. He has saved Daniel from the power of the lions."

▷ King Nebuchadnezzar writes a letter that shows he is finally praising God. Then he has another dream that only Daniel can explain to him.

▷ After the king dies, Belshazzar takes the throne. He throws a worship ceremony for false gods, using stolen cups from God's temple. Suddenly, a hand appears and writes a message on the wall. Daniel explains what it says, and the king dies that night.

▷ King Darius takes over and makes a rule that everyone must pray to him only. But Daniel continues to pray to God and is thrown into a lions' den. God sends His angel to shut the lions' mouths. Darius is amazed and praises Daniel's God.

TODAY'S GOD SHOT

God gave Daniel good character and the ability to affect the hearts of kings. But Daniel is not the hero of the story. Daniel didn't understand dreams or close lions' mouths on his own. God did it! He is the hero of every story. And He's where the joy is!

ACTIVITY

Fill in the blanks of Daniel 6:27.

"HE SETS PEOPLE .... AND .... THEM. HE

DOES MIRACULOUS .... AND .... HE DOES

THEM IN THE .... AND ON THE .... HE HAS

SAVED DANIEL FROM THE POWER OF THE ...." 335

Daniel 7–9

QUICK LOOK: Daniel 9:18—Daniel prayed, "Our God, please listen to us. The city that belongs to you has been destroyed. Open your eyes and see it. We aren't asking you to answer our prayers because we are godly. Instead, we're asking you to do it because you love us so much."

▷ Daniel has two strange dreams that he doesn't understand. In both dreams, an angel helps explain them, saying they are things that will happen in the future.

▷ Daniel asks God to bring His judgment on His people to an end—not because they deserve it, but because He is merciful.

▷ The angel Gabriel comes to Daniel and gives him some understanding and a timeline for when the exile will end and God's people will return to Israel.

TODAY'S GOD SHOT

God loves us and is in charge of all things. He hears our prayers and loves us so much. God loves you, and He's where the joy is!

ACTIVITY

Write a note to yourself from God.

DEAR ....,

    YOU ARE GREATLY LOVED. I AM AMAZED BY THE WAY

YOU .... I KNOW YOU

WORRY ABOUT ...., BUT

YOU DON'T NEED TO. I AM IN CHARGE OF YOUR LIFE.

                  YOUR FATHER,

                  GOD

Daniel 10–12

 QUICK LOOK: Daniel 10:12—A man dressed in linen continued, "Do not be afraid, Daniel. You decided to get more understanding. You made yourself humble as you worshipped your God. Since the first day you did those things, your words were heard. I have come to give you an answer."

 RECAP

▷ Daniel tells about a time when he was very sad for three weeks. Then, a man dressed in linen and gold, possibly an angel, came to him in a vision to tell him about the future.

▷ The angel encourages Daniel and tells him about how Israel will endure a terrible war but all of God's people will survive it.

▷ Two other angels come to Daniel. He tells them he doesn't understand what he has heard, but they encourage him to go on his way.

 TODAY'S GOD SHOT

When we know who God is, it's easy for us to trust Him, even when we don't understand what He is doing. One thing we do know is that He's where the joy is!

 ACTIVITY

As you are getting to know God, is it easier for you to trust Him?

Circle the emoji that shows how you feel trusting God even when you don't understand what He is doing.

Ezra 1–3

 QUICK LOOK: Ezra 3:11—"They sang to the LORD. They praised him. They gave thanks to him. They said, 'The LORD is good. His faithful love to Israel continues forever.'"

 RECAP

▶ King Cyrus of Persia has just defeated Babylon. God stirs up his spirit to rebuild the temple in Jerusalem. So King Cyrus sends fifty thousand exiles home along with the best provisions and the 5,400 stolen temple vessels.

▶ The newly returned exiles give generously to God to buy supplies in preparation for building the temple.

▶ They start laying a foundation for the temple according to the directions David gave Solomon when he built the First Temple. Many of the people are excited about this, and they have a worship service.

 TODAY'S GOD SHOT

The Israelites are back in their land after being driven into exile, and they give thanks to God! We're seeing the fulfillment of God's promises. He's been working even in the hearts of His enemies to bless His people. He's bringing them back to the land He gave them. He's restoring, He's remaking, and He's where the joy is!

 ACTIVITY

Think about what you've learned today and circle the answers.

TRUE   FALSE   The people are still in exile in Babylon.

TRUE   FALSE   The people are stingy, not giving toward the building of the temple.

TRUE   FALSE   God is blessing His people.

TRUE   FALSE   The people praise God because the temple would never be built.

TRUE   FALSE   God is faithful to keep His promises to me.

Ezra 4–6; Psalm 137

QUICK LOOK: Ezra 6:8—King Darius said, "Pay all their expenses from the royal treasures. Use the money you collect from the people who live west of the Euphrates. Don't let the work on the temple stop."

RECAP

▷ Zechariah and Haggai encourage Zerubbabel and Joshua, the current leaders of the returned exiles (the Israelites who have returned to their land), to rally the troops to start rebuilding the temple even though there are people trying to stop them from building.

▷ King Darius receives a letter from the governor asking if King Cyrus had really given the order to rebuild the house of God.

▷ Darius confirms that there is an order for the temple to be rebuilt, and the people are to be given the money and supplies to build it six times bigger than it was before. The people build until it is finished and dedicate it to God!

TODAY'S GOD SHOT

If the enemy hadn't tried to stop the temple from being rebuilt, the Jews would have had to pay for it all on their own. Instead, God works it out so that the enemy's plan to stop the temple created an even better outcome for His people! No one can pull off that kind of change except for God. He's where the joy is!

ACTIVITY

Circle the words that describe who God is from today's reading.

FAITHFUL   GOOD   ANGRY   TIRED   GENEROUS   FAR AWAY

Haggai 1–2

 QUICK LOOK: Haggai 2:9—"'The new temple will be more beautiful than the first one was,' says the LORD. 'And in this place I will bring peace,' announces the LORD who rules over all."

▷ Haggai has a conversation with Joshua and Zerubbabel about how the people are focusing on their own houses. Haggai tells them that rebuilding God's house is what they should be focused on.

▷ There is a problem with the people. Their hearts aren't clean, so the temple they are building isn't either. God doesn't want them to get to the end of this project and have it be an unclean building that He can't live in.

▷ God wants their hearts, not their hard work.

 TODAY'S GOD SHOT

After all God's people have done to break His heart through the years, He still promises that He'll dwell among them again and that the new temple will be more beautiful than the first one was. God can rebuild. And when God rebuilds something, He improves it. He's where the joy is!

 ACTIVITY

God cares about your heart. You are the temple that God is building now, and as you spend time with Him, He is making your heart more beautiful. Draw a ⭐ next to the ways you know God has changed your heart.

I am more generous.

I am more loving.

I am less angry.

I have more peace and don't have fear.

Zechariah 1–4

QUICK LOOK: Zechariah 3:3–4—"Joshua stood in front of the angel. He was wearing clothes that were very dirty. The angel spoke to those who were standing near him. He said, 'Take his dirty clothes off.' He said to Joshua, 'I have taken your sin away. I will put fine clothes on you.'"

RECAP

▷ Zechariah is one of two prophets to the returned exiles, and he's also a priest. He talks about how God wants the current generation to know how much their ancestors' sins impacted things, and He begs them not to walk the same path.

▷ Zechariah sees five visions in these chapters, and there are four more in the next chapters. These visions give a picture of what's to come.

▷ The high priest, Joshua, is a key figure in the fourth vision. He's standing in front of the Angel of the LORD (likely Jesus) in dirty clothes, and Satan is there too, accusing him. The LORD rebukes Satan for his accusations against Joshua and then gives him clean clothes.

TODAY'S GOD SHOT

God tells Joshua that He has taken his sin away. There isn't anything that Joshua does to remove his own sin. God Himself takes responsibility for it. We can't clean ourselves up, but God can, and by His grace, He does. He's where the joy is!

ACTIVITY

Pray and tell God you are thankful for how He took the responsibility for your sins.

Dear God, thank You for loving me and taking on the responsibility for my sins. I am clean because of what Jesus did for me on the cross, and it gives me joy! I love You. Amen.

Zechariah 5–9

 QUICK LOOK: Zechariah 9:9—The LORD's message said, "City of Zion, be full of joy! People of Jerusalem, shout! See, your king comes to you. He always does what is right. He has won the victory. He is humble and riding on a donkey. He is sitting on a donkey's colt."

 RECAP

▷ Zechariah has four more visions speaking to what's to come.

▷ Not all the promises God has made to His people have been fulfilled yet, and not all the things their ancestors lost have been restored yet.

▷ Zechariah gives a hint that Jesus is coming to bring peace to His people.

 TODAY'S GOD SHOT

Jesus shows up repeatedly in today's reading. Zechariah 9:9 is familiar to us because we know this is how Jesus rode through Jerusalem in Matthew 21. Jesus always does what is right. He won the victory over sin and death and brought peace, and He's where the joy is!

 ACTIVITY

Which one of these things is true about Jesus? Circle the answer.

    A. Jesus always does what is right.

    B. Jesus is humble.

    C. Jesus has won the victory.

    D. All of the above are true.

Zechariah 10–14

QUICK LOOK: Zechariah 10:3—"The LORD who rules over all says, 'I am very angry with the shepherds. I will punish the leaders. The LORD will take care of his flock. They are the people of Judah. He will make them like a proud horse in battle.'"

▷ God's sheep—His people—are under His care. He will bring them back from the nations where they've been scattered and multiply them in the promised land again.

▷ Zechariah initially takes pity on the sheep, firing wicked shepherds. He guides them with two staffs, which he names Favor and Union, representing not only his relationship to the sheep individually but also the relationship the sheep have as a flock.

▷ Zechariah gives messages about the future that include Jesus. He is the fountain who washes His people clean from their sins. Someday, Jesus will cut off all the idols and false prophets in the land.

TODAY'S GOD SHOT

Zechariah's prophecy points us to Jesus. He is the Good Shepherd to His flock. He was rejected by His sheep but also took their place when He became the Lamb who was sacrificed for sin. He's the shepherd *and* the sacrifice—because when it comes to His kids, God provides all He requires. He's where the joy is!

ACTIVITY

Draw a picture of a shepherd with some sheep. Thank God for being your Good Shepherd.

Esther 1–5

 QUICK LOOK: Esther 4:14—Mordecai said to Esther, "What if you don't say anything at this time? Then help for the Jews will come from another place. But you and your family will die. Who knows? It's possible that you became queen for a time just like this."

 RECAP

▷ Esther is the only book in the Bible that doesn't mention God's name, but we see Him in the shadows of every scene, working things out according to His plan and promises.

▷ When the king decides he wants a new queen, Esther is brought in with other girls to be offered to the king. Esther, a Jew, exercises wisdom and humility. God grants her favor with the king, who makes her his new queen.

▷ Esther's uncle Mordecai lets her know that Haman, a royal official to the king, wants to kill all the Jews. Esther comes up with a plan that includes inviting the king and Haman to dinner.

 TODAY'S GOD SHOT

Mordecai knows God has promised to preserve His people and lets Esther know that she may be the very tool God uses to accomplish His plans and fulfill His promises. Despite being under a death threat, Mordecai leans into what he knows to be true about God. God is our only hope, and He's where the joy is!

 ACTIVITY

Answer the questions with yes or no.

1. Is God's name mentioned in these chapters? YES NO

2. Did God have a plan for Esther's life? YES NO

3. Did the king select Esther to be his new queen? YES NO

4. Do you think Esther will help the Jews? YES NO

5. Is God our only hope? YES NO

Esther 6–10

 QUICK LOOK: Esther 8:3—"Esther made another appeal to the king. She fell at his feet and wept. She begged him to put an end to the evil plan of Haman, the Agagite. He had decided to kill the Jews."

 RECAP

▷ The king has trouble sleeping and asks his staff to read the events that have transpired during his reign. He recalls a man who had saved his life and wants to honor him. That man was Esther's cousin, Mordecai.

▷ At a dinner party, the king offers Esther whatever she wants. She tells him about Haman and how he has made an order to kill her people, the Jews. The king sentences Haman to death and makes Mordecai the leader in his place.

▷ Esther and Mordecai come up with a plan to save their people. Since they can't stop people from attacking the Jews, they'll give the Jews permission to fight back and plunder the goods of anyone who attacks them.

 TODAY'S GOD SHOT

God is at work even though He is never mentioned in this book. He is orchestrating every detail of this story to be the Rescuer of His people. Time will reveal how God is rescuing you in your current and future situations. He may appear to be absent, but He is always at work! He's where the joy is!

 ACTIVITY

Which one of these things has God rescued you from?

LYING   BULLIES   SICKNESS   FEAR   DISOBEYING

Ezra 7–10

 QUICK LOOK: Ezra 10:2—Shekaniah spoke to Ezra and said, "We haven't been faithful to our God. We've married women from the nations around us. In spite of that, there is still hope for Israel."

 RECAP

▷ King Artaxerxes sends Ezra and some other Jews back to Jerusalem, giving them everything they need.

▷ Ezra fasts and asks God to help them arrive safely back in Jerusalem.

▷ Ezra is sad because the people have disobeyed God by marrying women who worship other gods.

 TODAY'S GOD SHOT

God offers forgiveness to the people even though they have disobeyed Him. After Shekaniah confesses his sin, he says, "There is still hope for Israel." God is our hope, and He's where the joy is!

 ACTIVITY

List three things God has forgiven you for.

1. ....

2. ....

3. ....

Take some time to pray and thank Him!

Nehemiah 1–5

QUICK LOOK: Nehemiah 2:20—Nehemiah answered, "The God of heaven will give us success. We serve him. So we'll start rebuilding the walls."

RECAP

▷ Nehemiah is an Israelite official who works for the king of Babylon. God's people have been back in Jerusalem for a long time but have not rebuilt the city or its walls.

▷ Nehemiah is upset about this and prays. God puts a plan in his heart to rebuild the city and gives him favor with the king to work out the plan.

▷ Nehemiah goes to Jerusalem and leads the people to rebuild the wall. When their enemies come against them, Nehemiah asks God for help and sets up a guard for protection.

TODAY'S GOD SHOT

God works through His people—they're praying, working, and ready to defend His city.

It's key to stay tuned in to God like Nehemiah does, always asking Him for direction. Sometimes God calls us to be active, and sometimes He calls us to wait for Him to work, but He always has a plan. His plan is good, and He's where the joy is!

ACTIVITY

Ask someone you know about a time when they did something God asked them to do.

Nehemiah 6–7

 QUICK LOOK: Nehemiah 6:9—"All of them [Nehemiah's enemies] were trying to frighten us. They thought, 'Their hands will get too weak to do the work. So it won't be completed.' But I [Nehemiah] prayed to God. I said, 'Make my hands stronger.'"

 RECAP

▷ Sanballat and Geshem bully Nehemiah and send him a threatening letter accusing him of wanting to be king.

▷ Nehemiah is not afraid of them and continues his work, asking God to make him stronger. God hears his prayers and gives him the strength to finish rebuilding the wall of the city in fifty-two days!

▷ God has Nehemiah record all the heads of families who have returned from exile. Altogether, there are fifty thousand people and eight thousand animals.

 TODAY'S GOD SHOT

Nehemiah repeatedly seeks God for strength. It's clear that he knows God is the one who makes him strong. Nehemiah walks in confident humility not because he's awesome, but because he knows the source of his strength lies in the God who helps him. Nehemiah knows He's where the joy is!

 ACTIVITY

God gives us confident humility when we rely on Him to do it through us. Fill in the blank with something you have confident humility in.

I AM REALLY GOOD AT .... BECAUSE

GOD GIVES ME THE ABILITY TO DO IT WELL.

Nehemiah 8–10

 QUICK LOOK: Nehemiah 9:32—God's people said, "Our God, you are the great God. You are mighty and wonderful. You keep the covenant you made with us. You show us your love."

 RECAP

▷ The people gather together, and Ezra reads the Word, probably the five books of Moses, which are Genesis, Exodus, Leviticus, Numbers, and Deuteronomy.

▷ The people decide to celebrate the Feast of Booths, a seven-day fall festival they had forgotten about, thanking God for His provision for their people when they lived in the wilderness for forty years.

▷ Ezra prays and thanks God for all He has done for His people.

 TODAY'S GOD SHOT

God is committed to being known by His people and being in a relationship with them. He's so patient and persistent! After all this time, they're finally seeing how wonderful He is. And hopefully they realize He's where the joy is!

 ACTIVITY

Circle the words that describe who God is to you.

COMMITTED   KNOWN   UNFAIR   FAITHFUL

FAKE   GREAT   WONDERFUL

Nehemiah 11–13; Psalm 126

 QUICK LOOK: Nehemiah 12:43—"The people were glad because God had given them great joy. The women and children were also very happy. The joyful sound in Jerusalem could be heard far away."

 RECAP

▷ Nehemiah holds a grand opening ceremony celebrating the completion of the wall.

▷ God's people are not obeying God's laws, so Nehemiah takes matters into his own hands, literally. He pulls out their hair, curses at them, beats them up, and makes them promise to stop!

▷ Psalm 126 is a song of praise to God for the great things He has done.

 TODAY'S GOD SHOT

You can't force someone to have joy. You may be able to force someone to act joyful, but you can't force them to be joyful in their heart. God is the only one who can give us true joy because He's where the joy is!

ACTIVITY

Circle the word *joy* in Psalm 126. How many times do you see it? ....

Psalm 126

Our enemies took us away from Zion.
  But when the LORD brought us home,
  it seemed like a dream to us.
Our mouths were filled with laughter.
  Our tongues sang with joy.
Then the people of other nations said,
  "The LORD has done great things for them."
The LORD has done great things for us.
  And we are filled with joy.
LORD, bless us with great success again,
  as rain makes streams flow in the Negev Desert.
Those who cry as they plant their crops
  will sing with joy when they gather them in.
Those who go out weeping
  as they carry seeds to plant
will come back singing with joy.
  They will bring the new crop back with them.

Malachi 1–4

QUICK LOOK: Malachi 4:2—The LORD said, "But here is what will happen for you who have respect for me. The sun that brings life will rise. Its rays will bring healing to my people. You will go out and leap for joy like calves that have just been fed."

RECAP

▷ God tells Israel how much He loves them, but they don't believe Him.

▷ God begs His people to return to Him, but they want to know what it'll cost them. God says anything it costs will be repaid in ways they can't even imagine.

▷ A day is coming when God will judge all evil people. But for those who love Him, the sun that brings life will rise and its rays will bring healing to them.

TODAY'S GOD SHOT

God is both just and merciful. He will judge evil people, and He will forgive those who follow Him. When we show respect for God, He shines on us like the sun as it rises and brings life and healing to our hearts because He's where the joy is!

ACTIVITY

What is one way you show respect for God each day?

....

When you see the sun, tell God how much you love and respect Him. Thank Him for healing your heart and giving you joy.

Luke 1; John 1

QUICK LOOK: Luke 1:46–47—Mary said, "My soul gives glory to the Lord. My spirit delights in God my Savior."

▶ The first four books of the New Testament—Matthew, Mark, Luke, and John—are called the Gospels. Each gospel writer has a unique viewpoint on who Jesus is. Luke's primary perspective is "Jesus as man," and John's primary perspective is "Jesus as God." Jesus was 100 percent human and 100 percent God.

▶ Luke shares how the angel Gabriel tells a man named Zechariah and a woman named Mary the good news that Jesus is going to be born.

▶ John helps us see that Jesus was there at the beginning of time and was active in creating the world as God's Son.

TODAY'S GOD SHOT

God sent Jesus to fix our friendship with Him, and the songs of Mary and Zechariah show that they know what matters! They praise God because their long-awaited Savior, Jesus, has come to rescue the world from sin, and He's where the joy is!

ACTIVITY

Have you ever tried to write a song thanking God for His love through the gift of Jesus? Give it a try or play one of your favorite worship songs now.

Matthew 1; Luke 2

 QUICK LOOK: Luke 2:28–30—"Simeon took Jesus in his arms and praised God. He said, 'Lord, you are the King over all. Now let me, your servant, go in peace. That is what you promised. My eyes have seen your salvation.'"

 RECAP

▷ Matthew is another gospel writer, and his unique viewpoint on Jesus is "Jesus as King." His book opens by telling us the family line of Jesus, which includes women, Gentiles, and fourteen generations.

▷ God sends an angel to a man named Joseph and a virgin named Mary. They are two ordinary people God chose to fulfill His plan for Jesus to be born to fix our friendship with Him.

▷ Luke 2 tells us of Jesus's birth and the shepherds' visit, and about how Mary and Joseph take Jesus to the temple to dedicate Him to God. Anna, a widow, and Simeon, an old priest, praise God for fulfilling His promise to send Jesus.

 TODAY'S GOD SHOT

During the four hundred years of silence, the time between the end of the Old Testament and the beginning of the New Testament, God the Spirit speaks to an old priest named Simeon and promises that he will see Jesus before he dies. Simeon relies on that promise and clings to it when all seems lost. God keeps His promises, and Simeon knows He's where the joy is!

 ACTIVITY

How many days are left until you celebrate Christmas with your family?

....

God promised to send Jesus to save us from our sin, and we can celebrate that gift every day!

Matthew 2

QUICK LOOK: Matthew 2:13—"When the Wise Men had left, Joseph had a dream. In the dream an angel of the Lord appeared to Joseph. 'Get up!' the angel said. 'Take the child and his mother and escape to Egypt. Stay there until I tell you to come back. Herod is going to search for the child. He wants to kill him.'"

RECAP

▷ Jesus is born in a village called Bethlehem, in a kingdom called Judea that is under the Roman rule of King Herod.

▷ Wise men, possibly men who study the stars, are led to Jesus's location to worship Him and give Him gifts.

▷ King Herod makes it a law to kill all baby boys under two years old. An angel comes to Joseph in a dream to warn him to leave Bethlehem and go to Egypt.

TODAY'S GOD SHOT

God goes to great lengths to provide for and protect His people according to His plan. God's protective nature means that whatever comes our way, He can be trusted. And He's where the joy is!

ACTIVITY

Color the star beside the correct statement(s).

 Jesus was born in a nice hotel because He is God's Son.

 Wise men traveled a long way to worship Jesus and give Him gifts.

 An angel told Joseph to leave Bethlehem and go to Egypt.

Matthew 3; Mark 1; Luke 3

 QUICK LOOK: Matthew 3:16–17—"As soon as Jesus was baptized, he came up out of the water. At that moment heaven was opened. Jesus saw the Spirit of God coming down on him like a dove. A voice from heaven said, 'This is my Son, and I love him. I am very pleased with him.'"

 RECAP

▷ John the Baptist lives in the desert, eating locusts and honey. His message opens with a call for the people to turn away from doing wrong things and to be baptized.

▷ Jesus asks John to baptize Him. John the Baptist knows Jesus doesn't need to turn away from doing wrong things but obeys and baptizes him.

▷ After Jesus's baptism, God the Spirit leads Him into the wilderness. He's there for forty days, fasting and then being tempted by Satan. Then He launches His ministry when He's around thirty years old.

 TODAY'S GOD SHOT

At the moment Jesus is baptized, we can see all three persons of God. God the Son is in the water, God the Spirit comes down on Him like a dove, and God the Father's voice is heard approving of Jesus and identifying who He is. It's hard to understand how God can be three persons in one, but it's true! He's where the joy is!

 ACTIVITY

Fill in the blanks to name the three persons of God.

GOD THE ...., '

GOD THE ...., '

GOD THE ....

Matthew 4; Luke 4–5

 QUICK LOOK: Luke 4:18—"The Spirit of the Lord is on me. He has anointed me to announce the good news to poor people. He has sent me to announce freedom for prisoners."

RECAP

▷ After His baptism, the Spirit leads Jesus into the desert to be tempted. There, the devil tempts Him, but Jesus doesn't sin.

▷ After fasting there for forty days, Jesus begins preaching. The local leaders are excited about Jesus's teaching at first, but when He talks about the idea of loving their enemies, they want to throw Him off a cliff.

▷ Jesus calls some of His first disciples, saying, "Come and follow me!" Four fishermen and one tax collector leave everything behind to follow Him.

 TODAY'S GOD SHOT

Jesus sought out the people who were unwanted and unloved. He's bringing good news to the poor and bringing freedom to prisoners. He came to be rejected by the people He loved, to feel their pain so He could lead them into joy—to lead them to Himself. Because He's where the joy is!

 ACTIVITY

Jesus said, "Come follow me." Who are some people in your family, school, or neighborhood who need to know that Jesus loves them and wants them to follow Him? Write their names below.

....

....

John 2–4

QUICK LOOK: John 3:14–15—Jesus said to Nicodemus, "Moses lifted up the snake in the desert. In the same way, the Son of Man must also be lifted up. Then everyone who believes may have eternal life in him."

▷ Jesus performs His first public miracle by turning water into wine at a wedding.

▷ A teacher named Nicodemus comes to Jesus at night with his questions. Jesus teaches him about God's Spirit and being born again.

▷ Jesus talks to a Samaritan woman at a well and tells her everything about herself. He shows her love and offers her eternal life.

TODAY'S GOD SHOT

God sends Jesus to earth, and there are many similarities between Him and Moses. For example, Moses' first miracle was turning water into blood, which symbolizes death. Jesus's first miracle was turning water into wine, which symbolizes life. God is showing the world that a deliverer greater than Moses has arrived—Jesus. And He's where the joy is!

ACTIVITY

What do you remember about Moses and Jesus? Below you will see similarities in their lives. Draw lines from Moses and from Jesus to connect them to each characteristic.

MOSES   CHARACTERISTICS   JESUS

Saved as a baby

Sent by God

Performed miracles

Gave commands

Leader of people

Fed large number of people

Shepherd

Spent time in Egypt

Matthew 8; Mark 2

 QUICK LOOK: Mark 2:17—Jesus said, "Those who are healthy don't need a doctor. Sick people do. I have not come to get those who think they are right with God to follow me. I have come to get sinners to follow me."

 RECAP

▷ Jesus shows kindness and humility to a man with a skin disease when he kneels at Jesus's feet and asks for healing.

▷ Jesus says following Him will cost us our comfort and our control over our own lives.

▷ Jesus heals people who don't have anything to offer Him, not even their faith.

 TODAY'S GOD SHOT

Jesus has so much love for those who are sick and in need. Our only hope of finding the deep healing and joy of knowing Jesus is to realize we were born sick with our sin. Thank God He found us, because He's where the joy is!

 ACTIVITY

Circle the sins you want God to heal you from.

SELFISHNESS   PRIDE   DISOBEDIENCE   LAZINESS   JEALOUSY

John 5

 QUICK LOOK: John 5:8–9—"Then Jesus said to him, 'Get up! Pick up your mat and walk.' The man was healed right away. He picked up his mat and walked. This happened on a Sabbath day."

 RECAP

▷ Jesus heals a man who had not been able to walk for thirty-eight years. The man picks up his mat and goes straight to the temple to worship God.

▷ The Jewish leaders see the man and tell him he's not allowed to be healed on the Sabbath day of rest and that whoever healed him has broken the law.

▷ Jesus does whatever God the Father asks Him to do.

 TODAY'S GOD SHOT

God found the man who couldn't walk, and his entire world changed—but not because he got his legs fixed. It was because Jesus spoke to his heart and called him to a new life. And now that man knows for sure that He's where the joy is!

 ACTIVITY

Circle the emoji that shows how the healed man felt when he could walk again.

Matthew 12; Mark 3; Luke 6

 QUICK LOOK: Mark 3:2—"Some Pharisees were trying to find fault with Jesus. They watched him closely. They wanted to see if he would heal the man on the Sabbath day."

 RECAP

▷ Jesus teaches that the temple is important, but there's something more important than the dwelling place of God and that is God Himself.

▷ God made the Sabbath law to serve people, giving them a day of rest, so even the people's needs are greater than the Sabbath law.

▷ Jesus handpicks twelve disciples to follow Him closely.

 TODAY'S GOD SHOT

Jesus is falsely accused by religious leaders, and His closest friends and family turn against Him. He knows what it's like to be mistreated and has compassion for others who need gentleness, mercy, and healing. He comes near to us, and we can come near to Him because He's where the joy is!

 ACTIVITY

Do you remember the last time someone was mean to you and how it felt?

YES   NO

Always remember that Jesus knows exactly how it feels and will come near to you and help you.

Matthew 5–7

QUICK LOOK: Matthew 5:16—Jesus said, "In the same way, let your light shine so others can see it. Then they will see the good things you do. And they will bring glory to your Father who is in heaven."

RECAP

▷ This is Jesus's Sermon on the Mount, the famous sermon in which He describes God's kingdom. He opens with eight blessings.

▷ Life in God's kingdom begins with recognizing our desperate need for Him.

▷ God isn't just after the right actions. He's after a right heart.

TODAY'S GOD SHOT

When we do things for others, it shows them what God is like. His Spirit is producing good works in us. God gets the glory because He does the doing! But He doesn't leave us empty-handed. When we give Him glory, He gives us joy! And He's where the joy is!

ACTIVITY

God wants our lives to show others how good He is. Take some time to think about Matthew 5:16 while filling in the blanks. Try to memorize it!

"IN THE SAME ...., LET YOUR LIGHT

.... SO OTHERS CAN SEE IT. THEN THEY

WILL .... THE GOOD THINGS ....

DO. AND THEY WILL BRING .... TO YOUR

.... WHO IS IN ...."

Matthew 9; Luke 7

 QUICK LOOK: Matthew 9:22—"Jesus turned and saw her. 'Dear woman, don't give up hope,' he said. 'Your faith has healed you.' The woman was healed at that moment."

 RECAP

▷ The Jewish leaders (Pharisees) harass Jesus for eating with sinners, like tax collectors. He tells them that the people who sin are the reason He is here.

▷ Jesus heals a ruler's daughter, a woman who had an issue with bleeding, two blind men, and a widow's son.

▷ A sinful woman washes Jesus's feet to show her love and thankfulness to Him.

 TODAY'S GOD SHOT

Jesus says things like, "Your faith has healed you." Faith, no matter how big or strong, can't heal on its own. But faith in our God, who is powerful and loves us, can! He's where the joy is!

 ACTIVITY

Think of someone who needs healing: a friend with a broken arm, a sick grandparent, or even yourself. Pray this prayer.

> **God,** thank You for Your love and forgiveness. I put my faith in You,
>
> believing that You are powerful and can do anything! Please heal
>
> .... Thank You for being a Healer and for giving me joy!
> (name of person above)
> Amen.

Matthew 11

 QUICK LOOK: Matthew 11:28—Jesus said, "Come to me, all you who are tired and are carrying heavy loads. I will give you rest."

 RECAP

▷ John the Baptist is in prison. He sends messengers to ask Jesus to confirm or deny that He is the Messiah. Jesus confirms who He is and praises John the Baptist.

▷ Jesus speaks against the towns where He had done most of His miracles. The people there have not turned away from their sins.

▷ Jesus thanks His Father for the soft hearts of people who accept Him.

 TODAY'S GOD SHOT

Jesus says, "Come to me, all you who are tired and are carrying heavy loads. I will give you rest" (Matthew 11:28). Jesus wants you to tell Him anything that is hard or making you sad. Tell Him about what's in your heart. As we learn more about who Jesus is, it's evident how He gives us rest, and He's where the joy is!

 ACTIVITY

Rest looks different for everyone. It's anything you do that helps you to slow down and focus on God. Circle one of your favorite ways to rest.

READ A BOOK   RIDE A BIKE   WATCH A MOVIE

GO FOR A WALK   EAT ICE CREAM

Luke 11

 QUICK LOOK: Luke 11:9—Jesus said, "So here is what I say to you. Ask, and it will be given to you. Search, and you will find. Knock, and the door will be opened to you."

▷ The apostles ask Jesus to teach them how to pray. Prayer is simply talking to God.

▷ When Jesus performs miracles, it's to help people in need, not to prove who He is.

▷ The Father can be trusted to hear our prayers and answer with whatever He says is best.

 TODAY'S GOD SHOT

Jesus wants His followers to know how much the Father loves to talk with His kids, even about little things. God doesn't always give us what we ask for, because sometimes He has better ideas. But He always hears us and responds to us. And He's where the joy is!

 ACTIVITY

One way to pray is to use the acronym below. Practice praying like this today.

P—PRAISE God by telling Him how awesome He is, and thank Him for different things in your life.

R—REPENT is a fancy word for saying you're sorry. It's telling God you're going to stop doing the wrong thing and start doing what He says is right.

A—ASK God for whatever you want and need!

Y—Say YES to God and whatever He says is best, even if it's not what you want.

Matthew 13; Luke 8

 QUICK LOOK: Luke 8:15—Jesus said, "But the seed on good soil stands for those with an honest and good heart. Those people hear the message. They keep it in their hearts. They remain faithful and produce a good crop."

▷ Jesus likes to teach using parables, which are short stories that teach a lesson.

▷ Jesus tells a story about a farmer. He compares the good news of His love to a seed that is spread all around and falls on four different types of soil.

▷ Jesus doesn't explain His parable to the crowd, but He does explain it to His disciples. They have been blessed with open hearts to understand His teaching.

 TODAY'S GOD SHOT

Jesus had a lot of different followers who traveled with Him. Some were poor. Some were rich. Each one had a different kind of "soil" because of their different backgrounds. One of the beautiful things about God is that He can take the most unlikely soil and turn it into a garden. He's where the joy is!

ACTIVITY

Check the box below that represents the soil of your heart.

☐ Soil that is on the path where birds eat the seed. You don't understand what it means to follow Jesus, so your faith doesn't last long.

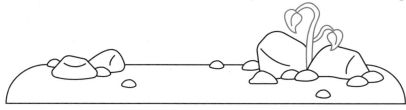

☐ Soil that is rocky and not deep. You are excited to follow Jesus at first but it gets too hard or you forget.

☐ Soil that is thorny and crowds out any plants. You get more caught up in what others have or do than in following Jesus.

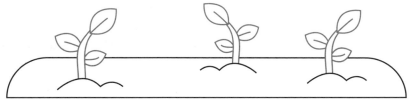

☐ Soil that is soft and good for growing. You hear about Jesus and choose to follow Him, even when it's tough.

Pray and ask God to help you keep a soft heart as you grow in your relationship with Him.

Mark 4–5

 QUICK LOOK: Mark 4:39—"He [Jesus] got up and ordered the wind to stop. He said to the waves, 'Quiet! Be still!' Then the wind died down. And it was completely calm."

 RECAP

▶ Jesus tells the story of the four soils and the purpose of a lamp. These help us know that Jesus wants the seed and the light to go everywhere!

▶ Jesus and His disciples are in a boat on the Sea of Galilee when a storm comes up. Jesus is asleep, but the disciples wake Him up because they are afraid.

▶ Jesus has compassion for His disciples and rebukes the storm, ordering it to stop.

 TODAY'S GOD SHOT

Our relationship with God is the most important thing in our lives. In the storm, the disciples learn something about Him they wouldn't know otherwise: He's in charge of whatever comes their way. He's so generous to let them see more of who He is! He's strengthening their faith because He's where the joy is!

 ACTIVITY

When you are going through something hard in your life, what truth about God can you remember to help get you through?

....

....

Matthew 10

QUICK LOOK: Matthew 10:10—Jesus said, "Do not take a bag for the journey. Do not take extra clothes or sandals or walking sticks. A worker should be given what he needs."

▷ Jesus sends His twelve disciples out to the people of Israel, who are like lost sheep. He wants them to preach about God's kingdom, heal the sick, and raise the dead.

▷ Jesus's disciples learn to trust Him for everything they need through the gifts of other people. This builds their faith as they rely on Him and others.

▷ Jesus says we should commit to God and love Him first, and then love our family.

TODAY'S GOD SHOT

God provides everything the disciples need, such as clothes, food, and places to stay. He even gives them words to speak. God cares about everything. He listens to all our prayers, no matter how big or small, and He always answers in one way or another. And He's where the joy is!

ACTIVITY

Check the boxes that describe something that is true about God.

☐ God gives me all I need.   ☐ God sees me.
☐ God hears my prayers.   ☐ God gives me joy.
☐ God cares about me.   ☐ God is in control.

Matthew 14; Mark 6; Luke 9

 QUICK LOOK: Mark 6:50—"They all saw him and were terrified. Right away Jesus said to them, 'Be brave! It is I. Don't be afraid.'"

 RECAP

▷ Herod has John the Baptist killed. Jesus most likely wants to grieve and talk to the Father about everything, so He and the disciples leave town.

▷ Five thousand men—and an unknown number of women and children—follow Jesus. He has compassion on them and tells His disciples to do something impossible like feed them!

▷ Jesus goes away to pray, and the disciples get into a boat. A storm comes up that terrifies them. Jesus walks on the water to where they are and calms the storm.

 TODAY'S GOD SHOT

When a storm comes up at sea, the disciples are exhausted. They even think they see a ghost coming toward them on the water! But what they perceive as tragic or terrifying is actually God moving in their lives to show them He is with them. Even in our storms in the middle of the night, He's where the joy is!

 ACTIVITY

Fill in the verse.

MARK 6:50—THEY ALL SAW HIM AND WERE

.... RIGHT AWAY JESUS SAID

TO THEM, "BE ....! IT IS I. DON'T BE

...."

Remember that whenever you are afraid you can ask God to help you!

John 6

QUICK LOOK: John 6:67–69—"'You don't want to leave also, do you?' Jesus asked the twelve disciples. Simon Peter answered him, 'Lord, who can we go to? You have the words of eternal life. We have come to believe and to know that you are the Holy One of God.'"

RECAP

▷ The people ask Jesus about what God's work requires of them. Jesus responds by telling them it is simply to believe in Him. The word *believe* means "to commit your trust, to place confidence in."

▷ Jesus explains how He is the bread of life. The people do not understand. He doesn't mean actual bread. He's talking about how He is the source of everything we need.

▷ God the Father has a plan, and God the Son submits to the will of God the Father.

TODAY'S GOD SHOT

Two of Jesus's twelve disciples—Simon Peter and Judas Iscariot—are going to walk away from their relationship with Him during the toughest moment of Jesus's life. Jesus knows it, but still, He keeps them close, submitting to the Father's plan. Even Peter knows Jesus's words have eternal life and that He's where the joy is!

ACTIVITY

Connect the dots to find the word that means "to commit your trust."

Matthew 15; Mark 7

 QUICK LOOK: Matthew 15:30—"Large crowds came to him. They brought blind people and those who could not walk. They also brought disabled people, those who could not speak, and many others. They laid them at his feet, and he healed them."

 RECAP

▷ Jesus is dealing with the complaints of the Pharisees, the religious teachers. They are upset that His disciples don't wash their hands before meals. Jesus says they aren't breaking God's law, just man's traditions.

▷ The Pharisees love being "right," but they don't know anything about being right with God. That only comes through having the right heart that is in a relationship with Him.

▷ Jesus is on a mountainside in what's considered a Gentile region. The locals bring sick people to Him. He heals them and feeds the large crowd.

 TODAY'S GOD SHOT

People are drawn to Jesus, and He welcomes them. He goes to a town and stays for three days to heal everyone who needs His help. What a compassionate Savior! He's where the joy is!

 ACTIVITY

Why do you think Jesus took the time to heal sick people?

....

....

Matthew 16; Mark 8

QUICK LOOK: Matthew 16:24—"Then Jesus spoke to his disciples. He said, 'Whoever wants to be my disciple must say no to themselves. They must pick up their cross and follow me.'"

RECAP

▷ Jesus compares the teachings of the Pharisees and Sadducees (Israelite religious leaders) to yeast, which is something that makes bread rise. He wants His disciples to understand that even a little wrong teaching can grow and impact everything they believe.

▷ Jesus heals a blind man by spitting on his eyes, something that most people would think is gross. Immediately, his eyes are opened and he can see again!

▷ Jesus asks His disciples who they think He is. Peter says He's the Christ, and Jesus says God blessed him with that information because there's no way he would've figured it out on his own.

TODAY'S GOD SHOT

Jesus knows He's going to die soon, so he's preparing His followers. He knows they will be tempted to wonder if what they are doing matters. He doesn't want them to quit whenever they are threatened. He encourages them that nothing can harm His kingdom because He's where the joy is!

ACTIVITY

Jesus says that whoever wants to be His disciple must say no to themselves. Circle the things that are hard for you to say no to.

CANDY   VIDEO GAMES   ANGER   LAZINESS

PRIDE   WANTING NEW THINGS

Saying no to yourself requires God's help. Stop right now and let Him know how much you need Him.

Matthew 17; Mark 9

QUICK LOOK: Mark 9:24—"Right away the boy's father cried out, 'I do believe! Help me overcome my unbelief!'"

▷ Jesus takes Peter, James, and John up on a mountain and lets them see things human eyes can't see. Moses and Elijah appear and talk with Jesus. A cloud covers them. They hear God speak, telling them Jesus is His Son and they should listen to Him.

▷ Jesus heals a boy who is controlled by an evil spirit.

▷ Jesus pays His tax bill in a miraculous way by having Peter catch a fish with a coin in its mouth. The fish has the exact amount to cover both of their taxes.

TODAY'S GOD SHOT

The father of the boy controlled by an evil spirit confesses his doubt and asks Jesus to help him believe. God can give us faith! God wants us to ask Him for help and to view Him as the source of all things. He's the source, and He's where the joy is!

ACTIVITY

Think about one thing you have a hard time believing God can do. Write it or draw a picture of it below. Pray and ask God to help you believe He can do it.

Matthew 18

QUICK LOOK: Matthew 18:12—Jesus said, "What do you think? Suppose a man owns 100 sheep and one of them wanders away. Won't he leave the ninety-nine sheep on the hills? Won't he go and look for the one that wandered off?"

RECAP

▷ The disciples ask Jesus which one of them is the greatest. Jesus says humility is connected to greatness.

▷ Jesus uses kids in His illustrations, showing how much He loves and values children.

▷ Jesus tells a parable about a man who has great debt and teaches that we should respond to the forgiveness He's given us by forgiving others.

TODAY'S GOD SHOT

God pays individual attention to His kids. He notices what's happening, and He acts because He cares. He moves toward us when we run away. He finds us and brings us back so that we can see He's where the joy is!

ACTIVITY

What are some of the things God pays attention to in your life?

- Friendships
- Fear
- Sports
- Thoughts
- Problems
- Feelings
- Grades
- Frustrations

Thank God for seeing you and coming after you when you forget He is there.

John 7–8

QUICK LOOK: John 8:12—"Jesus spoke to the people again. He said, 'I am the light of the world. Anyone who follows me will never walk in darkness. They will have that light. They will have life.'"

RECAP

▷ There are three feasts each year for which Jews travel to Jerusalem. Before one feast, Jesus's brothers say He should publicly demonstrate His power there, but their words are almost certainly mocking, because they don't believe in Him.

▷ Jesus teaches in the temple, and people are amazed by what He knows. He fills them in on the truth that He speaks with God's authority. A sinful woman is brought to Him, but He shows her love and tells her to leave her life of sin.

▷ The Pharisees question Jesus for things He is teaching and saying about Himself. He tells them that God has sent Him and that if they knew God they would know and love Him.

TODAY'S GOD SHOT

Jesus says He's the Light of the World, the very thing by which we can see. And He's where the joy is!

ACTIVITY

Answer the following by circling T for true and F for false.

T F   The Pharisees love Jesus and His teachings.

T F   Jesus teaches how He is the light. His presence gets rid of the darkness!

T F   Jesus will always show you the way because He is the Light of the World.

John 9–10

QUICK LOOK: John 10:28–30—Jesus said, "I give them eternal life, and they will never die. No one will steal them out of my hand. My Father, who has given them to me, is greater than anyone. No one can steal them out of my Father's hand. I and the Father are one."

RECAP

▷ In Jesus's day, people associate sickness or physical disability with sin. When His disciples ask about who sinned when they encounter a blind man, Jesus tells them that no one sinned but that his blindness will be used to glorify God.

▷ Jesus calls Himself the Good Shepherd. He willingly gives His life for us, His sheep.

▷ The Pharisees want Jesus to say if He is the Messiah or not.

TODAY'S GOD SHOT

For God's kids, the single most comforting thing is that nothing can snatch us from His hand. Nothing is stronger than His love for you. God promises us eternal life and eternal security in His hand. What He starts, He will finish. He's always working, and He's where the joy is!

ACTIVITY

Pray this prayer.

Heavenly Father, thank You for loving me and giving me eternal life. I am so happy to know that no one can snatch me away from Your hand. You are greater and stronger than anything in my life. I love You! Amen.

Luke 10

 QUICK LOOK: Luke 10:27—"He [Jesus] answered, "'Love the Lord your God with all your heart and with all your soul. Love him with all your strength and with all your mind.' (Deuteronomy 6:5) And, 'Love your neighbor as you love yourself.'" (Leviticus 19:18)."

 RECAP

▷ Jesus sends out seventy-two disciples. Their job is to let the towns know that Jesus the Messiah is coming to visit. They are agents of His healing power, bringing benefits and the truth of the kingdom to those far from the kingdom.

▷ A lawyer, who is probably a Pharisee, asks Jesus how to get eternal life. He wants to test Jesus and draw attention to how good he is.

▷ Two of Jesus's friends have Him over for lunch. Mary is talking to Jesus while Martha is trying to handle the details. Martha is frustrated that Mary is relaxing while she does all the work.

 TODAY'S GOD SHOT

In the parable of the Good Samaritan, Jesus is showing us what He has done. This story serves as a reminder that we are the ones in the ditch. It turns out the Good Samaritan isn't even the hero of his own parable—Jesus is! And He's where the joy is!

 ACTIVITY

Memorize Luke 10:27 this week. Write each word on its own note card. Make it a game by removing a note card each time you say the verse.

Luke 12–13

QUICK LOOK: Luke 12:32—Jesus said, "Little flock, do not be afraid. Your Father has been pleased to give you the kingdom."

RECAP

▷ Jesus is preaching about trusting God's provision and gets heckled by a man who asks Him to settle a financial dispute. He launches into a parable about a fool who builds new barns to hold his wealth.

▷ We have no idea when Jesus will return, and death can come at any moment, so Jesus tells us to be prepared. A relationship with Him is the only preparation possible and necessary. Do we know Him or not?

▷ Jesus tells a parable: A man plants a tree and has a gardener tend to it, but it's fruitless for three years. This is a metaphor for Israel at the time—Israel is the fig tree, Jesus is the gardener, and the Father owns the vineyard. It's been three years since Jesus began His ministry, but Israel shows no signs of repenting.

TODAY'S GOD SHOT

Jesus tells His disciples they don't need to be anxious, because their Father is attentive and is pleased with them. God delights to give good gifts to His kids. And there's no greater gift than Himself. He's where the joy is!

ACTIVITY

What is one good gift you have that you can thank God for?

....

Luke 14–15

 QUICK LOOK: Luke 15:31–32—"'My son,' the father said, 'you are always with me. Everything I have is yours. But we had to celebrate and be glad. This brother of yours was dead. And now he is alive again. He was lost. And now he is found.'"

 RECAP

▷ Jesus goes to dinner at a Pharisee's house, where He meets a man whose body is badly swollen. It's the Sabbath day of rest, so Jesus asks the Pharisees who are there if it's against the law for Him to heal the man. They don't reply, so Jesus heals Him.

▷ Jesus tells three parables about recovering lost things: a sheep, a coin, and a son.

▷ God rejoices at finding the lost, even when they may not seem valuable to anyone else.

 TODAY'S GOD SHOT

Jesus shows God celebrating our nearness to Him in the story of the lost son who comes home. The fact that God would celebrate us feels a little odd, but He calls it fitting. He's so merciful and gracious. And He's where the joy is!

 ACTIVITY

What do you learn about God through the stories Jesus told about the lost sheep, the lost coin, and the lost son?

....

....

Draw a picture of each lost thing on the next page.

The Lost Sheep

The Lost Coin

The Lost Son

Luke 16–17

QUICK LOOK: Luke 17:5–6—"The apostles said to the Lord, 'Give us more faith!' He replied, 'Suppose you have faith as small as a mustard seed. Then you can say to this mulberry tree, "Be pulled up. Be planted in the sea." And it will obey you.'"

RECAP

▷ Jesus tells His disciples a story to teach them they can't love their money and possessions and also love God.

▷ Jesus heals ten people who have a skin disease, but only one comes back to tell Him "Thank You!"

▷ Jesus encourages His disciples to be humble and to remember they're servants of the one true God.

TODAY'S GOD SHOT

Jesus is specific with how He speaks to different audiences. He meets them where they are—even in their unbelief. He encourages His disciples that a small amount of faith is powerful enough to move a mulberry tree into the sea. Jesus encourages His disciples, and He's where the joy is!

ACTIVITY

Do you want to have more faith?   YES   NO

Ask God to give you more faith and believe that He will do it!

John 11

QUICK LOOK: John 11:43–44—"Then Jesus called in a loud voice. He said, 'Lazarus, come out!' The dead man came out."

RECAP

▷ Jesus hears from Martha and Mary that His friend Lazarus is very sick. He chooses not to go to Bethany, where the family lives.

▷ Eventually, Jesus goes to Bethany, and Mary and Martha tell Him that Lazarus is dead, and everyone, including Jesus, is very sad.

▷ Jesus says to roll the stone away. He thanks the Father out loud and calls Lazarus out of the tomb. Lazarus comes back to life!

TODAY'S GOD SHOT

When Lazarus dies, Jesus intentionally waits for things to get worse in order for His power to be made known. From His intentional timing that somehow always seems too late, to His sweet, personal interaction with the sisters, to His power over death and the grave—He's where the joy is!

ACTIVITY

Think about something that you've been waiting on. Just like Mary and Martha, you can tell Jesus how you feel. Draw a face to show how it makes you feel to wait.

Luke 18

 QUICK LOOK: Luke 18:29–30—"'What I'm about to tell you is true,' Jesus said to them. 'Has anyone left home or wife or husband or brothers or sisters or parents or children for God's kingdom? They will receive many times as much in this world. In the world to come they will receive eternal life.'"

 RECAP

▷ Jesus encourages His disciples to pray by telling a story about a woman who doesn't stop asking for what she wants.

▷ Jesus tells a story to teach the people how God doesn't want the good things we do, He wants our hearts to belong to Him first.

▷ Jesus meets a rich ruler who wants to follow Him but won't make the choice to love God more than he loves his things.

 TODAY'S GOD SHOT

Jesus promises that what we gain in following Him is always better than what we lose. We gain eternal life, hope, peace, healing, freedom, justice . . . and joy! Because He's where the joy is!

 ACTIVITY

What are two things you have gained in following Jesus?

1. ....

2. ....

Matthew 19; Mark 10

 QUICK LOOK: Mark 10:44—Jesus said, "And anyone who wants to be first must be the slave of everyone."

RECAP

▷ Jesus answers the Pharisees' questions about marriage.

▷ Jesus continues to teach the disciples about heaven, which leads James and John to ask if they can sit next to Him in eternity.

▷ Jesus did not come to earth to be served. Instead, He came to serve others.

 TODAY'S GOD SHOT

In dying for the people, Jesus is taking Himself away from their physical presence but leaving them something that will last forever. By saying no to the requests of James and John, Jesus is giving them something better—they just don't understand at the time. Jesus is always serving us and giving the best gifts. He's where the joy is!

 ACTIVITY

Serving others isn't always easy. We have to choose to put other people before ourselves. Think about your day today and write the name of one person you can serve.

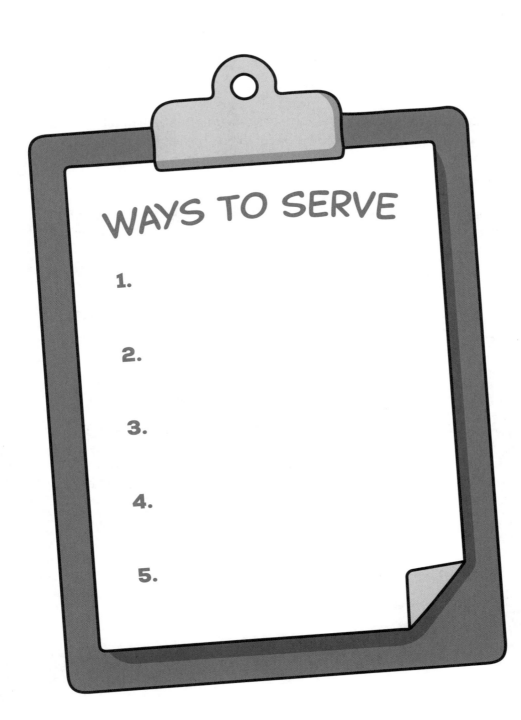

Matthew 20–21

QUICK LOOK: Matthew 21:19—"He saw a fig tree by the road. He went up to it but found nothing on it except leaves. Then he said to it, 'May you never bear fruit again!' Right away the tree dried up."

RECAP

▷ Jesus tells a parable about a vineyard and its workers and how much they get paid for the amount of work they did. He wants His followers to understand that everything God gives us is a gift we don't deserve.

▷ Jesus continues His journey to Jerusalem to celebrate the Passover and be crucified. He heals two blind men along the way.

▷ Jesus enters Jerusalem on a donkey, and a large crowd forms, waving palm branches. He knows His days on earth are limited and continues teaching with authority.

TODAY'S GOD SHOT

Jesus has the power to give life, like when He heals the blind men, but He also has power over death, like when He tells the fig tree to never bear fruit again. Jesus could have spoken death to those who wanted to kill Him, but instead He was humble, obeying His Father's plan to save us. His love is so great, and He's where the joy is!

ACTIVITY

When we follow Jesus, He gives us life! Just like the fig tree He spoke to, all of our sin is dead.

Draw a picture of what you think the fig tree looked like all dried up.

Luke 19

 QUICK LOOK: Luke 19:10—Jesus said to Zacchaeus, "The Son of Man came to look for the lost and save them."

 RECAP

▷ Zacchaeus is a rich and sinful man who has a life-changing encounter with Jesus that causes him to turn away from his wicked ways and start living for God.

▷ Jesus enters Jerusalem in a way that fulfills prophecies of the Messiah from the Old Testament.

▷ Jesus weeps over the people and their resistance to acknowledge Him as the Messiah they've been waiting for.

 TODAY'S GOD SHOT

Jesus came to seek and save the lost. You weren't alive back then, but you are in that story! Jesus came to save you too! Thank God that He knew we would need saving! He's where the joy is!

ACTIVITY

God made a way for you to be saved from the wrong things you do by sending Jesus to take the punishment for your sin. Have you made a decision to follow Jesus? It's as easy as A, B, C.

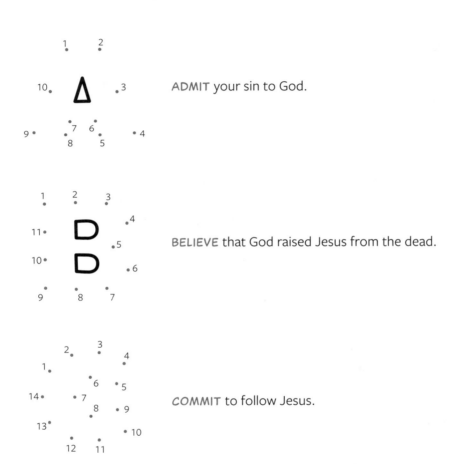

ADMIT your sin to God.

BELIEVE that God raised Jesus from the dead.

COMMIT to follow Jesus.

Mark 11; John 12

 QUICK LOOK: John 12:27–28—Jesus prayed, "My soul is troubled. What should I say? 'Father, keep me from having to go through with this'? No. This is the very reason I have come to this point in my life. Father, bring glory to your name!"

 RECAP

▷ Mary, Martha, and Lazarus invite Jesus and His disciples to dinner. Martha is busy doing the work, but Mary is spending time with Jesus.

▷ Mary takes an expensive jar of oil and uses it to wash Jesus's feet to show how much she loves Him. Jesus defends Mary's actions and says that she'll use the rest of the oil when she buries Him.

▷ Jesus worries over having to die but knows His death is the only way for us, the ones He loves, to have a friendship with God. He's the perfect sacrifice for sin because only He is perfect.

 TODAY'S GOD SHOT

Jesus is God the Son, not just a powerful prophet or a good teacher. He repeatedly claims to be God Himself, and God the Father affirms it. Jesus is God and still obeys God. He knows that God's plan is the best plan, even if it's hard. He's where the joy is!

 ACTIVITY

Jesus knew that good would come from His death. We can know good things will come when we face hard times too. Are you going through a hard time? If so, pray this prayer.

Father in Heaven, [hard thing you are facing] is very hard for me right now. Help me to trust Your plan for my life and see the good that You are doing. Like Jesus, I ask for You to bring glory to Your name. I love You. Amen.

Matthew 22; Mark 12

 QUICK LOOK: Matthew 22:37–39—"Jesus replied, "'Love the Lord your God with all your heart and with all your soul. Love him with all your mind.' (Deuteronomy 6:5) This is the first and most important commandment. And the second is like it. 'Love your neighbor as you love yourself.' (Leviticus 19:18).'"

 RECAP

▷ Jesus's enemies ask Him questions about taxes and death to trick Him, but He answers them with truth and kindness.

▷ Jesus teaches that all of the laws of the Old Testament can be combined into two. They are to love God and love others.

▷ Jesus says to be careful not to follow people who only do good things to show off. The right people to follow have humble hearts.

 TODAY'S GOD SHOT

God wants us to love Him and love others. We can't love God unless we know Him, and we can't love others without His help! God is so kind to show us how to love through Jesus's life, and He's where the joy is!

 ACTIVITY

God wants us to love Him and love others. Make a list of ways you can do that.

LOVE GOD

....

....

....

....

LOVE OTHERS

....

....

....

....

Matthew 23; Luke 20–21

QUICK LOOK: Luke 21:9—Jesus said, "Do not be afraid when you hear about wars and about fighting against rulers. Those things must happen first. But the end will not come right away."

RECAP

▷ Jesus gives the Pharisees seven warnings about their behavior.

▷ Jesus tells His followers that they will be able to endure life on the earth and will never die because they'll live forever in heaven.

▷ Jesus warns that we should not get caught up in anything that is from this world but focus on things that are eternal.

TODAY'S GOD SHOT

Jesus tells us to not be afraid of scary things in the future. He doesn't say things won't be scary or hard; He just promises that we don't go through those things alone and in the end we can live with Him forever. Whatever comes our way is no threat to Him. He's where the joy is!

ACTIVITY

What is something you are afraid of?

....

Read these verses and be reminded you have nothing to fear.

- Psalm 56:3—"When I'm afraid, I put my trust in you."
- Joshua 1:9—"Do not be afraid. Do not lose hope. I am the LORD your God. I will be with you everywhere you go."

Mark 13

 QUICK LOOK: Mark 13:13—Jesus said, "But the one who remains strong in the faith will be saved."

▷ Jesus warns His disciples not to put their trust in earthly things because even massive temples aren't stronger than God.

▷ Jesus says that the temple they see will crumble, and forty years later it does.

▷ Jesus teaches His disciples about a time when the world will end but encourages them that we have a role to play right now in making sure everyone hears about the good news of Jesus.

 TODAY'S GOD SHOT

Jesus promises that the people who belong to God will have hard times but He'll protect them from eternal harm. When we spend time with Him each day, we grow strong in our faith. God gives us what we need when hard times come because He's where the joy is!

 ACTIVITY

What is one thing you are doing each day to stay strong in your faith in God?

- Reading God's Word
- Praying
- Serving
- Loving others
- Other: ....

Matthew 24

QUICK LOOK: Matthew 24:42—Jesus said, "So keep watch. You do not know on what day your Lord will come."

RECAP

▷ Jesus teaches His followers about a time in the future, after His resurrection, when He will come back to earth.

▷ Jesus tells the people listening to Him not to guess when He will return. He also tells them not to be afraid of it happening.

▷ Jesus reminds His followers that His family will continue to grow until He comes back and that we should do our part in bringing people into His family.

TODAY'S GOD SHOT

Jesus tells His followers to "keep watch" because He wants them to continue to share the good news of His love. We should share the good news too! We don't know when Jesus will return or if it will happen in our lifetime, but we can trust that it will happen and it will be incredible because He's where the joy is!

ACTIVITY

Jesus said that He will come back on the clouds of heaven one day. Draw a picture of what you think that will look like.

Matthew 25

QUICK LOOK: Matthew 25:34—Jesus said, "The King . . . will say, 'My Father has blessed you. Come and take what is yours. It is the kingdom prepared for you since the world was created.'"

RECAP

▷ Jesus teaches His followers about the importance of waiting with a happy heart and especially in waiting for Jesus's return to earth.

▷ Jesus has a lot to say about how to best use our time, money, and talent. The more we have, the more we're responsible for.

▷ Jesus says that everyone will have an eternal life, but followers of God get to have eternal life with Him!

TODAY'S GOD SHOT

God has been preparing eternity for us for a long time! He is eager to share His blessings with His kids. The more we trust Him, the more we'll use what He's given us in ways that please Him and bless us. We get to share in His joy, and He's where the joy is!

ACTIVITY

We learned today that God has blessed us. He gives us gifts of talents, time, and money. Answer the questions about what He's given you.

What is my talent? ....

When do I have free time? ....

Do I have money I can give? ....

Matthew 26; Mark 14

 QUICK LOOK: Mark 14:22–24—"While they were eating, Jesus took bread. He gave thanks and broke it. He handed it to his disciples and said, 'Take it. This is my body.' Then he took a cup. He gave thanks and handed it to them. All of them drank from it. 'This is my blood of the covenant,' he said to them. 'It is poured out for many.'"

 RECAP

▷ The chief priest and elders make plans to arrest Jesus. A follower of Jesus named Judas takes money from them as a bribe for him to turn Jesus in.

▷ Jesus celebrates the Passover meal with His followers. It is His last supper with them. He takes the bread, gives thanks, and breaks it, giving it to them as "His body." Then, He takes a cup, gives thanks, and hands it to them to drink from as "His blood" poured out for many.

▷ Peter denies that he knows Jesus three times, which is exactly what Jesus told him would happen.

 TODAY'S GOD SHOT

The act of taking Communion, or the Lord's Supper, is a special time for us to look at our hearts and be thankful for what Jesus has done for us. When we eat the bread and drink the juice, we remember the truth that we are sinful and Jesus paid the price for all our sin. He loves us so much, and He's where the joy is!

 ACTIVITY

Taking Communion is an important part of your relationship with Jesus. If you have made a decision to follow Him, you can take Communion at home with your family using some bread and juice.

Luke 22; John 13

 QUICK LOOK: Luke 22:42—Jesus said, "Father, if you are willing, take this cup of suffering away from me. But do what you want, not what I want."

▷ Jesus washes the feet of each disciple as an example of serving others. He gives a new command: He says to love each other like He has loved them.

▷ Both Judas and Peter turn their backs on Jesus. Judas goes to the guards and receives money for telling them where to find Jesus. Shortly after, Jesus tells Peter that he will deny knowing Him three times.

▷ Jesus goes to the Mount of Olives, and His disciples follow. He prays to His Father, struggling over what He knows is about to happen. Soldiers come to arrest Jesus and take Him to be judged.

 TODAY'S GOD SHOT

The garden where Jesus is praying and struggling with God's plan is called Gethsemane, which means "olive press." Just like olives are pressed to produce oil, Jesus knew He had to be pressed for something good to happen for the whole world. He's where the joy is!

 ACTIVITY

God knows what's best, and Jesus is committed to obeying Him. In His prayer He says, "Do what You want, not what I want."

You can pray that prayer too!

> *Dear God,* I know that Your plans for me are good. Please do what You want and not what I want. I love You. Amen.

John 14–17

QUICK LOOK: John 14:27—Jesus said, "I leave my peace with you. I give my peace to you. I do not give it to you as the world does. Do not let your hearts be troubled. And do not be afraid."

▷ Jesus is about to go to heaven to be with His Father in the place He's prepared for us. He tells His disciples that He's the way, the truth, and the life. No one can go to heaven without following Jesus.

▷ Jesus says that after He dies, the Father will send the Holy Spirit, who will help them and teach them all things.

▷ Jesus prays for Himself, the disciples, and all of His future followers, which includes us!

 TODAY'S GOD SHOT

Jesus keeps reminding us about the peace He can give. Because He's with us, we have everything we need because He's where the joy is!

 ACTIVITY

Memorize today's verse by filling in the blanks.

JOHN 14:27—"I LEAVE MY .... WITH

YOU. I .... MY PEACE TO YOU. I DO NOT

.... IT TO YOU AS THE WORLD DOES. DO

NOT LET YOUR .... BE .... AND

DO NOT BE ...."

Matthew 27; Mark 15

 QUICK LOOK: Mark 15:20—"After they had made fun of him, they took off the purple robe. They put his own clothes back on him. Then they led him out to nail him to a cross."

 RECAP

▷ After Jesus is arrested, He is taken to trial and declared guilty, even though He didn't do anything wrong. He is sent to Pilate, a Roman official, to determine what His punishment will be. Jesus is sentenced to death.

▷ The soldiers beat Jesus and make fun of Him. They lead Him away to nail Him to a cross between two men who are criminals. The skies grow dark, and Jesus takes His last breath.

▷ A man named Joseph asks Pilate for Jesus's body. He buries Jesus in a new tomb made of rock and rolls a stone in front to seal it. Guards stand by the tomb to keep people from stealing His body.

 TODAY'S GOD SHOT

Jesus is humble as He submits to the Father's plans. It's very hard to hear how terrible Jesus's death was, knowing that it was the punishment we deserve. But ultimately, it was all part of God's plan to save us and to make us His! He loves us so much, and He's where the joy is!

 ACTIVITY

How does it make you feel to know what Jesus did for you?

....

If you have made a decision to follow Jesus, take some time to thank Him today for His sacrifice.

If you are still not sure about it, that's okay! Keep learning about Jesus and spending time with Him each day.

Luke 23; John 18–19

 QUICK LOOK: Luke 23:45–46—"The sun had stopped shining. The temple curtain was torn in two. Jesus called out in a loud voice, 'Father, into your hands I commit my life.' After he said this, he took his last breath."

 RECAP

▷ After Jesus's trial, He was beaten and the soldiers led Him to a place called the Skull. The soldiers put nails in His hands and in His feet as they placed Him on the cross.

▷ Jesus not only asks the Father to forgive the soldiers who do this to Him, but He spends His final moments inviting the two criminals beside Him into His kingdom.

▷ Jesus cries out to His Father and dies. The Roman commander watching it all praises God and says, "Jesus was surely a man who did what was right."

 TODAY'S GOD SHOT

Matthew, Mark, Luke, and John all wrote about the miraculous things God did during the events of Jesus's death. God shows His mighty power and fulfills His perfect plan to fix our friendship with Him forever! Praise Jesus, He saved us from our sin, and He's where the joy is!

 ACTIVITY

Circle the emoji that shows how you feel after reading about how much Jesus loves you.

Matthew 28; Mark 16

QUICK LOOK: Matthew 28:10—"Then Jesus said to them, 'Don't be afraid. Go and tell my brothers to go to Galilee. There they will see me.'"

▷ Some women go to visit Jesus's tomb and find an angel there who tells them that Jesus has risen from the dead. The angel invites them to see the empty tomb and tells them to go tell the disciples.

▷ The women leave to tell the disciples when Jesus appears to them! He tells them not to be afraid and to go tell His disciples to go to Galilee, where He will see them.

▷ Jesus's disciples go to Galilee, and Jesus comes to them. They worship Him, and He tells them to go and make other disciples. He promises to be with them until the end.

TODAY'S GOD SHOT

Jesus tells Mary to let His brothers, the disciples, know He's alive. The last time we saw them all together, He told them they'd turn their backs on Him. But even though they hurt Him, He still calls them His brothers, and He still can't wait to see them. What great love and forgiveness He has for the sinners in His family! He's where the joy is!

ACTIVITY

God's plan to bring Jesus back to life is miraculous! Draw a picture of what you think Jesus's friends looked like when He appeared to them.

Luke 24; John 20–21

 QUICK LOOK: Luke 24:32—"They said to each other, 'He explained to us what the Scriptures meant. Weren't we excited as he talked with us on the road?'"

 RECAP

▷ Jesus reveals Himself to two men on the way to Emmaus and again to His disciples.

▷ Jesus appears again to His disciples and proves to Thomas that He has risen from the dead by showing him the holes in His hands and feet.

▷ Jesus finds Peter fishing on the Sea of Galilee. He performs a miracle with Peter's catch and then asks Peter three times if he loves Him.

 TODAY'S GOD SHOT

The men on the road to Emmaus shared how Jesus explained what the Scriptures meant, and they got excited! Understanding God's Word opens our eyes to who He is. God is the one who makes His Word come alive! He's where the joy is!

 ACTIVITY

Can you list three things you have learned about God since you started this reading plan?

1. ....

2. ....

3. ....

God is opening your eyes to see more of Him! Keep going!

Acts 1–3

QUICK LOOK: Acts 2:2–4—"Suddenly a sound came from heaven. It was like a strong wind blowing. . . . They saw something that looked like fire in the shape of tongues. . . . All of them were filled with the Holy Spirit."

RECAP

▷ Jesus stays on earth for forty days after the resurrection, and He tells the apostles to stay in Jerusalem until the Holy Spirit comes to them. Then He goes back to heaven from the Mount of Olives.

▷ Later, the disciples are together celebrating Pentecost when a strong wind fills the house and tongues of fire appear over people's heads. All of them are filled with the Holy Spirit and begin to speak in languages they had not known before.

▷ Peter tells the people about Jesus's death and resurrection, which leads to over 3,000 people deciding to follow Jesus and getting baptized.

TODAY'S GOD SHOT

God doesn't usually do something exactly like we think He will. Even with His repeated promise to send the Holy Spirit, we probably never would've imagined an indoor tornado, fire, and different languages. He has the best ideas and the kindest heart, and He's where the joy is!

ACTIVITY

When you make a decision to follow Jesus, the Holy Spirit comes to live inside of you!

Here are a few ways the Holy Spirit works in our hearts:

1. He helps us.

2. He gives us gifts to use for God.

3. He helps us understand the Bible.

Acts 4–6

QUICK LOOK: Acts 4:11–12—Peter told them, "Scripture says that Jesus is 'the stone you builders did not accept. But it has become the most important stone of all.' (Psalm 118:22) You can't be saved by believing in anyone else. God has given people no other name under heaven that will save them."

▷ After healing a man who couldn't walk, Peter and John share the good news of Jesus. The religious leaders arrest them and put them in prison. They question Peter and John and let them go but tell them to stop talking about Jesus.

▷ All the believers share what they own to provide for the needs of the people.

▷ As the church grows, they have to solve problems like how to care for widows. Seven leaders are put in charge of these kinds of things, including Stephen, who can perform miracles in Jesus's name.

TODAY'S GOD SHOT

God's plan to save us is for us to believe in Jesus. He's our only hope for salvation, and He's where the joy is!

Connect the dots.

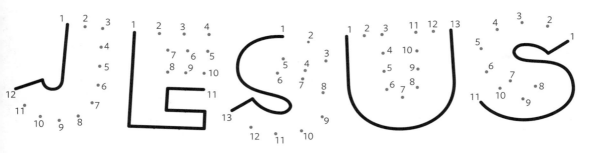

Acts 7–8

QUICK LOOK: Acts 8:4—"The believers who had been scattered preached the word everywhere they went."

▷ Stephen is falsely accused by unbelieving Jews and is on trial. Instead of talking about himself, he uses the trial to tell the crowd about Jesus's life, death, and resurrection, but the crowd still stones him to death.

▷ Saul, later named Paul, is introduced as the leader of the people against the followers of Jesus.

▷ An angel sends Philip to an Ethiopian official who is confused by the words of Isaiah. Philip shares the good news of Jesus with him. He believes and asks to be baptized. As soon as he comes out of the water, Philip disappears and then reappears at the coast.

TODAY'S GOD SHOT

What the enemy means for evil, God uses for good. They murdered Stephen to try to stop the spread of the gospel, but the exact opposite occurs. The believers of Jesus don't run and hide, but start telling people everywhere about Jesus because they know He's where the joy is!

ACTIVITY

If you could share the good news of God's love anywhere in the world, where would you go?

....

START HERE

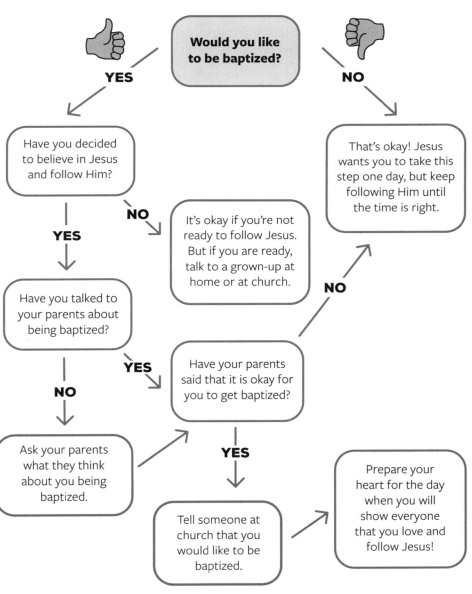

Would you like to be baptized?

YES

NO

Have you decided to believe in Jesus and follow Him?

That's okay! Jesus wants you to take this step one day, but keep following Him until the time is right.

YES

NO

It's okay if you're not ready to follow Jesus. But if you are ready, talk to a grown-up at home or at church.

Have you talked to your parents about being baptized?

NO

YES

Have your parents said that it is okay for you to get baptized?

NO

Ask your parents what they think about you being baptized.

YES

Tell someone at church that you would like to be baptized.

Prepare your heart for the day when you will show everyone that you love and follow Jesus!

Acts 9–10

QUICK LOOK: Acts 9:18—"Right away something like scales fell from Saul's eyes. And he could see again. He got up and was baptized."

RECAP

▷ Saul is blinded by a bright light from heaven and hears the voice of Jesus ask him why he is hurting His people. The voice then tells him to go to Damascus.

▷ God tells Ananias, who follows Jesus, to go to Saul and pray for him to receive his sight. Ananias obeys, and Saul can see! He is filled with the Holy Spirit and gets baptized, declaring that Jesus is Lord!

▷ God gives Peter a vision about eating animals that have been labeled unclean but uses the vision to show Peter that there is no racial divide in the family of God!

TODAY'S GOD SHOT

God is in control over the salvation of His people. Saul's story is proof that when God wants someone, they're His. If you've prayed for friends or family who don't show any interest in loving God, don't be discouraged. God is in charge, and He's where the joy is!

ACTIVITY

Is there someone in your life who needs Jesus? Take some time to pray for them right now.

Acts 11–12

QUICK LOOK: Acts 11:18—The Jewish believers said, "So then, God has allowed even Gentiles to turn away from their sins. He did this so that they could live."

▷ When Peter returns to Jerusalem, he helps the followers there understand God's heart to include everyone in His family.

▷ Barnabas goes to visit a church in Antioch to make sure everything is running smoothly, then he brings Saul with him, and they stay for a year, teaching and encouraging the people.

▷ Back in Jerusalem, Peter is arrested, but the church prays hard for him and an angel appears in the prison, removes his chains, and frees him from jail. Peter tells everyone about this miracle, and the church continues to grow!

TODAY'S GOD SHOT

God allowed the Gentiles to turn away from their sins, which means they repented. Repentance is admitting that you've done wrong and accepting God's forgiveness. What an incredible gift—to be given eyes to see, ears to hear, and a heart to know the truth! He's where the joy is!

ACTIVITY

What is one thing you need to repent from?

....

Tell God you are sorry and ask Him to help you stop doing that wrong thing in the future.

Acts 13–14

 QUICK LOOK: Acts 14:16–17—Paul and Barnabas said, "In the past, he let all nations go their own way. But he has given proof of what he is like. . . . He provides you with plenty of food. He fills your hearts with joy."

▷ The church at Antioch is worshipping God and fasting when they get direction from the Holy Spirit to send Barnabas and Saul to new places to tell people about Jesus.

▷ The first place Saul and Barnabus go is Cyprus, where Saul shares the gospel and stops a magician from being an evil influence on the governor there. The governor believes in Jesus. This is the first time the Bible refers to Saul as Paul.

▷ Paul and Barnabas continue to travel to different cities, telling the Gentiles about God's love, and many believe. When Paul and Barnabas return to Antioch, they give a report on everything that happened.

 TODAY'S GOD SHOT

Like our Quick Look verse says, God let His people walk in their own ways. And even though their complete rejection hurts Him, He still makes Himself known through His blessings—rain and fruit, food and gladness. What a generous God! He is where the joy is!

 ACTIVITY

We are a lot like the Israelites—we don't always follow God, but He still blesses us! Look around and name the first three things you see that God has blessed you with.

James 1–5

QUICK LOOK: James 1:5—"If any of you needs wisdom, you should ask God for it. He will give it to you. God gives freely to everyone and doesn't find fault."

RECAP

▷ The church is encountering trials, but James says they are growing stronger through those trials.

▷ Wisdom is the knowledge of God, and when we ask Him for it, He will give it to us.

▷ The way we treat others shows what is in our hearts. When we are wise, our actions are pure, peaceful, gentle, and kind.

TODAY'S GOD SHOT

Following Jesus doesn't mean we have to be perfect. We can feel like a failure when we focus on ourselves. But when we focus on who God is and ask for His help, He shapes us to be more like Him. He's where the joy is!

ACTIVITY

Do you need wisdom? Circle your answer.

YES   NO

Read James 1:5. What should you do if you need wisdom?

....

Take time right now to ask God to give you wisdom, and believe that He will!

Acts 15–16

QUICK LOOK: Acts 15:9—Peter said, "God showed that there is no difference between us and them. That's because he made their hearts pure because of their faith."

▶ Paul and Barnabas travel to different cities teaching how God has given the Holy Spirit to the Jews *and* the Gentiles.

▶ Paul and Silas travel and meet Timothy, who joins them in Lystra. God opens Lydia's heart to everything Paul is preaching, and she and her whole family decide to follow Jesus.

▶ Paul and Silas are thrown in jail. An earthquake frees them, but they don't go anywhere. Instead, they share the good news of God's love with the jail guard. He and his whole family believe in God.

TODAY'S GOD SHOT

God makes our hearts pure by faith in Him. He uses faith like a silversmith uses a furnace. It's like a fire that removes all of the wrong things we do. The presence of faith in your heart drives out whatever needs to go. Praise God! He's where the joy is!

ACTIVITY

What does it mean to have faith in Jesus?

....

....

....

Galatians 1–3

 QUICK LOOK: Galatians 2:16—"Here is what we know. No one is made right with God by obeying the law. It is by believing in Jesus Christ. So we too have put our faith in Christ Jesus."

 RECAP

▷ This is the first of Paul's letters to churches, and it's to a church he planted on his first missionary journey.

▷ Paul tells his story about how God set him apart before he was born to preach the good news about Jesus to everyone.

▷ Paul's message teaches that salvation is the gift of God, by grace alone, through faith alone, and in Jesus alone. That means there is absolutely nothing we can do to earn our salvation. We simply have to believe in Jesus.

 TODAY'S GOD SHOT

Paul makes sure we know that God's love and salvation are for everyone. It doesn't matter where you are from or what you have done. Because of the gift of Jesus's life, death, and resurrection, the door is open to everyone because He's where the joy is!

 ACTIVITY

God wants everyone around the world to believe in Him. On the next page, find the names of the five countries with the most people who have not heard the good news of God's love for them.

I	X	T	Z	Z	D	N	G	I	H
N	N	F	C	A	W	T	M	S	N
U	I	D	H	M	D	K	E	E	U
Q	E	C	I	R	B	D	P	Z	R
D	F	X	N	A	A	A	X	V	K
Y	F	P	A	L	L	Y	W	Z	W
W	K	O	G	S	T	U	W	W	P
N	Y	N	H	O	H	C	N	A	M
P	A	K	I	S	T	A	N	X	A
B	W	L	X	R	G	J	A	X	D

WORD BANK

INDIA   PAKISTAN   CHINA

BANGLADESH   NEPAL

If you need help, check out the Word Search Answer Key on page 471.

Galatians 4–6

QUICK LOOK: Galatians 5:22–23—"But the fruit the Holy Spirit produces is love, joy and peace. It is being patient, kind and good. It is being faithful and gentle and having control of oneself."

RECAP

▷ God adopts us as His children and gives us everything He gives to Jesus.

▷ Paul warns that when we start to rely on good works to save us, we become slaves to those works, trying to earn grace.

▷ Salvation comes through faith in Jesus. There isn't anything we have to do.

TODAY'S GOD SHOT

When the Holy Spirit produces fruit in our lives it shows others that we belong to God. Do others see love, joy, peace, patience, kindness, goodness, faithfulness, gentleness, and self-control increasing in your life? If so, thank God for it! That's His doing. He gets the glory, and you get the joy because He's where the joy is!

ACTIVITY

Begin to memorize Galatians 5:22–23 by filling in the blanks.

GALATIANS 5:......... — "BUT THE .... THE HOLY SPIRIT

PRODUCES IS LOVE, ... AND PEACE. IT IS BEING

PATIENT, ..., AND GOOD. IT IS BEING .... AND

.... AND HAVING .... OF ONESELF."

Acts 17

 QUICK LOOK: Acts 17:28—Paul said, "'In him we live and move and exist.' As some of your own poets have also said, 'We are his children.'"

 RECAP

▷ Paul spends three days in a place called Thessalonica going to the synagogue and telling the people how Jesus is the Messiah the prophets wrote about.

▷ Paul and Silas run into problems when many people decide to believe in Jesus.

▷ Paul is bold in preaching to various kinds of people. He hopes to always point to what is missing from their lives—a friendship with the one true God who made them.

 TODAY'S GOD SHOT

Paul uses a quote from a Greek poet in his conversation about God because it speaks to the truth of who God is. Look at how this quote reflects John 14:6: "In him we live" (He's the life), "and move" (He's the way), "and exist" (He's the truth at the core of who we are). He's the way, the truth, and the life, and He's where the joy is!

 ACTIVITY

Everything about you points to the truth that God is the one who gave you life. Pray this prayer as you spend time with Him.

Dear God, thank You for giving me life. You have placed me exactly where You want me to be on this earth. You give me everything I need to obey You. Help me live and move today knowing that I can depend on You. Amen!

1 Thessalonians 1–5;
2 Thessalonians 1–3

QUICK LOOK: 1 Thessalonians 1:2—"We always thank God for all of you. We keep on praying for you."

▷ Paul writes two letters to the church at Thessalonica. He shares how their lives demonstrate that God has chosen them to be a part of His family. They have received, lived out, and shared the gospel.

▷ The people in the church at Thessalonica were bullied and experienced a lot of hardship because of their passion to tell others about Jesus. Paul writes to encourage them.

▷ Other teachers tell lies about the church, and in his second letter Paul tells the church how God will protect them.

TODAY'S GOD SHOT

Paul consistently gives God the credit for the good works of the people. He thanks God, not them, for their growth in faith and love. Paul knows that it is God who is doing the work through them. He's where the joy is!

ACTIVITY

Paul wrote letters to encourage the church at Thessalonica. Who is someone you could encourage today by writing and giving them a letter?

....

What are you waiting for? Write them today!

Acts 18–19

QUICK LOOK: Acts 18:9—"One night the Lord spoke to Paul in a vision. 'Don't be afraid,' he said. 'Keep on speaking. Don't be silent.'"

RECAP

▷ Paul goes on his second missionary journey, where he meets Aquila and Priscilla, a married couple who are tentmakers like Paul. He stays with them and continues preaching the good news about Jesus.

▷ God speaks to Paul in a dream and encourages him to keep on sharing the gospel. God tells him not to be afraid and that He will protect him.

▷ God does uniquely miraculous things through Paul's ministry, and the good news of God's love is spread everywhere. It becomes more and more powerful.

TODAY'S GOD SHOT

God is in control over every detail of Paul's life. With each city he traveled to, more people heard the good news of Jesus, and the church grew! God had His hands in everything, which shows He's always at work on our behalf, and He's where the joy is!

ACTIVITY

Color the star next to one way God is working in your life.

☆ You are more loving to others.

☆ You are learning more about who God is and feel close to Him.

☆ You want to read God's Word every day.

☆ You think about God's ways and want to obey them.

1 Corinthians 1–4

QUICK LOOK: 1 Corinthians 3:7—"So the one who plants is not important. The one who waters is not important. It is God who makes things grow. He is the important one."

▷ Paul writes to the church in Corinth to remind them that God called them into His family and that He will continue to be with them.

▷ Paul plants a lot of seeds as he tells people about the good news of Jesus, but he's not the one who makes them grow. Only God can make someone grow in their understanding of Him.

▷ Paul talks about what it means to be a Christian leader. Leaders are servants to the people, but they're primarily accountable to God.

TODAY'S GOD SHOT

Paul shares three things God does in our past, present, and future that all point to the relationship God wants to have with us. He does all of the work forgiving our past sin, making us more like Jesus in the present, and promising us eternal life for our future. He's in all of it, and He's where the joy is!

ACTIVITY

As you read God's Word every day, seeds of truth are being planted in your heart. What is one thing you have learned this week?

....

....

1 Corinthians 5–8

 QUICK LOOK: 1 Corinthians 8:6—"But for us there is only one God. He is the Father. All things came from him, and we live for him."

 RECAP

▷ The Corinthians are sinning in big ways. They are using God's kindness and grace as an excuse to do whatever they want.

▷ Grace is God's favor on us to help us walk according to His ways. It's a gift we don't earn or deserve.

▷ In Paul's opinion, marriage is good but singleness is better. We find freedom in accepting the positions God has given us.

 TODAY'S GOD SHOT

All things are from God, through Him, and for Him. He starts and completes everything in our lives. God is all we need, and He's where the joy is!

 ACTIVITY

God has given you life and breath, and He's all you need! Stop and take three deep breaths. Each time you breathe in, say, "Thank you!" then as you breathe out, say, "God!"

On the next page, complete the color-by-number.

1	Yellow	**2**	Orange	**3**	Red
4	Blue	**5**	Gray	**6**	Purple

1 Corinthians 9–11

QUICK LOOK: 1 Corinthians 10:13—"You are tempted in the same way all other human beings are. God is faithful. He will not let you be tempted any more than you can take."

▷ God's people have always struggled with idolatry, despite His presence, protection, and provision. Paul addresses how their idolatry is leading them into sin.

▷ Paul compares marriage to God's relationship with the church.

▷ Jesus said to eat the bread and drink the cup in remembrance of Him, but it seems they're eating and drinking but forgetting His command to love others.

TODAY'S GOD SHOT

God will not let you be tempted any more than you can take. He will give you the strength to say no, so lean into His strength. Trust Him to provide what you need to obey Him. He's where the joy is!

ACTIVITY

Which one of these is the most tempting for you?

 Sneaking candy when my mom has told me I can't have any.

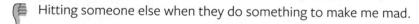 Lying to my teacher about what happened in the lunchroom.

Hitting someone else when they do something to make me mad.

Pray this prayer.

Father God, thank You for helping me when I am tempted to do the wrong thing. Give me the strength I need to obey You. Thank You for giving me joy when I do! Amen!

1 Corinthians 12–14

QUICK LOOK: 1 Corinthians 12:4–5—"There are different kinds of gifts. But they are all given to believers by the same Spirit. There are different ways to serve. But they all come from the same Lord."

▷ Paul teaches about the gifts of the Holy Spirit. When we decide to follow Jesus, God gives us a unique gift that helps to make His church better.

▷ Paul gives a good description of what love is and says it will outlast everything. Faith, hope, and love are important, but the greatest is love!

▷ When it comes to the gifts the Holy Spirit gives, Paul says you should want the gift of prophecy most of all. A person who has the gift of prophecy speaks to make people stronger, to give them hope, and to comfort them.

TODAY'S GOD SHOT

God works in and through us to show other people more of who He is! When we rely on His help, we actually make other people's lives better by using our spiritual gifts. God gives us all unique gifts to offer back to Him, and He pulls them all together like only He can do. He's where the joy is!

ACTIVITY

If you have made a decision to follow Jesus, the Holy Spirit lives inside of you! That means you also have a spiritual gift that you can use for God's glory.

With the help of a grown-up, go to focusonthefamily.com/parenting/take-this-spiritual-gifts-test-with-your-family. Ask your grown-up to read the article and then help you take the test so you can find out what your gift might be!

1 Corinthians 15–16

QUICK LOOK: 1 Corinthians 15:10—"But because of God's grace I am what I am. And his grace was not wasted on me. No, I have worked harder than all the other apostles. But I didn't do the work. God's grace was with me."

▷ Paul confronts some of the Corinthians who don't believe Jesus came back to life even though there are around five hundred eyewitnesses—many of whom are still alive to tell about it.

▷ The Corinthians who don't believe in the resurrection are doing wrong things because they feel like what they do doesn't matter. Paul tells them this life is not all there is.

▷ Paul asks the churches to give money on the first day of the week. That money is called an offering and is sent to the followers of Jesus in Jerusalem who are going through hard times.

TODAY'S GOD SHOT

Paul has a right view of himself and of God. God doesn't punish Paul for his wicked past; instead, He gives him a vital role in building the church. God supplies all Paul needs to do the work because He's where the joy is!

ACTIVITY

God has gifted you in a special way through His grace and kindness. How can you use that gift to show love to others at church this Sunday?

....

....

2 Corinthians 1–4

 QUICK LOOK: 2 Corinthians 4:6—"God said, 'Let light shine out of darkness.' (Genesis 1:3) He made his light shine in our hearts. His light gives us the light to know God's glory. His glory is shown in the face of Christ."

▷ In Paul's last letter to Corinth, he promised to visit, asked them to collect money for the needy believers in Jerusalem, and confronted many of their sin patterns and wrong beliefs.

▷ Paul asks the believers to pray for him and says that it helps. Prayer isn't pointless; it engages with God and encourages believers.

▷ Paul and his traveling companions are going through really hard things, but the light God put in their hearts is spilling out on the people they encounter.

 TODAY'S GOD SHOT

God made His light shine in your heart so you might know Him more! He doesn't hide anything from you but wants you to see who He is in the face of Jesus. Grow to know Him more because He's where the joy is!

 ACTIVITY

Unscramble the words that describe some of the things we know about God.

LHOY .... REOPFLUW ....

VOLGNI .... TSJU ....

NKDI ....

2 Corinthians 5–9

QUICK LOOK: 2 Corinthians 6:10—"We are sad, but we are always full of joy. We are poor, but we make many people rich. We have nothing, but we own everything."

▷ In the midst of all Paul's trials, it's not death he's wishing for—it's eternal life. He'll either be alive here or alive with Jesus, because everyone who follows Jesus lives forever.

▷ Paul urges the people to receive his message with open hearts. When our hearts love the right things, we won't fall prey to loving the wrong things. If we love Jesus most of all, it's easier to obey Him.

▷ Paul asked all of the churches to give generously. We're blessed in order to bless others so that God might be praised. We're conduits of His provision and praise!

TODAY'S GOD SHOT

Even though Paul and the others are experiencing hard times, they have joy! Trials have a way of revealing what matters—not only to us, but through us. In all our trials, we have the light and we have the joy, because He's where the joy is!

ACTIVITY

God gives us joy. What is one way you show the joy you have to others?

....

2 Corinthians 10–13

QUICK LOOK: 2 Corinthians 12:9—"But he said to me, 'My grace is all you need. My power is strongest when you are weak.' So I am very happy to brag about how weak I am. Then Christ's power can rest on me."

▷ Paul plans to visit Corinth again and wants them to deal with their sin. Through the power of the Spirit, he'll bring the truth to light, punish disobedience, and tear down the enemy's lies about him and his ministry.

▷ God helps Paul endure some really hard things, including beatings, jail, shipwrecks, and many other dangers.

▷ God allows Paul to have a "thorn in his flesh," which is something given to him to keep him humble. Three times he begs God to take it away, but God answers his prayer with a no.

TODAY'S GOD SHOT

God's power is strong when we are weak. Paul is happy to brag about how weak he is because Christ's power makes him strong. He uses his weakness to point to God, because He's where the joy is!

ACTIVITY

What is one area of your life where you feel weak? God wants you to depend on Him! He will make you strong. Pray this prayer.

Dear God, thank You for being strong and powerful when I need You most. When I am weak, I know You give me all I need. Amen!

Romans 1–3

QUICK LOOK: Romans 3:23–24—"Everyone has sinned. No one measures up to God's glory. The free gift of God's grace makes us right with him. Christ Jesus paid the price to set us free."

RECAP

▷ God has made the truth obvious—that there's a Creator in charge of everything—but many ignore the truth and live life on their own terms.

▷ Paul says, "When you look down on others, you act like you don't do these things too, but you do! So don't abuse God's kindness in not giving you over to your sins."

▷ We're all under the curse of sin and need God's rescue, and Jesus is the only Savior for all people of every race.

TODAY'S GOD SHOT

The free gift of God's grace makes us right with Him. He gives the best gifts! Everything we needed and everything we didn't know we needed—He gives it all. And He's where the joy is!

ACTIVITY

Fill in the blanks for Romans 3:23–24.

" .... HAS SINNED. NO ONE MEASURES

UP TO .... GLORY. THE FREE ....

OF GOD'S GRACE MAKES US .... WITH HIM.

CHRIST JESUS PAID THE .... TO SET US FREE."

Romans 4–7

QUICK LOOK: Romans 4:25—"Jesus was handed over to die for our sins. He was raised to life in order to make us right with God."

▷ Paul wants the Jewish people to embrace the Gentiles as God's family.

▷ Hard times help us to grow stronger in our ability to keep going.

▷ Paul lives in the struggle between who he was before believing in Jesus and who he is now. He wants to make sure his heart wants what God says is right.

TODAY'S GOD SHOT

Jesus was handed over to die for our sins, but God raised Him back to life. Not only does Jesus's death fix our friendship with God, but our sins aren't counted against us. We get blessings instead of punishment! What a Savior! He's where the joy is!

ACTIVITY

Which one of these would have been easier for God to do?

● Completely start over by wiping out all the sinful people and creating a new world

● Sending His only Son to take the punishment for the sins of all people

The easiest thing for God would have been to start over. But in His love, He did the hard thing. He took on the responsibility of fixing our friendship with Him.

Romans 8–10

QUICK LOOK: Romans 10:9—"Say with your mouth, 'Jesus is Lord.' Believe in your heart that God raised him from the dead. Then you will be saved."

▷ We must set our minds on the things God thinks about, choosing wisely what we think because our thoughts become our actions.

▷ The Holy Spirit helps and prays for us, always praying for things that align with the Father's will, which means His requests will always be granted.

▷ Paul wants everyone to know God and be saved.

TODAY'S GOD SHOT

Paul says we must share the gospel because the people God will adopt into His family have to hear the news. We must go, share, and tell. Spread the word that He's where the joy is!

ACTIVITY

There are two things in today's verse that let us know we are saved. What are they? Look at the verse and fill in the blank to find out!

1. SAY WITH YOUR ...., "JESUS IS LORD." When you say that Jesus is Lord, you are saying that you want Him to be the leader of your life.

2. BELIEVE IN YOUR .... THAT GOD RAISED HIM FROM THE DEAD. Following Jesus is very simple! You make Him your leader by saying it with your mouth and believing it in your heart.

If you are ready to start following Jesus, all you need to do is tell Him. Here's what you can say:

> **God,** I know that You love me. I admit that I have done wrong things and I am very sorry. I believe in my heart that Jesus, Your Son, died for me and that You brought Him back to life. I commit to following You, Jesus. You are the leader and Lord of my life!

Romans 11–13

 QUICK LOOK: Romans 11:33—"How very rich are God's wisdom and knowledge! How he judges is more than we can understand! The way he deals with people is more than we can know!"

 RECAP

▷ God wants His kingdom to be full and filled with every kind of person.

▷ Our lives should look different from other people's because we are more loving in the way we treat them. We should honor others more than we do ourselves.

▷ As people who trust God, we should be subject to people who are in charge, even if we don't like or respect them.

 TODAY'S GOD SHOT

God is so generous to give us wisdom and to help us know Him. There is no limit to how much we can learn! He's just and kind, and the more we spend time with Him, the more we know He's where the joy is!

 ACTIVITY

What is one new thing you have learned about God recently?

....

....

....

Romans 14–16

QUICK LOOK: Romans 16:20—"The God who gives peace will soon crush Satan under your feet. May the grace of our Lord Jesus be with you."

RECAP

▶ Paul reminds us that there's room for different opinions and preferences in the body of Christ.

▶ Paul challenges the people to hold firmly to their faith in God, to live out what they believe, letting their faith show up in everything. Our faith must be personal, but never private.

▶ Our harmony must be not only with each other but also with Jesus. We can learn not only from what God is teaching us but from what He's teaching other people as well.

TODAY'S GOD SHOT

In order to bring peace to any situation, you can't ignore chaos; you have to address it. God addresses the chaos of Satan and evil by crushing it. God crushes Satan under our feet. He does the crushing, and He's the one who makes us strong, moving our feet and crushing our enemy. He's where the joy is!

ACTIVITY

Circle two of the things that help to bring peace into your life and thank God for them.

GOD IS IN CONTROL   GOD IS POWERFUL

GOD KNOWS EVERYTHING   GOD IS STRONG

GOD HAS DEFEATED SATAN

Acts 20–23

QUICK LOOK: Acts 23:11—"The next night the Lord stood near Paul. He said, 'Be brave! You have told people about me in Jerusalem. You must do the same in Rome.'"

▷ While Paul is preaching in Troas, a man named Eutychus falls asleep and plummets three stories to his death. Paul raises him from the dead and goes on preaching until sunrise.

▷ God is the one who gives Paul this ministry, but it is full of threats from people who want the message of God's love for all people to stop.

▷ Paul speaks to many different people groups and ends up in jail. While he is in prison, God tells him he won't die there but will go to Rome to tell those people about His love.

TODAY'S GOD SHOT

God lined up everything in Paul's life, before he was even born, so that he would be the one to share the good news of God's love. God has always been in every detail of our lives. He's where the joy is!

ACTIVITY

Make a timeline of your life showing important events. God is lining up everything in your life for a purpose.

Here are some ideas of what you might include:

- Date you were born
- Date you started school
- Date you moved to a new city

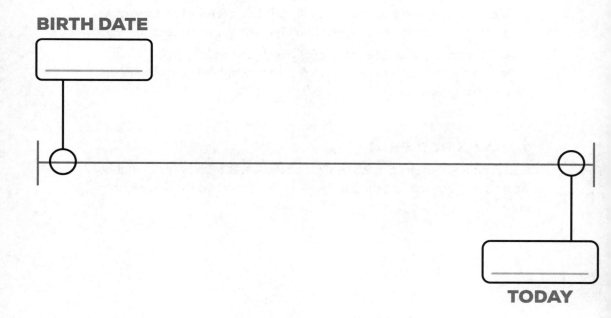

BIRTH DATE

TODAY

Acts 24–26

QUICK LOOK: Acts 26:22—Paul said, "But God has helped me to this day. So I stand here and tell you what is true."

RECAP

▷ Paul defends himself with the truth. He goes to great lengths to live with integrity and honor God.

▷ While Paul is in prison, Governor Felix keeps coming to learn about the ways of Jesus. Paul shares the gospel with him while obeying the rules.

▷ God helps Paul and gives him opportunities to share his story with King Herod Agrippa II. When Paul puts him on the spot concerning his belief in God, Agrippa says he needs more time to consider it. Paul wants everyone to know God.

TODAY'S GOD SHOT

Even though the road is hard and lonely and frustrating for Paul, God gives him all he needs. God is our helper, and He's where the joy is!

ACTIVITY

God helped Paul share the truth with everyone, and He can help you too! Who is someone you know who needs to hear the truth about God? It could be a friend, family member, coach, neighbor, or someone else. Write their name below and ask God to help you have the courage to tell them how much God loves them this week.

....

....

Acts 27–28

 QUICK LOOK: Acts 28:30–31—"For two whole years Paul stayed there in a house he rented. He welcomed all who came to see him. He preached boldly about God's kingdom."

RECAP

▷ Paul and some other prisoners are handed over to a Roman commander named Julius. They set sail, along with Paul's friends, to head toward Rome.

▷ Paul gives good advice to the sailors about how a storm will affect their travels. They shipwreck on an island called Malta, where Paul is bitten by a snake but is unharmed, and he heals many of the people on the island.

▷ After three months, Paul is taken to Rome, where he is able to live in a home but with a guard. He has leaders and other visitors come to him, and he shares the truth of God's love with them.

 TODAY'S GOD SHOT

God provided for Paul by appointing Julius to be his centurion—the one who would eventually come to listen to him and even save his life. God reaches across enemy lines to show mercy and save those who oppose Him. That's where He found all of us. He's where the joy is!

 ACTIVITY

Put a check mark beside the things Paul might be telling the people about God's kingdom.

☐ God's kingdom is no longer a thing.
☐ God's kingdom is full of people who believe in Him.
☐ God is the king of His kingdom.
☐ God doesn't allow new people into His kingdom.
☐ God's kingdom lasts forever.

Colossians 1–4; Philemon 1

 QUICK LOOK: Colossians 1:15—"The Son is the exact likeness of God, who can't be seen. The Son is first, and he is over all creation."

RECAP

▷ Paul wants people to love God with their minds. He wants their knowledge of God to show in the good things they do for others.

▷ The people who love God should live with compassion, kindness, humility, meekness, patience, self-control, forgiveness, love, peace, thankfulness, and the words of Jesus.

▷ Paul writes a letter to Philemon on behalf of Onesimus, a former slave, asking him to forgive and accept Onesimus. Onesimus had stolen from Philemon but later became a follower of Jesus.

 TODAY'S GOD SHOT

If we want to see what God the Father is like, we look to Jesus. He made everything, and everything serves His purposes. Jesus is God. He brings everything God is to the cross, and the impact of His sacrifice is seen through all of His creation because He's where the joy is!

 ACTIVITY

What are some things you've learned about Jesus that help you know what God is like?

JESUS IS . . .   GOD IS . . .

....

....

....

Ephesians 1–6

QUICK LOOK: Ephesians 6:11—"Put on all of God's armor. Then you can remain strong against the devil's evil plans."

RECAP

▷ God is an intentional and thoughtful Creator. He gave our lives purpose, and our good works are part of what He planned for us to do.

▷ Being grateful helps us see God in the right way, and that helps us love Him more. When we love God more, we want to sin less.

▷ God has equipped us with invisible armor that helps us fight spiritual battles where the devil tries to trick us into doing things that lead us to sin. God's armor helps us stand up against anything.

TODAY'S GOD SHOT

By being in God's Word every day, you gain strength for another day of fighting the lies of the devil. For every battle, God gives us each other and He gives us Himself. And during and after every battle, let's remember that He's where the joy is!

ACTIVITY

God tells us how to live in this explanation of His armor. Match the piece of armor to its description:

    ●   ●   **SHIELD OF FAITH**

    ●   ●   **SWORD OF THE SPIRIT**

    ●   ●   **HELMET OF SALVATION**

    ●   ●   **SHOES OF PEACE**

    ●   ●   **BREASTPLATE OF RIGHTEOUSNESS**

    ●   ●   **BELT OF TRUTH**

Philippians 1–4

QUICK LOOK: Philippians 4:8—"Finally, my brothers and sisters, always think about what is true."

▷ Paul writes an encouraging letter to the church in Philippi. He started this church and is happy to see how God is helping them grow.

▷ Paul is in prison when he writes, but he knows that even though some may think that's a bad thing, God can use it for good.

▷ Paul reminds them to get along with each other and to think of others as better than themselves.

TODAY'S GOD SHOT

What we think about changes our hearts and our actions. When we think about what is true, we are thinking the way God wants us to think. He can help us change the way we think and have peace and joy in our hearts because He's where the joy is!

ACTIVITY

We have so many thoughts going through our minds every day. We can change our minds to think the way God wants us to by using these three steps: Catch It, Check It, and Change It.

Catch your thought by pausing, then check it with God's Word. If your thought is not true, ask God to help you change it. Practice these steps today and see how right thinking can change how you feel and act to be more like Jesus.

1 Timothy 1–6

 QUICK LOOK: 1 Timothy 6:6–7—"You gain a lot when you live a godly life. But you must be happy with what you have. We didn't bring anything into the world. We can't take anything out of it."

 RECAP

▷ Paul is writing to encourage and teach Timothy about the church and how the church should work.

▷ Paul wants Timothy to learn the powerful lesson of humility. Humility means knowing that you are loved despite your sin. It's not puffing yourself up and not beating yourself up, because you know life isn't about you.

▷ Paul says money is a blessing that should be used to honor God, who wants us to be happy in the things He gives us. Money isn't the problem. The love of money is.

 TODAY'S GOD SHOT

When you live your life for God, you must be happy with what you have. Everything that is yours is given to you by God. Is knowing Him enough for you? God's Word says it is because He's where the joy is!

 ACTIVITY

Circle yes or no to answer these questions.

Are you happy with what you have?   YES   NO

Is knowing God all you really need?   YES   NO

Can you take anything on this earth with you when you die?   YES   NO

Is it best to be happy to know God and not worry about stuff?   YES   NO

Titus 1–3

QUICK LOOK: Titus 1:1–2—"God sent me to help them understand even more the truth that leads to godly living. That belief and understanding lead to the hope of eternal life. Before time began, God promised to give that life. And he does not lie."

RECAP

▷ Paul writes a letter to his friend and coworker, Titus, who leads the church on the Greek island of Crete. Titus faces many challenges with sharing the gospel.

▷ Paul wants the people in that church to show others how beautiful their faith is and how God's grace and gift of eternal life change everything.

▷ Paul reminds Titus and the church to live humbly with others, even when they disagree. He encourages them to say kind words, avoid arguing, and be gentle with everyone.

TODAY'S GOD SHOT

God made each of us with a soul that will live forever. Your soul is the part of who you are that only you and God can know. God promises eternal life, and that means when your body dies, your soul lives on forever! People who believe in Jesus and follow Him have the promise of living forever in heaven with Jesus! And that's great news because He's where the joy is!

ACTIVITY

Draw a picture of what you think heaven will be like.

1 Peter 1–5

QUICK LOOK: 1 Peter 5:10—"God always gives you all the grace you need. So you will only have to suffer for a little while. Then God himself will build you up again."

RECAP

▷ Paul is writing to the followers of Jesus who are under the evil Roman Empire and are going through bad times. He tells them that they can trust God because He always comes through for them.

▷ Because they are God's kids, they are called a royal priesthood. Every follower of Jesus can approach God directly like the priest used to do.

▷ The thing God wants people to notice about you is who you are on the inside. Let people see what it looks like to trust God in hard times.

TODAY'S GOD SHOT

Be on the lookout for God to give you all you need when you are being treated wrongly. He will always give you the grace (undeserved kindness) that you need because He's where the joy is!

ACTIVITY

In the left column are situations that might happen to you that are hard. In the right column are possible responses to a situation that come from God's gift of grace. Draw a line from the situation that is hard to the response that shows grace.

SITUATIONS THAT ARE HARD:

Someone takes your snack at school

You get pushed down on the playground

You can't find your homework

A friend talks bad about you to someone else

You invite a friend to church but they say no

GRACE-FILLED RESPONSES:

You say something nice about a friend who talked bad about you

You take two snacks to school

You pray for your friend

You tell the truth

You don't push back but forgive the person who hurt you

Hebrews 1–6

 QUICK LOOK: Hebrews 6:10—"God is fair. He will not forget what you have done. He will remember the love you have shown him. You showed it when you helped his people."

 RECAP

▷ God speaks to us through Jesus. Jesus shows us what God is like and holds the world together at all times. He made a way for us to be free of sin.

▷ We should be firm in our faith because it's proof that Jesus truly lives in us.

▷ If someone stops following Jesus, it's because they never let Him change their heart.

 TODAY'S GOD SHOT ~~~~~~~~~~~~~~~~~~~~~~~~~

God deals gently with those who are far away from Him. We've all been there, but He has patiently come close to us to teach us and love us. What a relief! He's where the joy is!

ACTIVITY

Draw two ways that you show God you love Him.

Hebrews 7–10

QUICK LOOK: Hebrews 10:22—"So let us come near to God with a sincere heart. Let us come near boldly because of our faith."

▷ The first covenant was made of rules the people had to obey, and when they sinned they had to make a sacrifice to fix their friendship with God.

▷ The new covenant got rid of the old one when God sent Jesus to take the punishment for all our sin once and for all. It changes our hearts.

▷ When we keep going during hard times, our faith gets tested and shows what we really believe.

TODAY'S GOD SHOT

The place where God's Spirit lived was no longer the temple. God's Spirit came to live in His people. This is how our hearts can be changed: by the presence of His Spirit in us! He lets us come near to Him, so let's continue to do that each day because He's where the joy is!

ACTIVITY

Fill this heart in with words that describe how you feel when you come near to God.

Hebrews 11–13

QUICK LOOK: Hebrews 11:6—"Without faith it is impossible to please God. Those who come to God must believe that he exists. And they must believe that he rewards those who look to him."

▷ Faith is being sure of what we hope for. It is being sure of what we do not see.

▷ Since God calls us His children, sometimes we'll have to endure His discipline.

▷ The things that bring a smile to God's face include loving each other well, being kind to strangers, caring for those in need, being happy with what we have, honoring our leaders, doing good, sharing, and holding to godly beliefs.

TODAY'S GOD SHOT

God rewards us when we seek Him. If you're seeking Him, the best reward you could get is more of Him. Nothing is better and nothing lasts longer and nothing else can't be taken away. He's the Rewarder, and He's the reward, and He's where the joy is!

ACTIVITY

Circle your answers to the following questions.

Have you spent the last 356 days looking for God?   YES   NO

If you have, would you agree that you now know more about who God is?   YES   NO

Does having a friendship with God help in your belief that God is real?   YES   NO

Will you spend time with Jesus every day to grow your faith in God?   YES   NO

459

2 Timothy 1–4

QUICK LOOK: 2 Timothy 3:16—"God has breathed life into all Scripture. It is useful for teaching us what is true. It is useful for correcting our mistakes. It is useful for making our lives whole again. It is useful for training us to do what is right."

▷ Paul writes a letter to remind Timothy that if we don't actively engage in the gift of our faith, we'll begin to have fear.

▷ God is at work in us to accomplish what He has promised.

▷ Paul tells Timothy to avoid certain kinds of people, including those who claim to believe but don't show that they have a real relationship with Jesus.

TODAY'S GOD SHOT

God spoke the words we read today for the following reasons: to correct us and to train us. He wants us to be ready to do every good work He has prepared for us. His Word helps us know who He is and points us to Jesus. He's where the joy is!

ACTIVITY

Circle T for statements that are true and F for statements that are false.

T F   The Bible is a book full of facts about ancient times.

T F   God breathed out the words we read in the Bible.

T F   God's Word teaches us how to go snorkeling.

T F   God's Word can correct our mistakes.

T F   The Bible shows us how to really mess up our lives.

2 Peter 1–3, Jude 1

 QUICK LOOK: Jude 1:5—"I want to remind you about some things you already know. The Lord saved his people. At one time he brought them out of Egypt."

 RECAP

▷ These two books deal with leaders in the church who are trying to stop false teachers' lies.

▷ God has given them everything they need for life and godliness. Because of this power, their lives should look different from everyone else's.

▷ Jude tells the believers that they should remain in God's love and watch out for false teachers.

 TODAY'S GOD SHOT

Jude says Jesus ("the Lord" in verse 5) rescued the Israelites out of Egypt. Even though He hadn't been born as a human at the time, Jesus has always existed. He showed up repeatedly in the Old Testament, doing miraculous things to save His people. He's always been rescuing His people. Then, now, and always, He's where the joy is!

 ACTIVITY

Put a check mark next to the stories you already know from the Old Testament that point to Jesus existing before He was born.

☐ Jesus created the world. (Genesis 1:26)

☐ Jesus appeared to Moses at his tent. (Genesis 18:1)

☐ Jesus called to Abraham when he was going to sacrifice Isaac. (Genesis 22:11)

☐ Isaiah talks about Jesus's birth. (Isaiah 7:14)

☐ Jesus appeared in the fiery furnace with Shadrach, Meshach and Abednego. (Daniel 3:25)

The whole Bible is a collection of stories and poems that were written to lead us to know Jesus.

1 John 1–5

 QUICK LOOK: 1 John 4:19—"We love because he loved us first."

 RECAP

▷ Jesus has always existed—He is truly God and truly human.

▷ Believing that Jesus is God is a sign of being one with Him, and being one with Him is evidence that He loves us!

▷ John wants believers to be confident their faith is real and that they belong to God.

 TODAY'S GOD SHOT

God's love came first, and then our love came from His. The only reason we can love Him at all is because all of this was His idea. We never would've sought Him out, but He loved us and made a way for us to be with Him forever! He's where the joy is!

 ACTIVITY

Memorize this verse this week by filling in the blanks.

1 .... 4:19—"WE .... BECAUSE

HE LOVED US ...."

Ask God to help you love others the way He does.

2 John 1; 3 John 1

 QUICK LOOK: 3 John 1:11 NIV—"Dear friend, do not imitate what is evil but what is good. Anyone who does what is good is from God. Anyone who does what is evil has not seen God."

▷ In 2 John, John starts out by saying he loves the church and its people.

▷ If we really believe that what Jesus says is truth, then love is living it out. Truth and love go together.

▷ John urges the church to stay strong and to be on the lookout for any teaching that is not the same as what Jesus and the Bible teach. In order to do that, you have to know what Jesus and the Bible say.

 TODAY'S GOD SHOT

God rescues those who oppose Him to bring them into His family. We are evidence of that. There is hope for everyone who doesn't know Him yet. May they come to know and believe that Jesus is the way, the truth, and the life and that He's where the joy is!

 ACTIVITY

Color the star next to the one good thing you could commit to doing today to help others see Jesus in you.

 I will tell three people something good about them that I see.

 I will pray for two people in my life and let them know that I prayed for them.

 I will help someone in my family with a chore they have to do.

Revelation 1–5

QUICK LOOK: Revelation 1:17—"When I saw him, I fell at his feet as if I were dead. Then he put his right hand on me and said, 'Do not be afraid. I am the First and the Last.'"

▷ John wrote Revelation from a tiny prison island to reveal something. When you're trying to reveal something to your reader, you try to make it known to them.

▷ John has a vision of Jesus, who says to write a letter to seven churches. He gives them warnings, encouragement, and hope.

▷ John gets a peek into God's throne room. God holds a scroll containing His purposes for mankind. It is shut with seven seals that no one can open.

TODAY'S GOD SHOT

This book could feel scary, but some of Jesus's first words in it are "Do not be afraid." Then He tells us who He is. If we first recognize who Jesus is, then we can understand and rightly view what He's going to do in this book, and we know He's where the joy is!

ACTIVITY

Revelation 1:17 tells us two things:

1. DO NOT BE ....

2. JESUS IS THE .... **AND THE** ....

Pray this prayer:

> *Jesus,* thank You for showing me more about who You are. You were present when the world began, making it a beautiful place for me to live. You will be present when the world ends, and I don't have to be afraid. I trust You. Amen.

Revelation 6–11

QUICK LOOK: Revelation 11:15—"The seventh angel blew his trumpet. There were loud voices in heaven. They said, 'The kingdom of the world has become the kingdom of our Lord and of his Messiah. He will rule for ever and ever.'"

RECAP

▷ Today Jesus opens the seals of the Father's scroll, one by one.

▷ Seven angels blow seven trumpets that bring different things upon the earth. The seventh trumpet will sound when the mystery of God is fulfilled, which some say is the return of Jesus.

▷ God gives His people power in the midst of very difficult times. When the enemy appears to be winning, God proves He can't be defeated.

TODAY'S GOD SHOT

Many people who talk about Jesus's return end up fearing it more than looking forward to it, but the kingdom of God is for people who love God! We can look forward to the day that Jesus will return, knowing and believing that He's where the joy is!

ACTIVITY

Have you ever thought about when Jesus will come back to make everything right on earth?

    A. Yes, I think about it.

    B. No, I've never heard about this.

    C. Sometimes, and I wonder what it will be like.

As followers of Jesus, we can look forward to the day Jesus will come back and can pray for it to be soon. Spend some time praying about that now.

Jesus, thank You for Your plan to come back to earth to bring Your perfect kingdom here. I know I don't have to be afraid but can look forward to the day when You will return. I love You. Amen.

Revelation 12–18

QUICK LOOK: Revelation 17:14—The angel said, "They will make war against the Lamb. But the Lamb will have victory over them. That's because he is the most powerful Lord of all and the greatest King of all. His appointed, chosen and faithful followers will be with him."

RECAP

▷ John's vision is filled with signs and symbols. There are wars, beasts, and angels with messages.

▷ John reminds us that the way to overcome hard times is to remain faithful to God.

▷ Jesus works out justice and vengeance on earth with the help of angels from the temple in heaven.

TODAY'S GOD SHOT

Babylon makes war on God and His people, but there is no need to be afraid. We can be confident that because of Jesus's death and resurrection, He has victory over all the enemies of light and life. He's our conqueror, and He's where the joy is!

ACTIVITY

Circle the words that describe who God is to you.

POWERFUL   RIGHT   LIGHT   LIFE

CONQUEROR   GREAT

Revelation 19–22

QUICK LOOK: Revelation 22:20—"Jesus is a witness about these things. He says, 'Yes. I am coming soon.' Amen. Come, Lord Jesus!"

▷ Jesus appears on a white horse, and He's followed by the armies of heaven.

▷ After this, heaven and earth pass away. They were affected by the sin of angels and the sin of men.

▷ We'll live in the new dwelling place of God and His people. It is the new Jerusalem, and it's amazing. It's a gold cube decorated with precious jewels. The gates are never shut, and it's always day, because God is the light.

TODAY'S GOD SHOT

Jesus says three times that He's coming back soon. John says God's kids will join with the Spirit and continually ask for Jesus to return. So when Jesus says, "Surely I am coming soon," John leads the response, "Amen. Come, Lord Jesus!" So we trust Jesus's promise and echo back our prayer, "Amen. Come, Lord Jesus!" You are where the joy is!

ACTIVITY

Congratulations! You made it through the entire Bible! Are you amazed at all you've learned about God? To celebrate, color the certificate and put it in a place where you can see it to remember how your friendship with Him grew this year!

CERTIFICATE OF COMPLETION

This certificate is granted to

_____

NAME

for successfully reading through the entire Bible

_____

DATE

THE
**BIBLE
RECAP**
KIDS' DEVOTIONAL

WORD SEARCH
Answer Key

DAY 17 (page 36)

```
J E H O V A H J I R E H U J
I O F S M J P U G M V A A V
I H M A H I L W X G X T H F
E E V G B J H O V H O W P X
L Y T S F B H Q R G J R I A
O O M R V O A M A M W Y R A
H D X T K D I R E X I Q H D
I W N A S O X A Y N G N A A
M G E I M M A N U E L R V H
D H U L I B O E Y C L O H S
F G K E R E L K V L G U H L
N I V A D O N A I X A W E E
H P U O C T I Z O V T M J E
```

DAY 73 (page 101)

```
G W A H S F R Z P G V C
G A S M O O N I E C X V
K L E Y O A G I O K O K
G Q E Z U R M E P W L O
X P R L T N D H L N D O
O T T D L U I N E I N C
H E A V E N S V D A I E
E A R T H L U T E R W A
V D B L K V N N I R L N
A V B I R D S Y P M S Y
V M O U N T A I N S E E
S T A R S V Q Y Q U H N
```

DAY 165 (page 221)

```
W X B M L D R P H W J V R S
G P R X N G W F M J I J L B
U G E P T E M J O V M U O Z
S R G C N X T K I C S Q V D
G A O X E J E U A C B M I N
W E T N K T V O I E M Y N I
P M N D N M D E J N W F G K
T E D E F J Q L H G G L G T
S K J A R B K P R E S E N T
U A I W J O T O Q G W Q X V
J E F E Q K U K T V E K S G
N T F B U L P S G J D X X L
C O M P A S S I O N A T E N
Z J L V C D X A U Z S M N C
```

DAY 189 (page 253)

```
F O R G I V I N G W O R
M T R K Q Q V Z E L L Z
J N F O N U L E G U V L
Y E J R O E G D G F I U
R I G H T E O U S I C F
W T Q L Q X J U U C T R
K A G U S M Y E W R O E
M P N F A T L I Q E R W
M H I Y P Q O Q R M I O
O W V O Y N H V O V O P
I A O J N F Q I V K U W
G H L W I S E Z Q L S L
```

DAY 227 (page 301)

```
K D L P G J B D Y X X O S R
Z L L I P I R L B Y F F T K
E N V N O F R J R F Q T N Z
B Q E I S N Q A I S R A B F
R M L U N M W E F J F N A H
A E C B Z L A K J F S N P E
T M F G P Z M E W Y A E C
A L L I G A T O R P U P L I
T J Y V K S V S Z V W O E P
L O K M H W R E A N N E Q S
U N C G Q Q L M O N K E Y H
T I G E R A S W B K E E C A
Z H Z S P O W A X Q P J T L
K R U S M R W E D N A R O N
```

DAY 231 (page 306)

```
H W C M M V K S A Y D I A R
L A S V B F J V F O D C Q C
S S I Q Q V X L O V E B L O
D R H R P Z R Y G Z I S O T
D G P E O T M C E M H D N H
E S H F L P X M M O Q N D E
D Y K Q G T H O G N J E T S
O T E Y L Z E F E Q I L
A E Q J X W Q R S B Z R W A
N F B R G S X P Z R N F N
W A T E R L F H A L U I R N
V S C Z A E U A Q M M A M J
D G N C V E E P W P B L T X
H B V F J P R L M Z H X H Z
```

DAY 328 (page 422)

```
I X T Z Z D N G I H
N N F C A W T M S N
U I D H M D K E E U
Q E C I R B D P Z R
D F X N A A A X V K
Y F P A L L Y W Z W
W K O G S T U W W P
N Y N H O H C N A M
P A K I S T A N X A
B W L X R G J A X D
```

ACKNOWLEDGMENTS

This project would not have been possible without the passion and dedicated work of Cherie Duffey and her team at KidSpring, the children's ministry of NewSpring Church. I'm forever grateful for your mentorship in my life! Your zeal for children to know the Lord will be a blessing to so many generations to come!

ABOUT the AUTHOR

TARA-LEIGH COBBLE'S zeal for biblical literacy led her to create and develop an international network of Bible studies called D-Group (Discipleship Group) International. Every week, hundreds of men's and women's D-Groups meet in homes and churches around the world to study Scripture.

She also writes and hosts a daily podcast called *The Bible Recap* designed to help listeners read and understand the Bible in a year. The podcast garnered over one hundred million downloads in its first three years, and more than twenty thousand churches around the world have joined their reading plan to know and love God better. It has been turned into a book published by Bethany House Publishers.

Tara-Leigh is a *Wall Street Journal* bestselling author, speaks to a wide variety of audiences, and regularly leads teaching trips to Israel because she loves to watch others be awed by the story of Scripture through firsthand experience.

Her favorite things include sparkling water and days that are 72 degrees with 55 percent humidity, and she thinks every meal tastes better when eaten outside. She lives in a concrete box in the skies of Dallas, Texas.

For more information about Tara-Leigh and her ministries, you can visit her online.

WEBSITES: **taraleighcobble.com** | **thebiblerecap.com** | **mydgroup.org** | **israelux.com**

SOCIAL MEDIA: **@taraleighcobble** | **@thebiblerecap** | **@mydgroup** | **@israeluxtours**